short

An International
Anthology of Five
Centuries of Short-
Short Stories, Prose
Poems, Brief
Essays, and Other
Short Prose Forms

short

Edited, with an
Introduction by Alan Ziegler

A Karen & Michael Braziller Book
PERSEA BOOKS / NEW YORK

Since this page cannot legibly accommodate all copyright notices, pages 301–316 constitute an extension of the copyright page.

Persea Books, Inc.
277 Broadway, Suite 708
New York, New York 10007

Library of Congress Cataloging-in-Publication Data

Short : an international anthology of five centuries of short-short stories, prose poems, brief essays, and other short prose forms / edited with an introduction by Alan Ziegler.—First edition.
    pages cm
"A Karen and Michael Braziller Book."
ISBN 978-0-89255-432-4 (alk. paper)
1. Literature—Collections. I. Ziegler, Alan, editor of compilation.
PN6014.S5116 2014
808.8—dc23
        2013023115

Designed by Rita Lascaro. Typeset in Minion.
Manufactured in the United States of America

First Edition

For Richard Howard

I'd like to capture an individual in a single sentence, a soul-stirring experience on a single page, a landscape in one word!
—PETER ALTENBERG

Stories that make a point of going no further than they go, this being their point.
—LAURA (RIDING) JACKSON

Since time immemorial, short prose . . . has been liminal, ludic and disruptive . . . short prose has a way of indicating paths into alternative universes just around the corner.
—CHRISTOPHER MIDDLETON

Contents

Precursors
SIXTEENTH TO EIGHTEENTH CENTURIES

Modern Shorts

NINETEENTH TO TWENTY-FIRST CENTURIES

A Personal Note

As an undergraduate at Union College in the late 1960s I wrote journalism and song lyrics, and although the campus poets had fewer readers (and listeners) than I had, I envied their literary legitimacy. I attempted to venture into their rarefied air by publishing a poem in the campus literary magazine. The poem was written in colloquial language organized into standard sentences, with line breaks. The reviewer in the school newspaper called it a prose poem.

I detected a hint of genre inferiority in the adjective *prose*, but I was relieved to be inoculated from comparisons with the *real* poems in the magazine. I felt more legitimate when I heard about Charles Baudelaire's prose poem collection *Paris Spleen* (published posthumously in 1869). But Baudelaire's book contained page after page of paragraphs with justified right-hand margins. I had published a prosy poem in verse, not a prose poem.

Thumbing through *Paris Spleen* had an immediate effect on me. I wanted to do that. Free verse gives poets the option not to work with rhyme and meter; the prose poem further permits us to use the shape we grew up with, the paragraph.

A couple of years later, David Ignatow introduced me to prose poems by James Wright, Robert Bly, Russell Edson, and others. In 1975 I had a prose poem published in *The Paris Review*—selected by poetry editor Michael Benedikt, who was editing *The Prose Poem: An International Anthology*, a volume that would do more for prose poetry than any single publication since *Paris Spleen*.

I enjoyed writing prose poems so much that I tried to increase my yield by de-lining my prosy verse poems. This only worked occasionally, and I started to get a feel for whether or not a poem should run ragged on the right.

Meanwhile, another genre option was becoming increasingly available. Writers who preferred the arena of fiction rather than poetry could publish short-short stories. Anthologies started appearing with names like *Sudden Fiction*, *Micro Fiction*, and *Flash Fiction*. These books—along with Benedikt's anthology and special prose poem issues of literary magazines—both reflected and begat an exponential growth of writers working in short prose.

I tried to base my genre designations on a sense of how much "air" was in a text—I was more likely to call denser pieces prose poems than short-short stories—but marketplace considerations sometimes came into play. Was I submitting to the prose-poem issue of *Poetry Now* or to the PEN-NEA Syndicated Fiction Project? Over the years, the distinction between prose poems and short-short stories—indeed, the terms themselves—became less meaningful for my work. In 2004, I subtitled *The Swan Song of Vaudeville*—a collection of short prose—*Tales and Takes*.

In my Short Prose Forms classes at Columbia University—which I instituted in 1989—I encourage students to explore multiple forms. They have the option to label any piece they write by genre, or they can eschew genre designation. The published texts I bring in for discussion also come with various—or no—formal labels.

Short prose forms belong together in my own writing, in a classroom, and in an anthology. I do not advocate eliminating the option to use genre nomenclature (discussed in the Introduction) for short forms; indeed, we might consider adding to the mix *short* as an über-genre for prose. My objective in *Short* is to offer a reading experience made richer by setting aside categorical imperatives.

A. Z., New York
August, 2013

Introduction

Most anthologies of short prose are confined to stories, prose poems, or essays. Pieces of flash fiction are excluded from collections of prose poems; and prose poems are ineligible for books of stories or essays. But a study of short forms—spanning centuries and languages—reveals that the concept of genre is slippery, shape-shifting, and sometimes nonexistent. One writer's prose poem may be another's flash fiction or brief essay. And what's an editor to do about pieces of short prose left uncategorized by their authors or given names like "anecdote" or "picture": Can we justifiably place them in an anthology of prose poems, short-short stories, or essays?

The answer in *Short* is to put them all together. With distinctions among short prose forms blurry at best, *Short* opts for formal inclusiveness, presenting prose poems by Stéphane Mallarmé and Harryette Mullen alongside short-short stories by Luisa Valenzuela and Diane Williams, brief essays by Edgar Allan Poe and Joe Wenderoth, fragments by Friedrich Schlegel and E. M. Cioran, and unclassified pieces by Robert Musil and W. S. Merwin.

Total inclusiveness would lead to a mighty big book, so *Short* is limited to pieces with fewer than 1250 words from Western literature. A great deal of wonderful material out there isn't in here, including ancient texts and examples from a strong Eastern tradition (Sei Shonagon's *The Pillow Book*, Pu Songling's *Strange Tales from a Chinese Studio*, Yasunari Kawabata's *Palm-of-the-Hand Stories*).

Once we get to the mid-twentieth century, the authors are predominately from the United States, where there has been a rich bounty of short prose. Compelling short pieces are being written elsewhere (especially in Latin America) with a great deal yet to be translated into English. (*Short* does include recent pieces from Argentina, Canada, France, Israel, Mexico, and Slovenia.)

Texts are arranged by the year of the author's birth. The Notes on the Authors (in the back of the book) are arranged alphabetically. Determining the nationality of some authors can be problematic. More than one country is listed for some writers who were reared in one place and eventually settled in another.

To give a sense of the long tradition of the short form, *Short* opens with a cohort of precursors from the sixteenth through the eighteenth centuries. Louis-Sébastien Mercier's "Balcony" is a piece from *Le Tableau de Paris*, which influenced Baudelaire. Michel de Montaigne paved the way for the personal essay. The short takes of Baltasar Gracián have the size and flavor of prose poems, and fragments by François de La Rochefoucauld and Friedrich Schlegel set the stage for E. M. Cioran and Malcolm de Chazal.

Modern authors begin with Louis "Aloysius" Bertrand (born in 1807) and Edgar Allan Poe (1809), who were separated by an ocean and a language and never read each other, but shared an admirer, Charles Baudelaire. Bertrand's posthumously-published (and little-known) *Gaspard de la nuit* (*Gaspard of the Night*) provided Baudelaire with a formal model for the pieces in *Paris Spleen*. Bertrand called the short prose pieces in *Gaspard* "fantasies," and the critic Sainte-Beuve referred to them as "little *ballades* in prose."

What Baudelaire found in Poe (whom he translated into French and championed ardently) was perhaps even more valuable—a kindred spirit: "The first time I opened one of his books, I saw, with horror and delight, not only topics I'd dreamed of, but *sentences* I'd thought of, and that he'd written twenty years before." Baudelaire was instrumental in the surge of interest in Bertrand and the burgeoning influence of Poe in Europe.

Some critics consider only a portion of the prose poems in Baudelaire's *Paris Spleen* to be truly poetic, the rest being closer to stories, fables, essays, memoirs, and anecdotes. But by appropriating these modes of expression for his *petits poèmes en prose,* Baudelaire provided us with a mix of models that makes *Paris Spleen* an exemplar for the whole gamut of short prose forms.

Many influence-trails stem from the Bertrand / Poe / Baudelaire nexus. Here's one: Baudelaire read Bertrand and Poe in Paris;

Peter Altenberg read Baudelaire in Vienna; Franz Kafka read Altenberg in Prague (admiring how "in his small stories his whole life is mirrored"); in the United States, Russell Edson said he found a good example "in the works of Kafka, who explored the vaunted dreamscape, and yet was able to report it in rational and reasoned language"; for Lydia Davis, Edson "jolted me out of my stuckness in long conventional stories and into one-paragraph freedom"; and Deb Olin Unferth has expressed "supreme admiration" for Davis. Similar paths wend through other countries in Western Europe and Latin America.

WHAT'S IN A NAME?

If the subtitle for this book contained even a partial list of nomenclature for short prose forms, it might include:

Anecdotes, Aphorisms, Briefs, Brief Essays, *Casos, Crônicas/ Chronicas, Denkbilder,* Espresso Stories, Feuilletons, *Ficciones Relámpagos,* Figures, Flash Fiction, Fragments, *Greguerías,* Hint Fiction, *Kurzprosa,* Maxims, Microstories/*Microcuentos,* Monostichs, Nanofiction, Napkin Stories, Notes, Paragraphs, *Pensées/Pensieri,* Prose Poems, Quick Fiction, Sentences, Shorts, Short-Short Stories, Situations, Sketches, Sudden Fiction, Tableaus, Transmutations, Tropisms, Utterances, Very Short Stories.

Let's look at four terms that encompass most of the others. Prose poem, short-short story, brief essay, and fragment are the wild cards in the writer's deck. How they are defined depends on the dealer and can change from hand to hand. The names *prose poem, short-short story,* and *fragment* scream challenge— appearing to be, respectively, self-contradictory, redundant, and downright misleading. Many prose poems are indistinguishable from short-short stories; brief essays from prose poems; and fragments from prose poems and brief essays.

Although there is no absolute answer to "What is it?" let us go and make our visits.

THE PROSE POEM

The prose poem is "the monster child of two incompatible strategies, the lyric and the narrative" (Charles Simic), "characterized by the intense use of virtually all the devices of poetry" (Michael Benedikt), except when it uses "very prosy elements, conversation or journalese" (John Ashbery). Although the prose poem has "no obvious elegant shape, the reader nevertheless asks it to arrive at elegance" (Robert Bly) as it arouses "an unconquerable desire to reread" (Charles Simic), inviting "both a forward and backward motion of the eye" (Naomi Shihab Nye).

Prose poems can be compact (Henri Michaux's "Insects") or expansive (Luis Cernuda's "The Teacher"), dreamlike (David Ignatow's "The Diner") or reportorial (Carolyn Forché's "The Colonel"); they can proceed through leaps of imagery (Arthur Rimbaud's "After the Flood") or memory (Stéphane Mallarmé's "The Pipe").

The only universally valid definition of *prose poem* is quite simple: A prose poem is a piece without line breaks that the author calls a poem. (The prose poet is not totally bereft of breaks: the end of each sentence offers the opportunity for a new paragraph.)

Essentially, a piece is a prose poem *because the writer says so*, making it easy to write a prose poem. The challenge—as with any piece of writing—is to write a good one. Robert Frost compared writing free verse to "playing tennis with the net down"; writing a prose poem is like playing tennis with no net in an open field—and making an interesting game of it.

THE SHORT-SHORT STORY

The closest I can come to defining a short-short story (and I wouldn't want to come any closer) is that it must be short (unlike a prose poem, which can be any length, though the vast majority are very short) and contain a narrative element. But it doesn't need to develop everything we expect from a conventional short story (such as plot, character, setting, conflict, change). Indeed, the short-short story often achieves its power by the lack of some or most of these elements.

In a conventional story, something happens and something changes; in a short-short story, one or the other can be sufficient. In Fielding Dawson's "Double Vision—*The Rewrite*," a bartender and customer exchange anecdotes about seeing a stranger (not the same one) twice that day in different locations. No change takes place, but a moment of human connection is revealed through snippets of dialogue and imagery. In Augusto Monterroso's eight-word story "The Dinosaur" ("When he awoke, the dinosaur was still there."), we don't know what happened, but we know that someone's life has changed.

In a longer story the writer has more room to engage the reader than in a short-short, where the reader is barely past the entrance when the exit beckons. A novel can be composed of many plot ropes, each with multiple strands; a short story can have one rope with several strands; a short-short story may be held together by a thread—but it must be one powerful thread.

THE BRIEF ESSAY

Brief essays (perhaps designated as lyric or personal essays) are often akin to prose poems and short-short stories in length and style. Although the brief essay has not achieved the formal recognition (and is not as prevalent) as short-short stories and prose poems, unlike these forms it does offer the reader an explicit promise of truth—however the author defines it.

A breed of brief essays has historically been published in European and Latin American newspapers under such names as feuilletons, *Denkbilder, ocherks,* and *crônicas/chronicas* (each with variable denotations).

These pieces can blend memoir, observation, and opinion, often with a strong first-person voice, and they may embody literary aspirations beyond what might otherwise be expected from their host publications. Joseph Roth (see "Rest While Watching the Demolition") wrote to his editor, "You can't write feuilletons with half a mind or one hand tied behind your back . . . I am *not* an encore, not a pudding, I am the main dish . . . I don't write 'witty glosses.' *I paint the portrait of the age.*"

Other contributors to this book who wrote such pieces for popular periodicals include Peter Altenberg, Walter Benjamin, Ernst Bloch, Karl Kraus, Clarice Lispector, António Lobo Antunes, and Mikhail Zoshchenko.

Similar pieces have appeared in the United States on newspaper Op-Ed pages, in the front or back sections of popular magazines, and in literary publications (print and online).

THE FRAGMENT

The literary term *fragment* does not always refer to an enticing piece of literary flotsam that has felicitously washed up on shore, such as a shard of Sappho's poetry. *Fragment* is used here for a complete piece with a fragmentary quality (like a chef 's amuse bouche—which is not scooped out of a pot—or Chopin's Prelude No. 9). Such pieces include aphorisms, epigrams, maxims, *pensées*, figures, and *greguerías*.

The Precursors section includes posthumously published fragments (not extracted from completed works) that relied on "curators" to identify their literary worth and place the work in front of readers. Joseph Joubert's fragments were initially mined from his notebooks by Chateaubriand. Chamfort jotted down maxims, anecdotes, and eavesdrops on little squares of paper, tossing them into boxes; they were rescued by his friend Guingené.

The brothers Friedrich and August Schlegel—influenced in part by Chamfort—sought to recognize the fragment as a genre. In 1798, Friedrich wrote, "Many of the works of the ancients have become fragments. Many modern works are fragments as soon as they are written."

Malcolm de Chazal, Gertrude Stein, and E. M. Cioran—among others in this anthology—composed in fragments, which often travel in packs. Charles Simic curated his own notebook entries into discrete pieces, sampled here. One of the form's appeals for E. M. Cioran—who called himself "a fragment man" with a "dislike of developing things"—was that he could "put two aphorisms that are contradictory right next to each other."

DISTINCTIONS AND DIFFERENCES

Emotions can run high regarding nomenclature; the claim implicit in a name may raise the hackles and bring out the shackles. Diane Williams recalls being shocked at the vehemence of an early reaction to her short-short stories: "If only you called this poetry... I wouldn't be so angry with you..." And some writers and readers have demanded irregular line lengths as a requirement for earning the moniker *poem*. Poet and essayist Tom Montag offered this admittedly "cranky" opinion: "Prose poems are not poems: let's stop pretending they are."

Almost everyone now accepts poems without lines and stories without length, but is there a distinction without a difference between them? The problem / opportunity is that genre-designation is fungible. "There may be a difference between flash fiction and prose poems, but I believe the researchers still haven't found the genes that differentiate them," says Denise Duhamel, who writes both. James Tate finds it useful to have both designations available. His prose poems "may have qualities of fiction... but I limit myself in space so that I am forced into a tremendous compression," while his stories are "a little more relaxed in their method... In a story you can be just a little bit more circuitous."

Ray Gonzalez's *The Religion of Hands: Prose Poems and Flash Fictions* has discrete sections of each ("El Bandido"—his contribution here—is flash fiction), while Margaret Atwood's *Murder in the Dark: Short Fictions and Prose Poems* doesn't identify which is which. (On the back jacket, the book is described as Atwood's "seventh work of fiction or her tenth work of poetry, depending on how you slice it.")

Authors may designate a genre depending on how they want a piece to be read. Readers might approach a story with greater expectations of plot and character development than they bring to a piece labeled a prose poem. And they might expect the language of a prose poem to require—and deserve—a closer reading. Or a writer's home genre may determine how a piece is designated. Diane Williams and Lydia Davis are primarily story writers, and they call even their shortest pieces stories; David Ignatow and Joy Harjo are primarily poets and publish prose poems.

With terms such as flash fiction taking hold in the last couple of decades, writers and publishers have more options for genre designation. Who knows how many earlier prose poems might have entered literary society under different names, had they been available?

Some pieces go on to live double lives. Jayne Anne Phillips's piece "Happy" was first published as a prose poem in *The Paris Review* and subsequently included in her collection of stories *Black Tickets*. Bernard Cooper's collection *Maps to Anywhere* received a Hemingway Foundation / PEN Award for fiction, although many of the pieces were originally published as nonfiction. Prose poems from Anne Carson's *Short Talks* appeared in a volume of *Best American Essays*.

Pieces can be sent into the world without a passport from any genre. The book jacket text of the first edition of W. S. Merwin's 1970 *The Miner's Pale Children* begins, "It is not easy to characterize this book"; and Merwin writes in his preface to the 1994 edition, "I am still not certain what to call the pieces that took shape . . . this seems to me a valuable condition." Merwin did not want "these writings to qualify for membership in some recognizable genre. I hoped that they would keep raising some questions about accepted boundaries and definitions of genres altogether . . . I recalled what I thought were precedents—fragments, essays, journal entries, instructions and lists, oral tales, fables."

One advantage of not designating a genre—or of using a nondescript term like *paragraph, piece,* or *text*—is that readers cannot respond that they like the work but it is just not a *poem story/essay* because it is too *prosaic/static/lacking verisimilitude*. Each piece makes a *prima facie* case for itself, with no room for rebuttal based merely on formal expectations.

SUBVERSIVE PROCLIVITIES

"To expect the unexpected shows a thoroughly modern intellect," wrote Oscar Wilde, and short prose pieces often flaunt their modernity through surprise and subversion. Perhaps space constriction lends itself to work that subverts expectations, or maybe when writers work in a renegade form they feel free to throw caution to the winds of imagination.

Prose poems and short-short stories can be literary tricksters, appropriating qualities of other forms. Shape-changing pieces in this anthology include Jack Anderson's "Phalaris and the Bull: A Story and an Examination," Apollinaire's "Little Recipes from Modern Magic," W. S. Merwin's "Make This Simple Test," Robert Walser's "The Job Application," and Traci Brimhall's "Rookery" (in the form of a dictionary entry). Sometimes the appropriation is a nod (with a wink) to another genre (Robert Hass's "Novella" and Macedonio Fernández's "A Novel for Readers with Nerves of Steel").

Marcel Schwob's "Cyril Tourneur: Tragic Poet" subverts the expectation that a biographer will at least *try* to be faithful to the facts of the subject's life; and Jorge Luis Borges cleaves autobiography in "Borges and I." Paul Colinet's "The Lobster" sounds so authoritative, you might think for a second that the "lobster's calcified eye" really is "used, in shoemaking, to fasten half-boots." Charles Simic adopts the guise of a raconteur by opening one of his prose poems with "Everybody knows the story..." when in fact no one knows the story he is about to tell.

Not surprisingly, short prose writers have subverted book terminology. The burgeoning of creative contributors' notes in the back matter of literary periodicals and anthologies engendered the pieces herein by Michael Martone and Stacy Harwood. Paul Violi turns "Acknowledgments" on its head; and Augusto Monterosso offers an "Errata and Final Notice."

The expectation of closure can be thwarted by letting readers know they are barking up the wrong tree if they expect a definitive ending. "The surprise, at times, is that the story has no ending," writes Enrique Anderson Imbert. The final sentence of Gary Lutz's "Steep" is "I make it sound as if I know an answer"; Rae Armantrout's "Imaginary Places" closes with "But this is getting us nowhere"; and "But no more about it" ends Beckett's "One Evening."

This apparent flippancy must be earned. Anderson Imbert cautions that it would be "too mechanical a procedure" if "within the artifice there were not beating a conception of the world: ironic, perhaps poetic." David Lehman writes, "There is beauty in the inconclusive anecdote terminating in ellipses"; such beauty can be found in Max Jacob's "The Beggar Woman of Naples."

Authors can subvert the very notion of freedom in short prose forms by self-imposing patterns and restrictions. Dionisio D. Martínez's "Homage to Li Po" is a prose version of a sestina, and David Lehman's "But Only . . ." uses the title phrase throughout as a kind of anaphora. Writers of the Oulipo movement—co-founded by Raymond Queneau in 1960—conceive of linguistic and mathematical constraints that can demystify the creative process while producing inventive writing.

Harryette Mullen's "Bleeding Hearts" is "constructed with letters and sounds, graphemes and phonemes, derived from the word Crenshaw" (a neighborhood in Los Angeles). One doesn't have to pledge rigid adherence to constraints; Mullen advocates that writers "use and then lose the constraint at different points in the creative process."

Authors may choose to limit the size of the real estate on which they build. Giorgio Manganelli had a surplus of extra-large typing paper and decided to write a "series of narratives," each of which "would never exceed the length of a single page"; he called the results "ouroboric novels." Ann DeWitt's "Influence" was a response to *Esquire's* call for stories that could fit on a napkin.

The bottomless pit of the internet—so far removed from the pay-by-the-character letterpress—has brought about a blossoming of constricted-form publishing. Cyberspace expands the solar system of the computer into a galaxy of free space, yet many choose to use only a speck at a time. (Twitter's 140-character limit seems to have hit a sweet spot for writers and readers.) Online publications often specify length limits or exact word counts: Build it and they will post. The title of Lou Beach's collection *420 Characters* refers to the old limit on Facebook, where the stories initially appeared. Two are included here.

Do short forms *have* to be linguistically loopy or use structural restrictions or legerdemain? Can they be staid and conventional, relying on accessible tropes and straightforward narrative?

The answers are, of course: *No* and *Yes*.

In inconclusion: I make it sound as if I know an answer but this is getting us nowhere so no more about it.

short

A Note on Reading the Texts

An asterisk (*) indicates that what follows is a new piece by the same author; a tilde (~) marks a section break intended by the author within a continuing piece; and a bullet (·) alerts the reader to a line space occurring at the top of a page in a continuing piece. To preserve the distinctiveness and integrity of the individual texts, each one is reprinted as in its source publication, including variations in spelling and punctuation.

Precursors

SIXTEENTH TO EIGHTEENTH CENTURIES

GIROLAMO CARDANO (Italy, 1501–1576)

Those Things in Which I Take Pleasure

Among the things which please me greatly are stilettos, or *stili* for writing; for them I have spent more than twenty gold crowns, and much money besides for other sorts of pens. I daresay the writing materials which I have got at one time and another could not be bought for two hundred crowns. Besides these, I take great pleasure in gems, in metal bowls, in vessels of copper or silver, in painted glass globes and in rare books.

I enjoy swimming a little and fishing very much. I was devoted to the art of angling as long as I remained at Pavia and I am sorry I ever changed.

The reading of history gives me extraordinary satisfaction, as well as readings in philosophy, in Aristotle and Plotinus, and the study of treatises on the revelations of mysteries, and especially treatises on medical questions.

In the Italian poets, Petrarch and Luigi Pulci, I find great delight.

I prefer solitude to companions, since there are so few men who are trustworthy, and almost none truly learned. I do not say this because I demand scholarship in all men—although the sum total of men's learning is small enough; but I question whether we should allow anyone to waste our time. The wasting of time is an abomination.

Translated from the Latin by Jean Stoner

MICHEL DE MONTAIGNE (France, 1533–1592)

Something Lacking in Our Civil Administrations

My late father, a man of a decidedly clear judgement, based though it was only on his natural gifts and his own experience, said to me once that he had wished to set a plan in motion leading to the designation of a place in our cities where those who were in need of anything could go and have their requirements registered by a duly appointed official; for example: "I want to sell some pearls"; or "I want to buy some pearls." "So-and-so wants to make up a group to travel to Paris"; "So-and-so wants a servant with the following qualifications"; "So-and-so seeks an employer"; "So-and-so wants a workman"; each stating his wishes according to his needs.

It does seem that this means of mutual advertising would bring no slight advantage to our public dealings; for at every turn there are bargains seeking each other but, because they cannot find each other, men are left in extreme want.

I have just learnt something deeply shameful to our times; under our very eyes two outstanding scholars have died for want of food, Lilius Gregorius Giraldus in Italy and Sebastian Castalio in Germany; and I believe that there are hundreds of people who would have invited them to their houses on very favourable terms or sent help to them where they were, if only they had known.

The world is not so completely corrupt that we cannot find even one man who would not gladly wish to see his inherited wealth able to be used (as long as Fortune lets him enjoy it) to provide shelter for great men who are renowned for some particular achievement but who have been reduced to extreme poverty by their misfortunes; he could at least give them enough assistance that it would be unreasonable for them not to be satisfied.

In his administration of his household affairs my father had a rule which I can admire but in no ways follow. In addition to keeping a record of household accounts entrusted to the hands of a domestic bursar (making entries for small bills and payments or transactions which did not need the signature of a lawyer) he told the man who acted as his secretary to keep a diary covering any noteworthy event and the day-to-day history of his household. It is very pleasant to consult, once time begins to efface memories; it is also useful for clearing up difficulties. When was such-and-such a job begun? When was it finished? Who called at Montaigne with their retinues? How many came to stay? It notes our journeys, absences, marriages and deaths, the receipt of good or bad news; changes among our chief servants—things like that: an ancient custom which I would like to be revived by each denizen in his own den. I think I am a fool to have neglected it.

Translated from the French by M. A. Screech

BALTASAR GRACIÁN (Spain, 1601–1658)

Earlids

We have eyelids but not earlids, for the ears are the portals of learning, and Nature wanted to keep them wide open. Not content with denying us this door, she also keeps us, alone among all listeners, from twitching our ears. Man alone holds them motionless, always on alert. She did not want us to lose a single second in cocking our ears and sharpening our hearing. The ears hold court at all hours, even when the soul retires to its chambers. In fact, it is then that those sentinels ought to be most wide awake. If not, who would warn of danger? When the mind goes lazily off to sleep, who else would rouse it? This is the difference between seeing and hearing. For the eyes seek out things deliberately, when and if they want, but things come spontaneously to the ears. Visible things tend to remain: if we don't look at them now, we can do so later; but most sounds pass by quickly, and we must grab that opportunity by the forelock. Our one tongue is twice enclosed, and our two ears are twice open, so that we can hear twice as much as we speak. I realize that half, perhaps more, of all things heard are unpleasant and even harmful, but for this there is a fine solution, which is to pretend not to hear, or to hear like a shopkeeper or a wise man. And there are things so devoid of reason that one walls up the ears with the hands. For if the hands help us to hear, they can also defend us from flattery. The snake knows a way to escape the charmer: he keeps one ear to the ground and plugs the other with his tail.

Cancel the Dedication

Those praised in a book take that praise, and more, as their due. What you meant as a gift is accepted as an obligation. In a second printing of one of his books, a writer listed the misprints in the first. Among them was the dedication.

Translated from the Spanish by Christopher Maurer

FRANÇOIS DE LA ROCHEFOUCAULD
(France, 1613–1680)

Passion often turns the cleverest man into a fool, and often makes the worst fools clever.

*

In the human heart, passions are perpetually being generated—so that the downfall of one is almost always the rise of another.

*

Self-interest speaks all kinds of languages and plays all kinds of parts—even that of disinterestedness.

*

We often forgive those who bore us, but we cannot forgive those whom we bore.

Translated from the French by E. H. Blackmore and A. M. Blackmore

JOHN AUBREY (England, 1626–1697)

William Shakespeare

Mr. William Shakespeare was borne at Stratford upon Avon in the County of Warwick. His father was a Butcher, and I have been told heretofore by some of the neighbours, that when he was a boy he exercised his father's Trade, but when he kill'd a

Calfe he would doe it in a high style, and make a Speech. There was at this time another Butcher's son in this Towne that was held not at all inferior to him for a naturall witt, his acquaintance and coetanean, byt dyed young.

This William, being inclined naturally to Poetry and acting, came to London, I guesse about 18: and was an Actor at one of the Play-houses, and did acte exceedingly well: now B. Johnson was never a good Actor, but an excellent Instructor.

He began early to make essayes at Dramatique Poetry, which at that time was very lowe; and his Playes tooke well.

He was a handsome, well-shap't man: very good company, and of a very readie and pleasant smoothe Witt.

The Humour of the Constable in Midsomernight's Dreame, he happened to take at Grendon, in Bucks (I thinke it was Midsomer night that he happened to lye there) which is the roade from London to Stratford, and there was living that Constable about 1642, when I first came to Oxon. Ben Johnson and he did gather Humours of men dayly where ever they came. One time as he was at the Tavern at Stratford super Avon, one Combes, an old rich Usurer, was to be buryed. He makes there this extemporary Epitaph:

> *Ten in the Hundred the Devill allowes,*
> *But Combes will have twelve he sweares and vowes:*
> *If anyone askes who lies in this Tombe,*
> *Hoh! quoth the Devill, 'Tis my John o' Combe.*

He was wont to goe to his native Countrey once a yeare. I thinke I have been told that he left 2 or 300 pounds per annum there and thereabout to a sister.

I have heard Sir William Davenant and Mr. Thomas Shadwell (who is counted the best Comoedian we have now) say that he had a most prodigious Witt, and did admire his naturall parts beyond all other Dramaticall writers.

His Comoedies will remaine witt as long as the English tongue is understood, for that he handles *mores hominum* [the ways of mankind]. Now our present writers reflect so much on particular persons and coxcombeities that twenty yeares hence they will not be understood.

Though, as Ben Johnson sayes of him, that he had little Latine and lesse Greek, He understood Latine pretty well: for he had been in his younger yeares a schoolmaster in the countrey.

He was wont to say that he never blotted out a line in his life. Sayd Ben: Johnson, I wish he had blotted-out a thousand.

JEAN DE LA BRUYÈRE (France, 1645–1696)

There is nothing that brings a man more suddenly into fashion, or attracts so much attention to him, as playing for high stakes; it's on a par with drunkenness. I should be surprised if the most cultured, witty and vivacious of men, Catullus himself or one of his disciples, could stand comparison with one who has just lost eight hundred *pistoles* at a sitting.

*

If you could go into those kitchens where the secret of flattering your taste and making you eat more than you need is practised as an art and a method; if you could examine in detail the preparation of the foodstuffs which are to make up the feast in store for you; if you should see through what hands they pass, and what various forms they take before becoming an exquisite dish and acquiring that daintiness and elegance that delight your eyes, make choice difficult and induce you to sample everything; if you could see the whole meal anywhere else than on a well-laid table, how nasty, how loathsome it would seem! If you go behind the scenes at a theatre and count the weights, the wheels, the ropes which make the machines work and the actors fly, if you consider how many people are involved in making the things move, and what strength of arms, what muscular exertion they display, you will say: `Are these the principles and the secret springs of that splendid spectacle that seems so natural, as though it were alive and moved of its own accord?' You will protest: 'What strenuous and violent efforts!' In the same way, do not seek to look deeply into the fortune of the *partisans*.

*

The people of Paris keep a tacit, but most punctual, rendezvous every evening on the Cours or in the Tuileries, to stare each other in the face and disapprove of one another.

They cannot do without their fellow-citizens, whom they dislike and scoff at.

On a public promenade people wait to see one another pass; they file past for mutual inspection: carriages, horses, liveries, coats of arms, nothing escapes observation, everything is curiously or maliciously noted; and according to the size of the equipage, the owner is either respected or despised.

*

It is harder to make one's name by means of a perfect work than to win praise for a second-rate one by means of the name one has already acquired.

*

What's that you say? I beg your pardon? I don't follow; would you mind beginning again? I'm even more at a loss. At last I guess: you're trying to tell me, *Acis*, that it is cold; why can't you say 'It's cold'? You want to inform me that it is raining or snowing; say: 'It's raining, it's snowing.' You think I am looking well, and you would like to congratulate me; say: 'I think you're looking well.' But, you may reply, all that is very simple and straightforward; anyone could say as much. What does that matter, Acis? Is it such a great misfortune to be understood when one speaks, and to speak like everybody else? There is just one thing, Acis, that all you phrasemongers are lacking in; you never suspect it, and I'm going to astonish you; there's one thing you are lacking in, and that is wit. Moreover, there's another thing that you could well do without, namely your belief that you are wittier than others: hence your pompous nonsense, your involved phrases and your long words that mean nothing. When I see you accosting someone, or entering a room, I shall pull you by the coat-tails and whisper in your ear: 'Don't aim at wit, don't be witty, it doesn't suit you; speak, if you can, in simple language, like those in whom you find no wit; perhaps, then, people will credit you with having some.'

*

The things we have most longed for do not happen; or if they do, it is never at the time nor under the circumstances when they could have made us happiest.

Translated from the French by Jean Stewart

LOUIS-SÉBASTIEN MERCIER (France, 1740–1814)

Balcony

One of the more curious sights of Paris may be seen without trouble; you have only to lean over your balcony and look down into the street below, upon carriages crossing and blocking each other's way, and pedestrians, like game that flees before the menace of the gun, dodging in and out among the wheels of stationary juggernauts; one leaps the gutter to escape a shower of mud, miscalculates an inch, and finds himself in mud up to the eyes, while another, more lucky, goes mincing along unscathed, parasol under arm.

In a gilded chariot, velvet-lined, with glass windows and a pair of horses exquisitely bred and matched, a duchess in all her regalia reclines; and there she remains, unable to get forward or back by reason of an old filthy cab, with boards on straps instead of glass, which is blocking the way. One of the horses is blind, and the other lame; the cabman whips up both impartially, and quite ineffectually; but blind and halt though his pair may be, they contrive without difficulty to hold up any number of thoroughbreds until the whole procession reaches a cross-roads where there is room to pass; then the gilded equipage flashes by, striking sparks from the stones as it goes. Compare this vehicle and its pace with the huge market wagons that lumber slowly along, taking up the whole street, leaving no room for the pedestrian, who goes in terror of one of their great hubs catching him amidships and plastering him into a wall.

A poorly paid lawyer in his cab at twenty-four sous the hour may hold up the Lord Chancellor; a marshall of France must wait while the recruiting sergeant's party drags its slow length along, and a call girl yields no ground to an archbishop. All these different interests in motion, perched up behind coachmen whose vocabulary respects neither ducal, nor clerical, nor legal ears; and the porters at the street-corners, giving in their own lingo as good as they get; what a sight, what a blend of splendour, and poverty, and riches, and wretchedness.

Listen to Madame la Marquise; she is in a hurry, and her shrill little voice sings soprano to the bass of the wagoner calling on all the powers of heaven and hell. But this moving picture is full of such oddities, what with berlins, and sulkies, and cabriolets and whiskies, and carriages jobbed by the week; there is always something queer, or strange, or laughable for the observer to ponder.

You see, for instance, the woman of birth in her coach, ugly as sin, but covered with diamonds, and rouge, and her face shining with some fashionable concoction; compare her with the little fresh, plump nobody in her simple dress. Then the bishop, leaning back upon his cushions, empty-headed but magnificent, a jewelled cross upon his breast, and some grey-headed magistrate in a shabby berlin, reading the affidavits in some case or other. A young fashionable thrusts his head out of the carriage-window, and bawls till his throat aches: "Well, you pack of rascals, have I got to wait here all day?" Nobody heeds him. He makes some poor attempt at swearing, but his meagre voice has about as much effect as the buzzing of a fly upon the hardened tympanums of carters. A neighbouring doctor eyes him solicitously, but the plethoric double-chinned financier on the other side takes no notice of him, or of his surroundings, or the waste of time.

Confusion becomes worse confounded; six hundred vehicles are involved by this time, and there is no help for it, they all must wait until somehow or other they are disentangled. Now, what can have been the preoccupation of that elegant young-ster who could not make himself heard? Meeting a lady, per-haps? Not a bit of it. The trouble was, he wished to be seen that night at all three theatres, the Comédie française, the Opéra, and the italienne.

Translated from the French by Helen Simpson and Jeremy D. Popkin

CHAMFORT (France, 1741–1794)

"Considering the general level of literature during these last ten years," M—said, "literary celebrity, it seems to me, is by now a kind of disgrace which is not quite so damaging as the pillory, but soon will be."

*

During a siege a water carrier cried through the town, "Water! Six sous a bucket." A cannonball carried away one of his two buckets. Unperturbed, and without losing a moment, he cried, "Water! Twelve sous a bucket."

*

The Comtesse de Boufflers told the Prince de Conti that he was the best of tyrants.

*

In M. de Machaut's time the King was presented with a pro-spectus for a royal audience, as they wished to see it enacted. Everything was agreed upon beforehand by the King, Mme. de Pompadour, and the ministers. The King was prompted as to what he should say, in each instance, to the president. It was all set out in a memorandum, complete with: "Here the King will look stern. Here the King will assume a gentler expression. Here the King will make such–and–such a gesture, etc." The memo-randum still exists.

*

Society is made up of two great classes: those who have more dinners than appetite, and those who have more appetite than dinners.

Translated from the French by W. S. Merwin

JOSEPH JOUBERT (France, 1754–1824)

The silence of the fields. How everything hushes imperceptibly with the fall of night. How everything seems to be gathered up: men and animals, by the work of unanimous silence; plants and all things that move, for the wind falls when evening comes near, and the air holds only a single, frail breath. It is from this immobility of all things, and because the remaining light is reflected more during these tranquil hours by the earth and its rocks than by the trees and plants, that the hills and fields seem to lift up the earth and to stand in wonder.

*

The soul paints itself in our machines.

*

Dreams. Their lantern is magical.

*

Pleasures are always children, pains always have wrinkles.

*

Forgetfulness of all earthly things, desire for heavenly things, immunity from all intensity and all disquiet, from all cares and all worries, from all trouble and all effort, the plenitude of life without agitation. The delights of feeling without the work of thought. The ravishments of ecstasy without medication. In a word, the happiness of pure spirituality in the heart of the world and amidst the tumult of the senses. It is no more than the gladness of an hour, a minute, an instant. But this instant, this minute of piety spreads its sweetness over our months and our years.

*

Those useless phrases that come into the head. The mind is grinding its colors.

*

To finish! What a word. We finish nothing when we stop, when we say we have come to the end.

Translated from the French by Paul Auster

WILLIAM BLAKE (England, 1757–1827)

The road of excess leads to the palace of wisdom.

*

A fool sees not the same tree that a wise man sees.

*

Eternity is in love with the productions of time.

*

No bird soars too high, if he soars with his own wings.

*

The fox condemns the trap, not himself.

*

Exuberance is Beauty.

AUGUST WILHELM SCHLEGEL
(Germany, 1767–1845)

Notes to a poem are like anatomical lectures on a piece of roast beef.

*

Nothing is more pitiful than to sell oneself to the devil for nothing; for example, to write lascivious poems that aren't even very good.

*

The story goes that Klopstock met the French poet Rouget de Lisle, who was paying him a visit, with this greeting: how did he dare appear in Germany after his *Marseillaise* had cost the lives of fifty thousand brave Germans? This was an undeserved reproach. Didn't Samson defeat the Philistines with the jawbone of an ass? And even if the *Marseillaise* really does have a share in the victories of France, then Rouget de Lisle exhausted the murderous power of his poetry in this one piece: with all the others put together you couldn't kill a fly.

Translated from the German by Peter Firchow

NOVALIS (Germany, 1772–1801)

Monologue

There is really something very foolish about speaking and writing; proper conversation is merely a word game. One can only marvel at the ridiculous mistake that people make when they think—that they speak for the sake of things. The particular quality of language, the fact that it is concerned only with itself, is known to no one. Language is such a marvelous and fruitful secret—because when someone speaks merely for the sake of speaking, he utters the most splendid, most original truths. But if he wants to speak about something definite, capricious language makes him say the most ridiculous and confused stuff. This is also the cause of the hatred that so many serious people feel toward language. They notice its mischief, but not the fact that the chattering they scorn is the infinitely serious aspect of language. If one could only make people understand that it is the same with language as with mathematical formulae. These constitute a world of their own. They play only with themselves, express nothing but their own marvelous nature, and just for this reason they are so expressive—just for this reason the strange play of relations between things is mirrored in them. Only through their freedom are they elements of nature and only in their free movements does the world soul manifest itself in them and make them a sensitive measure and ground plan of things. So it is too with language—on the one hand, anyone who is sensitive to its fingering, its rhythm, its musical spirit, who perceives within himself the delicate working of its inner nature, and moves his tongue or his hand accordingly, will be a prophet; on the other hand, anyone who knows how to write truths like these but does not have ear and sense enough for it will be outwitted by language itself and mocked by people as Cassandra was by the Trojans. Even if in saying this I believe I have described the essence and function of poetry in the clearest possible way, at the same time I know that no one can understand it, and I have said something quite foolish because I wanted to say it, and in this way no poetry comes about. What would it be like though if I had to speak? and this instinct of language to speak were the hallmark of what inspires language, of the efficacy of language within me? and were my will to want only everything that I was obliged to do, in the end could this be poetry without my knowledge or belief and could it make a secret of language understandable? and thus I would be a born writer, for a writer is surely only a language enthusiast?

Translated from the German by Margaret Mahony Stoljar

FRIEDRICH SCHLEGEL (Germany, 1772–1829)

Many of the works of the ancients have become fragments. Many modern works are fragments as soon as they are written.

*

One can only become a philosopher, not be one. As soon as one thinks one is a philosopher, one stops becoming one.

*

Publishing is to thinking as the maternity ward is to the first kiss.

*

Beautiful is what is at once charming and sublime.

The history of the first Roman Caesars is like a symphony—striking up the theme that runs through the history of all the subsequent ones.

Translated from the German by Peter Firchow

GIACOMO LEOPARDI (Italy, 1798–1837)

Man or bird or four-legged creature killed in the countryside by hail.

*

He put on eyeglasses made of half the meridian connecting the two polar circles.

*

A house hanging in the air held by ropes to a star.

*

For the *Manual of Practical Philosophy*. Patience, how it mitigates physical pain, makes it easier, more bearable, even lighter—as I myself experienced and observed during chest spasms I suffered in Bologna on May 29, 1826, where impatience and restlessness increased my pain. It's a question of non-resistance, mental resignation, a certain quieting of mind while suffering. You can sneer at this virtue or call it cowardice if you like. But it's still necessary to mankind, which is born, fated—inexorably, inevitably, irrevocably—to suffer, suffer greatly, with few reprieves. A virtue born or acquired (unwillingly sometimes) along with the necessity of enduring arduous or nagging experiences. Patience and quietude are largely what renders tolerable over a long term (to a prisoner for example) the awful tedium of solitude or idleness. A tedium almost unbearably grating because of how hard a man resists his troubles, because of his impatience and vehemence, his anxious craving to escape it. When resistance ceases, troubles and suffering become easier, lighter.

*

If a good book hasn't become famous, the best way to make it happen is to say it has already happened, to speak of it as a famous book, famous everywhere, etc. These things become true by force of saying they're true. Let many people affirm and repeat it and they'll make it true beyond all doubt. And if for some reason this tactic doesn't work, the best play is to keep quiet, seem indifferent, and wait for time to do its work. There's nothing worse than *de se fâcher avec la public*, to rail against injustice, against contemporary bad taste for not paying attention to the book. Even if these complaints make perfect sense, even if the book is a classic, once its failure is publicly acknowledged the best it can hope for is to be seen as one of those pretenders who, for lack of an army, have only their rights and legitimacy to back their claim.

*

We do not just become impervious to praise though never to denigration (as I say elsewhere) but in all kinds of circumstances the praise of thousands of esteemed people do not console us or counterbalance the pain inflicted by the derision, ill words, or disrespect by those most looked down upon, by a porter.

Translated from the Italian by W. S. Di Piero

Modern Shorts

NINETEENTH TO TWENTY-FIRST CENTURIES

LOUIS ("ALOYSIUS") BERTRAND

(France, 1807–1841)

Haarlem

While Amsterdam's golden cockerel doth sing and spin,
Haarlem's golden chicken dwells within."

—*THE CENTURIES* OF NOSTRADAMUS

Haarlem, that fine free-hand sketch, birthplace of the Flemish school, Haarlem as painted by Breughel the Elder, Peter Neefs, David Teniers and Paul Rembrandt.

With its canal full of shimmering blue water, and its church with flaming, golden windows, and the stone porches with bed-linen drying in the sun, with its roofs, green with straw.

And the storks sailing around the town clock, stretching out their necks to catch raindrops in their beaks.

And the slow-moving burgomeister stroking his double chin, and the lovelorn florist growing thinner and thinner, her eye battened upon a tulip.

And the gypsy leaning over his mandolin, and the old man playing upon the Rommelpot, and the child filling up his wineskin-bladder.

And the drinkers smoking in some dark dive, and the hotel-keeper's servant hanging up a dead pheasant in the window.

Translated from the French by Michael Benedikt

Ondine

. . . I thought I heard a delicate harmony troubling my sleep; beside my side I heard a murmur like some tender, sweet, interrupted song.

—*TRILBY,* CHARLES NODIER

"Listen!—Listen!—it's me, me, Ondine, flicking these droplets against the trembling panes of your window, your window aglow in the moon's regretful light; and here, in her silken dress, is the lady of the castle upon her balcony, staring at the starry night and the lovely, sleeping lake.

"Each ripple is a faerie creature, swimming with the current; every current of this stream is a path winding toward my palace, and my palace is built from the waters, waters you will find at the bottom of the lake, located in the triangle of fire, earth, and air.

"Listen!—Listen!—My father stirs the croaking stream with a green birch branch, and my sisters with their foaming arms embrace iris, water lilies, and glistening islands of grass; or, to make mock of the ancient, bearded willow, giggle as he goes on bending his back and fishing."

~

When her song was through, she begged me to slip her ring on my finger, to become an Ondine's husband; and to visit her palace with her, to become king of the lakes.

And when I told her I loved a mortal woman, resentful and sullen, she wept a teardrop or two; but then burst out into laughter, to disappear among the gleaming raindrops streaming down my blue-black window.

Translated from the French by Michael Benedikt

The Song of the Mask

Venice with the face of a mask.

It is not with the frock and the rosary beads; it is with the tambourine and the fool's habit that I, life, undertake this pilgrimage to death!

Our noisy band has hastened to Saint-Mark's Square from the Inn of Signor Arlecchino, who invited us all to a feast of macaroni with oil and polenta with garlic.

Let us join hands, you, ephemeral monarch, who assumes the crown of gilded paper, and you, his grotesque subjects, who form his retinue with your coats of a thousand patches, with your faded beards and wooden swords.

Let us join hands to sing and dance a roundelay, forgotten by the inquisitor, to the magic splendor of the fireworks of this night laughing like the day.

Let us sing and dance, we who are joyous, while the melancholy go down to the canal on the gondoliers' bench and weep watching the stars.

Let us sing and dance, we who have nothing to lose; while behind the curtain, where boredom is outlined on their sloping foreheads, our patricians gamble palaces and mistresses on a turn of the cards!

Translated from the French by John T. Wright

EDGAR ALLAN POE (United States, 1809–1849)

Instinct vs. Reason—A Black Cat

The line which demarcates the instinct of the brute creation from the boasted reason of man, is, beyond doubt, of the most shadowy and unsatisfactory character—a boundary line far more difficult to settle than even the North-Eastern or the Oregon. The question whether the lower animals do or do not reason, will possibly never be decided—certainly never in our present condition of knowledge. While the self-love and arrogance of man will persist in denying the reflective power to beasts, because the granting it seems to derogate from his own vaunted supremacy, he yet perpetually finds himself involved in the paradox of decrying instinct as an inferior faculty, while he is forced to admit its infinite superiority, in a thousand cases, over the very reason which he claims exclusively as his own. Instinct, so far from being an inferior reason, is perhaps the most exacted intellect of all. It will appear to the true philosopher as the divine mind itself acting *immediately* upon its creatures.

The habits of the lion-ant, of many kinds of spiders, and of the beaver, have in them a wonderful analogy, or rather similarity, to the usual operations of the reason of man—but the instinct of some other creatures has no such analogy—and is referable only to the spirit of the Deity itself, acting *directly*, and through no corporal organ, upon the volition of the animal. Of this lofty species of instinct the coral-worm affords a remarkable instance. This little creature, the architect of continents, is not only capable of building ramparts against the sea, with a precision of purpose, and scientific adaptation and arrangement, from which the most skillful engineer might imbibe his best knowledge—but is gifted with what humanity does not possess—with the absolute spirit of prophecy. It will foresee, for months in advance, the pure accidents which are to happen to its dwelling, and aided by myriads of its brethren, all acting as if with one mind (and *indeed* acting with only one—with the mind of the Creator) will work diligently to counteract influences which exist alone in the future. There is also an immensely wonderful consideration connected with the cell of the bee. Let a mathematician be required to solve the problem of the shape best calculated in such a cell as the bee wants, for the two requisites of strength and space—and he will find himself involved in the very highest and most abstruse questions of analytical research. Let him be required to tell the number of sides which will give to the cell the greatest space, with the greatest solidity, and to define the exact angle at which, with the same object in view, the roof must incline—and to answer the query, he must be a Newton or Laplace. Yet since bees were, they have been continually solving the problem. The leading distinction between instinct and reason seems to be, that, while the one is infinitely the more exact, the more certain, and the more farseeing in its sphere of action—the sphere of action in the other is of the far wider extent. But we are preaching a homily, when we merely intended to tell a short story about a cat.

The writer of this article is the owner of one of the most remarkable black cats in the world—and this is saying much; for it will be remembered that black cats are all of them witches. The one in question has not a white hair about her, and is of a demure and sanctified demeanor. That portion of the kitchen which she most frequents is accessible only by a door, which closes with what is termed a thumb-latch; these latches are rude in construction, and some force and dexterity are always requisite to force them down. But puss is in the daily habit of opening the door, which she accomplishes in the following way. She first springs from the ground to the guard of the latch (which resembles the guard over a gun-trigger,) and through this she thrusts her left arm to hold on with. She now, with her right hand, presses the thumb-latch until it yields, and here several attempts are frequently requisite. Having forced it down, however, she seems to be aware that her task is but half accomplished, since, if the door is not pushed open before she lets go, the latch will again fall into its socket. She, therefore, screws her body round so as to bring her hind feet immediately beneath the latch, while she leaps with all her strength from the door—the impetus of the spring forcing it open, and her hind feet sustaining the latch until this impetus is fairly given.

We have witnessed this singular feat a hundred times at least, and never without being impressed with the truth of the remark with which we commenced this article—that the boundary between instinct and reason is of a very shadowy nature. The black cat, in doing what she did, must have made use of all the perceptive and reflective faculties which we are in the habit of supposing the prescriptive qualities of reason alone.

*

I believe that Hannibal passed into Italy over the Pennine Alps; and if Livy were living now, I could demonstrate this fact even to him.

*

I make no exception, even in Dante's favor:—the only thing well said of Purgatory, is that a man may go farther and fare worse.

*

The Swedenborgians inform me that they have discovered all that I said in a magazine article, entitled "Mesmeric Revelation," to be absolutely true, although at first they were very strongly inclined to doubt my veracity—a thing which, in that particular instance, I never dreamed of not doubting myself. The story is pure fiction from beginning to end.

*

Words—printed ones especially—are murderous things. Keats did (or did not) die of a criticism, Cromwell of Titus' pamphlet "Killing no Murder," and Montfleury perished of the "Andromache." The author of the "'Parnasse Réformé" makes him thus speak in Hades—"*L'homme donc qui voudrait savoir ce dont je suis mort, qu'il ne demande pas s'il fût de fievre ou de podagre ou d'autre chose, mais qu'il entende que ce fut de L'Andromache.*" As for myself, I am fast dying of the "*Sartor Resartus.*"

*

All that the man of genius demands for his exhaltation is moral matter in motion. It makes no difference *whither* tends the motion—whether for him or against him—and it is absolutely of *no* consequence "*what* is the matter."

*

After reading all that has been written, and after thinking all that can be thought, on the topics of God and the soul, the man who has a right to say that he thinks at all, will find himself face to face with the conclusion that, on these topics, the most profound thought is that which can be the least easily distinguished from the most superficial statement.

*

An infinity of error makes its way into our Philosophy, through Man's habit of considering himself a citizen of a world solely— of an individual planet—instead of at least occasionally contemplating his position as a cosmopolite proper—as a denizen of the universe.

CHARLES BAUDELAIRE (France, 1821–1867)

The Stranger

Whom do you love best? do tell, you enigma: your father? your mother, sister, brother?
—I have no father, no mother, neither sister nor brother.
—Your friends?
—That is a word I've never understood.
—Your country?
—I don't know at what latitude to look for it.
—Beauty?
—Immortal goddess, I would gladly love her.
—Gold?
—I hate it as much as you hate God.
—Well then, you puzzling stranger, what do you love?

—I love clouds . . . clouds that go by . . . out there . . . over there . . . marvelous clouds!

Translated from the French by Keith Waldrop

Dog and Flask

"—My beautiful dog, good dog, dear bow-wow, come closer and sniff an excellent perfume, purchased at the best scent shop in town."

And the dog, wagging his tail, which I suppose, in these poor creatures, the sign corresponding to laugh and to smile, approaches and, curious, puts his moist nose to the unstoppered flask; after which, drawing back in fright, barks at me, clearly a reproach.

"—Ah! wretched dog, if I had offered you a bundle of excrement, you would have sniffed its scent with delight and perhaps devoured it. So you too, unworthy companion of my sad life, you are like the public, to whom one must not present the delicate perfumes which exasperate them, but carefully selected crap."

Translated from the French by Keith Waldrop

The Bad Glazier

There are natures purely contemplative, completely unsuited for action, who nevertheless, under mysterious unknown impulses, act sometimes with a rapidity of which they would suppose themselves incapable.

Those for instance who, afraid their concierge may have bad news for them, pace an hour timorously before daring to go in; those who hold letters for two weeks before opening them, or wait six months to take some step that has been immediately necessary for a year already—but sometimes abruptly feel precipitated into action by an irresistible force, like an arrow leaving the bow. Moralists and doctors, who claim to know everything, fail to explain from whence so sudden a mad energy comes to these lazy, voluptuous souls and why, incapable of the simplest and most necessary things, they find at certain moments a spurt of first class courage to execute the most absurd and even most dangerous actions.

A friend of mine, as harmless a dreamer as ever was, one day set a forest on fire, in order to see, he said, if a fire would catch as easily as generally claimed. Ten times the experiment failed; but the eleventh it was all too successful.

Another lit a cigar next to a powder keg, *to see, to see if, to tempt fate,* to force himself to prove his own energy, to gamble, to feel the pleasures of anxiety, for nothing, caprice, to kill time.

This sort of energy springs from ennui and reverie; and those in whom it so unexpectedly appears are in general, as I have said, the most indolent and dreamy of mortals.

Another, timid to the extent of lowering his eyes before any-body's gaze, to the point of having to pull together his poor will to enter a café or go past the ticket office of a theater (where the managers seem to him invested with the majesty of Minos, of Aeacus and of Rhadamanthus) will all of a sudden fall on the neck of some geezer and embrace him enthusiastically, to the astonishment of passers-by.

Why? Because . . . because of an irresistibly sympathetic physiognomy? Maybe, but we may well suppose that he himself has no idea.

More than once I have been victim to these crises, these out-bursts, that give some authority to the notion that malicious Demons slip into us and make us unwittingly accomplish their most absurd wishes.

One morning I got up on the wrong side, dejected, worn out from idleness, driven it seemed to me to perform some grand, some brilliant action. And, alas! I opened the window.

(Please note that the urge to practical jokes, in certain per-sons, the result neither of work nor planning, but of mere chance inspiration, belongs largely, even if only through the eagerness of desire, to that temper—hysterical according to doctors; by rather better minds than a doctor's, satanic—which drives us irresistibly towards a host of dangerous or indecent acts.)

The first person I noticed in the street was a glazier whose cry, piercing, discordant, came up to me through the oppressive and dirty Parisian atmosphere. Impossible for me to say why this poor fellow roused in me a hatred as sudden as despotic.

"—Hey there!" and I yelled for him to come up, meanwhile reflecting, not without amusement, that, my room being on the sixth floor and the stairs very narrow, the man would find it difficult to effect his ascent, to maneuver at certain spots the corners of his fragile merchandise.

Finally he appeared: I examined curiously all his glass and said to him: "What? you have no colored glass? pink, red, blue glass, magical glass, the glass of paradise? Shameful! you dare promenade this poor district and you don't even have glass to suggest a better life!" And I pushed him smartly towards the staircase where he stumbled growling.

I went to the balcony, picked up a little pot of flowers, and when the man came out of the door below, I let my war machine fall straight down, onto the edge of his hooks. The shock sending him over backwards, he smashed under his back the whole petty fortune he carried, from which burst the sound of a crystal palace shattered by a bolt of lightning.

And, drunk with my folly, I shouted at him, madly, "The beauty of life! the beauty of life!"

These nervous pleasantries are not without danger, and sometimes quite costly. But what's an eternity of damnation to one who has found in such an instant infinite satisfaction?

Translated from the French by Keith Waldrop

Get Drunk

You must get drunk. That's it: your sole imperative. To avoid the backbreaking, body-bending burdens of time, you must get drunk and stay that way.

On what? On wine, on poetry, or on virtue, your choice. But get drunk.

And if sometimes, while on the steps of a palace, on the green grass beside a marsh, in the morning solitude of your room, you snap out of it, your drunkenness has worn off, has worn off entirely, then ask the wind, ask an ocean wave, a star, a bird, a clock, every evanescent thing, everything that flies, that groans, that rolls, that sings, that speaks, ask them what time it is; and the wind, the wave, the star, the bird, the clock, will tell you: "It's time to get drunk! To avoid being the martyred slaves of time, get drunk, get drunk and stay that way. On wine, on poetry, or on virtue, your choice."

Translated from the French by David Lehman

AMBROSE BIERCE (United States, 1842–1914?)

The Pavior

An Author saw a Laborer hammering stones into the pavement of a street, and approaching him said:

"My friend, you seem weary. Ambition is a hard taskmaster."

"I'm working for Mr. Jones, sir," the Laborer replied.

"Well, cheer up," the Author resumed; "fame comes at the most unexpected times. To-day you are poor, obscure and disheartened, but to-morrow the world may be ringing with your name."

"What are you telling me?" the Laborer said. "Can not an honest pavior perform his work in peace, and get his money for it, and his living by it, without others talking rot about ambition and hopes of fame?"

"Can not an honest writer?" said the Author.

STÉPHANE MALLARMÉ (France, 1842–1898)

The Pipe

Yesterday I found my pipe while pondering a long evening of work, of fine winter work. Thrown aside were my cigarettes, with all the childish joys of summer, into the past which the leaves shining blue in the sun, the muslins, illuminate, and taken up once again was the grave pipe of a serious man who wants to smoke for a long while without being disturbed, so as better to work: but I was not prepared for the surprise that this abandoned object had in store for me; for hardly had I drawn the first puff when I forgot the grand books I was planning to write, and, amazed, moved to a feeling of tenderness, I breathed in the air of the previous winter which was now coming back to me. I had not been in contact with my faithful sweetheart since returning to France, and now all of London, London as I had lived it a year ago entirely alone, appeared before my eyes: first the dear fogs that muffle one's brains and have an odor of their own there when they penetrate beneath the casements. My tobacco had the scent of a somber room with leather furniture sprinkled by coal dust, on which the thin black cat would curl and stretch; the big fires! and the maid with red arms pouring coals, and the noise of those coals falling from the sheet-iron bucket into the iron scuttle in the morning—when the postman gave the solemn double knock that kept me alive! Once again I saw through the windows those sickly trees of the deserted square—I saw the open sea, crossed so often that winter, shivering on the deck of the steamer wet with drizzle and blackened from the fumes—with my poor wandering beloved, decked out in traveller's clothes, a long dress, dull as the dust of the roads, a coat clinging damply to her cold shoulders, one of those straw hats with no feather and hardly any ribbons that wealthy ladies throw away upon arrival, mangled as they are by the sea, and that poor loved ones refurbish for many another season. Around her neck was wound the terrible handkerchief that one waves when saying goodbye forever.

Reminiscence

Orphan, I was wandering in black and with an eye vacant of family: at the quincunx, the tents of a fair were unfolded; did I experience the future and that I would take this form? I loved the odor of the vagabonds, and was drawn toward them, forgetting my comrades. No cry of a chorus clamoring through the canvas rift, nor distant tirade, the drama requiring the holy hour of the footlights, I wanted to speak with an urchin too unsteady in his wavering to figure forth among his people, in a nightcap cut like Dante's hood—who was already returning to himself, in the guise of a slice of bread and soft cheese, the snow of mountain peaks, the lily, or some other whiteness constitutive of internal wings: I would have begged him to admit me to his superior meal, which was quickly shared with some illustrious older boy who had sprung up against a nearby tent and was engaged in feats of strength and banalities consistent with the day. Naked, he pirouetted in what seemed to me the surprising nimbleness of his tights and moreover began: "Your parents?—I have none.—Go on, if you knew what a farce that is, a father . . . even the other week when he was off his soup, he still made faces as funny as ever, when the boss was flinging out smacks and kicks. My dear fellow!" and triumphantly raising a leg toward me with glorious ease, "Papa astounds us"; then, biting into the little one's chaste meal: "Your mama, maybe you don't have one, maybe you're alone? Mine eats rope and everyone claps his hands. You have no idea what funny people parents are, how they make you laugh." The show was heating up, he left: myself, I sighed, suddenly dismayed at not having parents.

Translated from the French by Henry Weinfield

BOLESŁAW PRUS (Poland, 1847–1912)

Mold of the Earth

I happened one time to be in Puławy with a certain botanist. We were seating ourselves by the Temple of the Sibyl on a bench next to a boulder grown over with mosses or molds which my learned companion had been studying for some years.

I asked what he found of interest in the irregular splotches of beige, grey, green, yellow or red?

He looked at me doubtfully but, persuaded that he had before him an uninitiate, he proceeded to explain:

"These splotches that you see are not inanimate dirt but— collections of living beings. Invisible to the naked eye, they are born, carry out movements imperceptible to us, enter into matrimonial bonds, produce offspring, and finally die.

"More remarkably, they form as it were societies which you see here in the form of the variously colored splotches—they cultivate the ground beneath them for the next generations—they proliferate, colonize empty places, even fight one other.

"This grey splotch, large as the palm of a man's hand, two years ago was no larger than a penny. This tiny grey spot, a year ago, did not exist and comes from the great splotch that occupies the summit of the boulder.

"These two again, the yellow and the red, are fighting. At one time the yellow was the larger, but slowly it has been displaced by its neighbor. And look at the green one—how its grizzled neighbor is making inroads into it—how many grey streaks, spots, clumps you can see against the green background . . ."

"A bit as among people," I said.

"Well, no," replied the botanist. "These societies lack language, art, learning, consciousness, feeling—in a word, they lack souls and hearts, which we human possess. Here everything happens blindly, mechanically, without sympathy or antipathy."

A few years later I found myself at night beside that same boulder, and by the light of the moon I regarded the changes that had taken place in the shapes and sizes of the various molds.

Suddenly somebody nudged me. It was my botanist. I invited him to have a seat; but he stepped before me in such a way that he hid the moon, and he whispered something in a hollow voice.

The Temple of the Sibyl, the bench and the boulder vanished. I sensed about me a faint luminosity and an immense void. And when I turned my head, I saw something like a schoolroom globe that shone with a faint light, a globe as large as the boulder beside which we had been the moment before.

The globe slowly revolved, showing successive new areas. There was the Asian landmass with the little peninsula, Europe; there was Africa, the two Americas . . .

Looking intently, I made out on the inhabited lands the same kinds of splotches—beige, grey, green, yellow and red—as on the boulder. They comprised myriads of infinitesimal points, ostensibly motionless but actually moving very lazily: an individual point moved at most by a two-minute arc in an hour, and that not in a straight line but as it were oscillating about its own center of motion.

The points converged, separated, vanished, came to the surface of the globe: but all these things merited no particular attention. What was of consequence was the movements of entire splotches, which diminished or grew, appeared in new places, infiltrated or displaced one another.

Meanwhile the globe kept making its rounds and seemed to execute hundreds of thousands of revolutions.

"Is that supposed to be the history of mankind?" I asked the botanist, who stood beside me.

He nodded in confirmation.

"All right—but where are the arts and knowledge? . . ."

He smiled sadly.

"Where is consciousness, love, hate, yearning? . . ."

"Ha! ha! ha! . . ." he laughed softly.

"In short—where are the human souls and hearts? . . ."

"Ha! ha! ha! . . ."

I was offended by his demeanor.

"Who are you? . . ." I asked.

Just then I found myself back in the garden beside the boulder, whose shapeless splotches swam in the moonlight.

My companion had vanished, but now I knew him by his mockery and melancholy.

Translated from the Polish by Christopher Kasparek

KATE CHOPIN (United States, 1850–1904)

Ripe Figs

Maman-Nainaine said that when the figs were ripe Babette might go to visit her cousins down on the Bayou-Lafourche where the sugar cane grows. Not that the ripening of figs had the least thing to do with it, but that is the way Maman-Nainaine was.

It seemed to Babette a very long time to wait; for the leaves upon the trees were tender yet, and the figs were like little hard, green marbles.

But warm rains came along and plenty of strong sunshine, and though Maman-Naiaine was as patient as the statue of la Madone, and Babette as restless as a humming-bird, the first thing they both knew it was hot summer-time. Every day Babette danced out to where the fig-trees were in a long line against the fence. She walked slowly beneath them, carefully peering between the gnarled, spreading branches. But each time she came disconsolate away again. What she saw there finally was something that made her sing and dance the whole long day.

When Maman-Nainaine sat down in her stately way to breakfast, the following morning, her muslin cap standing like an aureole about her white, placid face, Babette approached. She bore a dainty porcelain platter, which she set down before her godmother. It contained a dozen purple figs, fringed around with their rich, green leaves.

"Ah," said Maman-Nainaine, arching her eyebrows, "how early the figs have ripened this year!"

"Oh," said Babette, "I think they have ripened very late."

"Babette," continued Maman-Nainaine, as she peeled the very plumpest figs with her pointed silver fruit-knife, "you will carry my love to them all down on Bayou-Lafourche. And tell your Tante Frosine I shall look for her at Toussaint—when the chrysanthemums are in bloom."

ROBERT LOUIS STEVENSON (Scotland, 1850–1894)

The Tadpole and the Frog

"Be ashamed of yourself," said the frog. "When I was a tadpole I had no tail."

"Just what I thought!" said the tadpole. "You never were a tadpole."

The Penitent

A man met a lad weeping. "What do you weep for?" he asked.

"I am weeping for my sins," said the lad.

"You must have little to do," said the man.

The next day they met again. Once more the lad was weeping. "Why do you weep now?" asked the man.

"I am weeping because I have nothing to eat," said the lad.

"I thought it would come to that," said the man.

ARTHUR RIMBAUD (France, 1854–1891)

After the Flood

No sooner had the notion of the Flood regained its composure,

Than a hare paused amid the gorse and trembling bellflowers and said its prayer to the rainbow through the spider's web.

Oh the precious stones that were hiding,—the flowers that were already peeking out.

Stalls were erected in the dirty main street, and boats were towed toward the sea, which rose in layers above as in old engravings.

Blood flowed in Bluebeard's house,—in the slaughterhouses, —in the amphitheaters, where God's seal turned the windows livid. Blood and milk flowed.

The beavers built. Tumblers of coffee steamed in the public houses.

In the vast, still-streaming house of windows, children in mourning looked at marvelous pictures.

A door slammed, and on the village square, the child waved his arms, understood by vanes and weathercocks everywhere, in the dazzling shower.

Madame xxx established a piano in the Alps. Mass and first communions were celebrated at the cathedral's hundred thousand altars.

The caravans left. And the Splendide Hotel was built amid the tangled heap of ice floes and the polar night.

Since then the Moon has heard jackals cheeping in thyme deserts,—and eclogues in wooden shoes grumbling in the orchard. Then, in the budding purple forest, Eucharis told me that spring had come.

—Well up, pond,—Foam, roll on the bridge and above the woods;—black cloths and organs,—lightning and thunder,—rise and roll;—Waters and sorrows, rise and revive the Floods.

For since they subsided,—oh the previous stones shoveled under, and the full-blown flowers!—so boring! and the Queen, the Witch who lights her coals in the clay pot, will never want to tell us what she knows, and which we do not know.

Departure

Enough seen. The vision has been encountered in all skies.

Enough had. Sounds of cities, in the evening, and in sunlight, and always.

Enough known. The stations of life.—O Sounds and Visions!

Departure amid new noise and affection!

Phrases

Once the world has been reduced to a single dark wood for our four astonished eyes,—and to a beach for two loyal children,—and to a musical house for our clear sympathy,—I'll find you.

When there's nothing on earth but a single old man, calm and handsome, surrounded by "unheard-of luxury,"—I'll kneel down and worship you.

When I've realized all your memories,—when I am she who knows how to garrotte you,—I'll smother you.

~

When we're very strong,—who's backing down? very merry, who collapses in ridicule? When we're very nasty, what would they do with us.

Adorn yourselves, dance, laugh,—I'll never be able to throw Love out the window.

~

—My friend, beggar girl, monstrous child! how little it all matters to you, these unhappy women and these machinations, and my embarrassment. Fasten yourself to us with your impossible voice, your voice! sole flatterer of this vile despair.

Translated from the French by John Ashbery

OSCAR WILDE (Ireland, 1854–1900)

The Artist

One evening there came into his soul the desire to fashion an image of *The Pleasure that abideth for a Moment*. And he went forth into the world to look for bronze. For he could only think in bronze.

But all the bronze of the whole world had disappeared, nor anywhere in the whole world was there any bronze to be found, save only the bronze of the image of *The Sorrow that endureth for Ever*.

Now this image he had himself, and with his own hands, fashioned, and had set it on the tomb of the one thing he had loved in life. On the tomb of the dead thing he had most loved had he set this image of his own fashioning, that it might serve as a sign of the love of man that dieth not, and a symbol of the sorrow of man that endureth for ever. And in the whole world there was no other bronze save the bronze of this image.

And he took the image he had fashioned, and set it in a great furnace, and gave it to the fire.

And out of the bronze of the image of *The Sorrow that endureth for Ever* he fashioned an image of *The Pleasure that abideth for a Moment*.

Theater Evening

She couldn't take the poodle with her into the theater. So the poodle stayed with me in the café and we awaited the mistress.

He stationed himself so as to keep an eye on the entrance, and I found this very expedient, if a bit excessive, since, honestly, it was only half past seven in the evening and we had to wait till a quarter past eleven.

We sat there and waited.

Every carriage that rattled by awakened hope in him, and every time I said to him: "It's not possible, it can't be her yet, be reasonable, it's just not possible!"

Sometimes I said to him: "Our beautiful, kind-hearted mistress—!"

He was positively sick with longing, twisted his head in my direction: "Is she coming or isn't she?!"

At one point he abandoned his guard post, came close to me, lay his paw on my knee and I kissed him.

As if he'd said to me: "Go ahead, tell me the truth, I can take anything!"

At ten o'clock he began to whine.

So I said to him: "Listen pal, don't you think I'm antsy? You've got to control yourself!"

But he didn't put much stock in control and whined.

Then he started softly weeping.

"Is she coming or isn't she?!"

"She's coming, she's coming—."

Then he lay himself perfectly flat on the floor and I sat there rather stooped over in my chair.

He wasn't whining any more, just stared at the entrance while I stared ahead of me.

It was a quarter to twelve.

She came at last. With her sweet, soft, sliding steps, she came quietly and collected, greeted us in her mild manner.

The poodle whined, sang out and leapt.

But I helped her off with her silken coat and hung it on a hook.

Then we sat down.

"Were you antsy?!" she asked.

As if one said: "How's life, my friend?" or: "Yours truly, N.N.!"

Then she said: "Oh, it was just wonderful in the theater—!"

But I felt: Longing, longing that flows and flows and flows from the hearts of man and beast, where do you go?! Do you perhaps evaporate in the heavens like water in the clouds?! Just as the atmosphere is full of water vapor so must the world be full and heavy with longings that came and found no soul to take them in! What happens to you, dear emotion, the best and most delicate thing in life, if you don't find willing souls greedy to soak you up and derive their own strength from yours?

Longing, longing, that flows from the hearts of man and beast, flooding, flooding the world, where do you go?

Traveling

There's one dirt cheap pleasure I know that's altogether free of disappointments, to study the train schedule from mid-May on and pick out the very train with which you would, if only.... So, for instance, at 8:45, you're already up and about and even shaved (to travel unshaven is only half a pleasure, better, if need be, to go without washing); so at 8:45 with the southbound express to Payerbach, and from there by one-horse carriage (my favorite driven by Michael Ruppert, Jr.) to the heavenly idyllic Thalhof Hotel. Once there you do nothing at all for the moment, seeing as you're actually still seated in your room in Vienna poring over your travel plans. Enough, everything's fine as it is, facing the forest, the cowshed, the horse stable, the bubbling trout brook, the laundry yard, the woodshed, where once, thirty years ago, with Anna Kaldermann—you gathered wood, and in the distance the hills near the Payerbachgräben where my father wanted to acquire a plot of land planted with sour cherry trees to flee to the holy refuge of nature, while my mother said: "Not until our two daughters are wed, my dear!" So there you sit before your travel plans, 8:45 departure time, dreaming sweet dreams free of the burdens of reality, and you just saved, conservatively speaking, at least twenty Crowns. For every change of place taxes the cost of your stay!

Translated from the German by Peter Wortsman

FÉLIX FÉNÉON (France, 1861–1944)

On the doorstep of the rectory in Suippes, Marne, a harmless box nevertheless caused excitement on account of its lit fuse and its wires.

*

Discharged Tuesday by his employer, 13-year-old Godillot, of Bagnolet, has not dared go home. Go there, son; they're waiting for you.

*

Satagnan, grape picker, declared, "I have struck grape picker d'Ay with a 22-cent knife. Bat d'Af and Cyrano are innocent."

*

A bottle floated by. Mauritz, of Sèvres, leaned over to grab it and fell into the Seine. He is now in the morgue.

Translated from the French by Luc Sante

JULES RENARD (France, 1864–1910)

The Mouse

As I sit under the lamp, writing out my daily page, I hear a faint noise. If I stop, it stops too. It begins again, as soon as I scratch my way across the paper.

It is a mouse waking up.

I sense her comings and going around the dark corner where the maid keeps her rags and brushes.

The mouse jumps onto the floor and trots across the kitchen tiles. She passes near the fireplace, under the sink, vanishes into the dishes, and by a series of reconnaissance missions which she extends farther and farther, approaches me.

Each time I set down my pen, the silence alarms her. Each time I use it, she thinks, I suppose, that there is another mouse somewhere, and this reassures her.

Then I lose sight of her. She is under my table, at my feet. She circulates from one chair leg to the next. She brushes against my shoes, nibbles the sole, or, boldly, gets up on top!

And now I must not move my leg, or breathe too hard: she would vanish.

But I have to go on writing, or else she would abandon me to my solitude—I write, I doodle, little things, tiny, dainty, the way she nibbles.

The Glow-Worm

What's going on? Nine o'clock and there's still a light on up there!

The Butterfly

This love-letter folded in two is looking for a flower's address.

The Kingfisher

They weren't biting, this evening, but I came home with a rare emotion.

While I was sitting there, holding out my line, a kingfisher came and perched on the rod.

We have no bird more brilliant.

He looked like a big blue flower on the end of a long stem. The rod bent under his weight. I held my breath, proud of being taken for a tree by a kingfisher.

And I'm sure he didn't fly away because he was frightened, but because he thought he was merely passing from one branch to another.

The Cage Without Birds

Felix does not understand how people can keep birds in cages.

"It's a crime," he says, "like picking flowers. Personally, I'd rather sniff them on their stems—and birds are meant to fly, the same way.

Nonetheless he buys a cage, hangs it in his window. He puts a cotton-wool nest inside, a saucer of seeds, and a cup of clean, renewable water. He also hangs a swing in the cage, and a little mirror.

And when he is questioned with some surprise:

"I pride myself on my generosity," he says, "each time I look at that cage. I could put a bird in there, but I leave it empty. If I wanted to, some brown thrush, some fat bullfinch hopping around outside, or some other bird of all the kinds we have here would be a captive. But thanks to me, at least one of them remains free. There's always that . . ."

Translated from the French by Richard Howard

RUBÉN DARÍO (Nicaragua, 1867–1916)

Juan Bueno's Losses

This is the story of a fellow called Juan Bueno—"Johnny Goodfellow," you see. People called him that because from the time he was a boy, when someone would give him a smack on one side of the head, he would turn his cheek for another. His schoolmates would take away his candies and cakes, strip him almost naked in the street, and when he got home, his parents, one on one side, one on the other, would pinch him and slap him until his ears rang. And so he grew up, until he became a man. How this poor Juan suffered! He got smallpox, but he didn't die, though his face was left looking as though a dozen hens had been pecking at it. He was sent to jail in the place of another Juan—Juan Lanas. And he suffered all this with such patience that all the townspeople, when they said *"There goes Juan Bueno!"* would laugh out loud.

And then the day came when this fellow got married.

One morning St. Joseph, in excellent humor, with his halo of glory upon his head, a new cloak upon his back, bright new sandals upon his feet, and his long flowering staff to aid him, went out for a walk through the village in which Juan Bueno lived and suffered. Christmas night was near, and St. Joseph was thinking about his baby, Jesus, and the preparations for his birth; he strolled along blessing the good believers and from time to time softly humming some carol or another. As he was walking along one street he heard a great racket, and much moaning and lamenting, and he found—oh, grievous sight!—Juan Bueno's wife, *bam, bam, bam,* giving her wretched spouse what-for.

"Halt!" called out the putative father of the divine Savior. I'll have no such rows in my presence!"

Just that short and sweet. The fierce Gorgon grew calmer, the couple made their peace, and when Juan told his tale of woe good St. Joseph consoled him, gave him a pat or two on the back, and as he bade him good night, he said to him:

"It will all be all right, my son. Soon your troubles will be over. In the meantime, I'll help you as much as I can. You know, with whatever comes along. You can find me in the parish church, the altar to the right. So long, now."

Happy as could be, was good Juan Bueno at these tidings. And it may well be imagined that he went off, day after day, almost hour after hour, to visit the shoulder he knew he could cry on.—Lord, this has happened! Lord, this other! Lord, can you imagine what's happened now! He asked for everything, and everything was granted. Well, not quite everything, because he was too embarrassed to tell the saint that his tyrant of a wife had not lost the habit of boxing his ears. So when St. Joseph would ask him, "What's that bump on your head there?" he would laugh and change the subject. But St. Joseph knew very well . . . and he admired Juan's forbearance.

One day Juan came in terribly sad and downcast.

"I've lost," he moaned, "a bag of silver I'd put away. Could you find it for me?"

"Well, that's really St. Anthony's job, but we'll see what we can do."

And indeed when Juan returned to his house, he found the little bag of silver.

Another day Juan came in with his face all swollen and one eye practically falling out of its socket.

"The cow you gave me has disappeared!"

And the kind saint replied:

"Go home, you'll find it."

And another time:

The mule you were so kind as to give me has run off!

And the saint replied:

"Now, now, off home with you, the mule will come back."

And so on, for many months.

Until one day the saint was not in the cheeriest of moods, and Juan Bueno came in with his face looking like an overripe tomato and his head all squashed out of shape. When the good saint saw him, he went, "Hm, hm."

"Lord, I come to ask another favor of you. My wife has left me, and since you are so good . . ."

St. Joseph's patience with Juan Bueno had reached its limit. He lifted his flowering staff and smacked Juan Bueno on the very top of his head, at a spot exactly between his ears.

"To hell with you—where you'll find her for yourself, you blockhead!"

Translated from the Spanish by Andrew Hurley

MARCEL SCHWOB (France, 1867–1905)

Cyril Tourneur: Tragic Poet

Cyril Tourneur was born out of the union of an unknown god with a prostitute. Proof enough of his divine origin has been found in the heroic atheism to which he succumbed. From his mother he inherited the instinct for revolt and luxury, the fear of death, the thrill of passion and the hate of kings. His father bequeathed him his desire for a crown, his pride of power and his joy of creating. To him both parents handed down their taste for nocturnal things, for a red glare in the night, and for blood.

The exact date of his birth is not known, though we are told that he appeared one dark day during a pestilential year.

No celestial protector watched over the woman whose body was swollen with this infant god, for the plague touched her several days before her confinement, and the door of her little house was marked with a red cross. At the moment when Cyril Tourneur was coming into the world the sexton at the cemetery began to toll the bell for the burial of the dead. Then, quite as his father had disappeared into that heaven common to all gods, so a green cart dragged his mother away to the common grave of men.

That night is said to have been so dark that the sexton had to hold a torch by the pesthouse door while the grim carter gathered his load. Another historian tells us how the mists upon the river Thames (by Cyril Tourneur's birthplace) were shot with scarlet rays while the sound of the bells was like the barking of cynocephales. There is little doubt but that a real star rose flaming over the house tops. The new born child shook his feeble fists as its fiery, malevolent gleams mottled his upturned face. So came Cyril Tourneur into the empty vastness of the Cimmerian night.

It is impossible to discover what were his thoughts or habits before he reached the age of thirty. The signs of his latent divinity had no record, nor do we know how he first recognized his hidden sovereignty. An obscure list of his blasphemies has come to light. From this document we know that he declared Moses nothing more than a juggler, while one named Heriot, he said, was an infinitely cleverer juggler than Moses. The beginning of religion, according to Cyril, consisted in terrorizing man. Christ, he held, merited death more than Barabbas, though Barabbas were thief and murderer. Should he, Cyril Tourneur, write a new religion, he said, he could vow to establish it upon a finer, more admirable basis. He thought the style of the New Testament wholly repugnant. He declared that his right to coin money was as good as the queen of England's, and furthermore, that he knew a man named Poole, a prisoner at Newgate, with whose aid he meant some day to strike gold pieces in his own image. A pious soul has erased the more terrible affirmations from this document.

Cyril Tourneur's words have been overheard and his gestures thought to indicate an atheism even more vindictive. He has been represented to us cloaked in a long black robe, a glorious twelve-starred crown on his head, his feet resting on the celestial sphere while he holds the terrestrial globe in his right hand. Pale as a wax taper on an altar, with eyes deeply aglow like burning incense, he walked the streets on stormy nights when the pest was over the city. Some have said he had a strange mark like a seal on his right thigh, but the point will never be verified since no one saw his body naked after death.

For mistress he took a prostitute from Bankside, a girl who had haunted the waterfront streets. He called her Rosamonde. His love for her was unique. On her blonde, innocent face the rouge spots burned like flickering flames, and she was very young. Rosamonde bore Cyril Tourneur a daughter whom he loved. Having been looked at by a prince, Rosamonde died tragically, drinking emerald-coloured poison from a transparent cup.

Vengeance merged with pride in Cyril's soul. Night came ... he walked the Mall, down the full length of that royal promenade, flourishing a torch of burning horsehair to illuminate his face, this poisoner prince. Hatred of all who reign was in his mouth and on his hands. So he became a highwayman, not to steal but to assassinate kings. Various princes who disappeared in those days were lighted to their death by Cyril Tourneur's torch before he killed them.

He would lie in wait along the queen's highway, hiding near some gravel pit or lime kiln. Selecting his victim from a group of travellers, he would offer to guide the gentleman through the quagmires. At the mouth of the pit he would extinguish his torch and hurl the unsuspecting man into the black hole. The gravel always gave way under their feet and Cyril would roll two enormous stones down to stifle the cries. In the dull glow of the kiln, he would sit through the night watching the cadaver as the lime consumed it.

When Cyril Tourneur had thus satisfied his hatred for kings he was assailed by his hatred of the gods. The divine spark within him urged him on to original creation. He dreamed of founding an entire generation out of his own blood—a race of gods on earth. He looked at his daughter. She was pure and desirable. To carry out his plan under the eyes of heaven he chose a cemetery as the most appropriate scene. Vowing to brave death and create a new humanity in the heart of that destruction decreed by the gods, Cyril Tourneur sought among old, dead bones to engender new ones. He carried out this project on the roof of a charnelhouse.

The end of his life is lost in a haze of obscurity. We may not be sure what pen has given us *The Athiest's Tragedy* and *The Revenger's Tragedy*. One legend pretends that the pride of Cyril Tourneur went still farther. He is said to have raised a black throne in his garden. Several persons have seen him sitting there with his gold crown on his head, though they all ran away, frightened by the long blue aigrettes waving to and fro above him. He read the poems of Empedocles in the manuscript. He often expressed his admiration for the manner in which the ancient poet died. No one saw the manuscript of Empedocles after Cyril Tourneur disappeared. That year the plague was come again, and the people of London took refuge on barges floating midstream in the Thames. One night a meteor flashed across the face of the moon. Moving with a sinister roar it whirled like a globe of white fire toward Cyril Tourneur's house. On his black throne, in his black robes and his golden crown, the man waited for the comet. Like a battle on the stage, an ominous blast of trumpets sounded a funereal fanfare across the night. In a shimmering, sanguine blaze, Cyril Tourneur was borne away to some unknown god in the somber, stormy regions of the sky.

Translated from the French by Lorimer Hammond

PAUL VALÉRY (France, 1871–1945)

Last Visit to Mallarmé

I saw Stéphane Mallarmé for the last time on the 14th of July, 1898, at Valvins. When lunch was over, he took me into his study. Four paces long by two paces wide; the window opening onto the Seine and onto the forest through foliage rent apart by light, and the smallest movements of the shining river faintly reflected on the walls.

Mallarmé was worried about the finishing touches to the construction of the *Coup de Dés*. The inventor was contemplating and touching up with a pencil this new machine which the Lahure Press had agreed to construct.

Nothing had so far been undertaken—or even considered—to give the form of the text a significance and an effect comparable to those of the text itself. Just as the everyday use of our limbs makes us almost forget their existence and neglect the variety of their resources, and just as it happens that an artist in the use of the human body sometimes points out to us all their suppleness, at the cost of his life which he consumes in exercises and which he exposes to the dangers of his addiction, so the habitual use of language, the practice of reading at random, and the use of everyday expressions, weaken the understanding of these too familiar acts and banish the very conception of their power and of their possible perfection, unless some person survives and dedicates himself who is particularly disdainful of the easy ways of the mind, but singularly attentive to what he can produce that is most unexpected and most subtle.

I was in the presence of such a person. Nothing told me that I should never see him again. On this golden day there was no raven to foretell it.

Everything was calm and certain.... But while Mallarmé was talking to me, with his finger on the page, I remember that my mind began to contemplate this particular moment. Absent-mindedly I gave it an almost absolute value. Near him while he was still alive, I thought of his destiny as already realized. Born for the delight of some and to the dismay of others, and to the amazement of all; for the latter a madness and an absurdity; for his own kind a marvel of pride, elegance and intellectual modesty, a few poems had sufficed for him to put in doubt the very purpose of literature. His work, difficult to understand and impossible to neglect, divided literate people. Poor and without honors, the nakedness of his condition disgraced all the advantages that others had; but he was assured, without having looked for it, of extraordinary loyalty. As for him, whose wise, disdainful victim's smile quietly disposed of the universe, he had never asked anything of the world but the most precious and rarest things it contained. He found them in himself.

~

We went into the country. The 'artificial' poet gathered the simplest flowers. Our arms were filled with corn-flowers and poppies. The air was on fire; the splendor absolute; the silence full of intoxication and communication; death impossible or unimportant; everything amazingly beautiful, afire and asleep; and the landscape trembled.

In the sun, in the immense arc of the cloudless sky, I dreamed of an incandescent space where nothing distinct exists, where nothing lasts, but where nothing ends, as if destruction itself was destroyed before it was accomplished. I lost my perception of the difference between being and not-being. Sometimes music gives us this impression, which is beyond all others. Is not poetry, I thought, the supreme pastime of transmuting ideas? . . .

Mallarmé pointed out to me the plain which summer was already beginning to turn to gold; "Look," he said, "it is the first drum-beat of autumn on the earth."

When autumn came, he was no more.

Translated from the French by Anthony Bower

MACEDONIO FERNÁNDEZ (Argentina, 1874–1952)

A Novel for Readers with Nerves of Steel

A Sunday rain was falling, completely by mistake, since it was Tuesday, the dry day of the week par excellence. Even so, nothing was happening: the all-out-strike order of things was carried out without incident.

Without disturbing this embroiled state of affairs I pushed back my chair, making the noise with which a petty tyrant under-assistant-bureaucrat sets twenty underlings quaking in their boots and yawning. I took my rack from its hat and, putting both arms into the sleeves, wound the calendar, ripped that day's leaf from the clock, put some coal in the icebox, added ice to the stove, supplemented the wall thermometer with all the thermometers I had handy just to ward off an approaching cold spell, and, as a streetcar ran catchably by, I sprang to the sidewalk and fell comfortably into my desk easy chair.

Here was a matter for thought: the days were going by all at once and yet no light was shed on the mystery (no one knew that there was one) of the forthcoming bridge. First: we were shown a diagram of the bridge, showing how far construction had progressed, before anyone had even thought of bringing it into existence; second: a sketch of what the bridge was like when somebody was thinking of it; third: a photograph of someone crossing the bridge; fourth: construction is begun on the first span. In short: the bridge was already finished, but it had to be extended over to the opposite bank, since due to an oversight the bridge had been built to go from one bank to the same bank of the river.

And why was it that the government official, whose carefully-considered speech was dedicated, with throat-clearing eloquence, to the bridge, since one or the other of them had a slight cold, I'm not sure which one, accuse it of ingratitude toward the government?

You don't need to be reminded how humanity has suffered from the ingratitude of bridges. Yet, in this case, where did the ingratitude lie? Surely not over on the other side of the river, because the bridge didn't lead to that side and, in truth, the great labor that lay at hand was to get the water to flow under the bridge. It was the least that could be demanded and expected of a river that had so far played no part in the bridge effort.

Translated from the Spanish by Jo Anne Engelbert

KARL KRAUS (Austria, 1874–1936)

A pretty little girl hears a pawing noise at the wall of her room. She is afraid it is mice, and only becomes calm when she is told there is a stable next door and a horse is moving around. "Is it a stallion?" she asks, and goes to sleep.

*

Aphorisms are never congruent with the truth: they are either half-truths or one-and-a-half.

*

My wish that my things be read twice has aroused great bitterness. Unjustly so; the wish is modest. It is not as if I asked that they be read once.

Translated from the German by Jonathan McVity

GERTRUDE STEIN (United States / France, 1874–1946)

A Cloth

Enough cloth is plenty and more, more is almost enough for that and besides if there is no more spreading is there plenty of room for it. Any occasion shows the best way.

A Drawing

The meaning of this is entirely and best to say the mark, best to say it best to show sudden places, best to make bitter, best to make the length tall and nothing broader, anything between the half.

Water Raining

Water astonishing and difficult altogether makes a meadow and a stroke.

A Petticoat

A light white, a disgrace, an ink spot, a rosy charm.

Shoes

To be a wall with a damper a stream of pounding way and nearly enough choice makes a steady midnight. It is pus.

A shallow hole rose on red, a shallow hole in and in this makes ale less. It shows shine.

SHERWOOD ANDERSON (United States, 1876–1941)

Man Walking Alone

The nights in the valley of the Mississippi River have the eyes of an owl. I have risen from the place where I slept under a tree but cannot shake the sleep out of my eyes. The nights in the valley of the Mississippi River are staring nights. They look at men with the pupils extended. The skies are empty over the cities and the plains. The skies have not formulated a thought that I can breathe into my being. In the whole valley of the Mississippi River there is no bed of thought in which I can lie.

·

There are farm women living in houses that stand beside dusty roads in Illinois and Iowa. In Indiana and Ohio there are many towns. In Michigan—far up where the valley is no more and where the cold finger of the north touches the earth in September—there are men living who wear heavy boots and fur caps and who walk all day under naked trees.

Everywhere are men and women who arouse wonder in me. I have awakened the feeling of wonder in myself. I have awakened from sleeping under a tree.

MAX JACOB (France, 1876–1944)

Fake News! New Graves!

During a performance at the Opéra of *For the Crown*, when Desdemona sings "My father is in Goritz and my heart is in Paris," a shot was heard in a box on the fifth balcony, then another in the orchestra and instantly rope ladders were uncoiled; a man climbed down from the top of the house: a bullet stopped him on the balcony level. The whole audience was armed and it turned out the hall was filled with nothing but . . . and . . . Then neighbors were murdered, jets of liquid fire. There was the siege of the boxes, the siege of the stage, the siege of a folding chair and the battle lasted eighteen days. Maybe the two camps were resupplied, I don't know, but what I know for sure is the newsmen all came for the grim performance, that one of them, being sick, sent his dear mother and she was deeply impressed by the sang-froid of a young French gentleman who held out for eighteen days in a proscenium box on nothing more than a little bouillon. This episode of the War of the Balconies did a lot for voluntary enlistments in the provinces. And I know of three brothers in brand-new uniforms, on my river bank, under my trees, who embraced each other dry-eyed while their families searched for sweaters in attic armoires.

Translated from the French by William T. Kulik

The Beggar Woman of Naples

When I lived in Naples there was always a beggar woman at the gate of my palace, to whom I would toss some coins before climbing into my carriage. One day, surprised at never being thanked, I looked at the beggar woman. Now, as I looked at her, I saw that what I had taken for a beggar woman was a wooden case painted green which contained some red earth and a few half-rotten bananas. . . .

Translated from the French by John Ashbery

Literature and Poetry

It was near Lorient, the sun shone brightly and we used to go for walks, watching through those September days the sea rising, rising to cover woods, landscapes, cliffs. Soon there was nothing left to combat the blue sea but the meandering paths under the trees and the families drew closer together. Among us was a child in a sailor suit. He was sad and took me by the hand: "Sir," he said, "I have been in Naples; do you know that in Naples there are lots of little streets; in the streets you can stay all alone without anyone seeing you: it's not that there are many people in Naples but there are so many little streets that there is never more than one street for each person." "What stories is the child telling you now," said the father. "He has never been to Naples." "Sir, your child is a poet." "That's all right, but if he is a man of letters I'll wring his neck." The meandering paths left dry by the sea had made him think of the streets of Naples

Translated from the French by John Ashbery

Loving Thy Neighbor

Who's watched a toad cross the street? He looks like a very small man: no bigger than a doll. He crawls along on his knees: do we say he looks ashamed?...no! That he's got rheumatism. A leg drags behind, he pulls it forward. Where's he headed like this? He came up out of the sewer, poor clown. No one noticed him on the street. Long time ago no one noticed me. Now the children mock my yellow star. Lucky toad, you don't have a yellow star.

Translated from the French by William T. Kulik

Reconstruction

All it takes is a five-year-old in pale blue overalls drawing in a coloring book for a door to open into the light, for the house to be built again and the ochre hillside covered with flowers.

Translated from the French by William T. Kulik

FILIPPO TOMMASO MARINETTI
(Egypt / Italy, 1876–1944)

The Automotive Kiss (10th Letter to Rose of Belgrade)

Believe me, the only kiss worthy of our futurist generation is the automotive kiss. Yes, kissing while speeding. You, defiant driver, with your left hand on the steering wheel, will lean out of the right side of the car. And I? . . . In another car sitting next to my young driver, who naturally will fall madly in love with you, I will lean out of the left side, looking for your lips. In flight!

Piston of desire. The oil of fortune circulates in the gear of thought. The tension of our wills shapes the road whose touching or threatening undulations can, at any moment, merge into a crashing mortal kiss . . .

To be avoided, of course! Especially since my driver will feel his own hands trembling from the vibrations of the steering wheel. Jealousy, his and mine. The road ferocious.

With all the spice of danger, it is nonetheless necessary to accelerate the motor and to concentrate all our thousand souls in our tendered lips. Finally, finally, let the spark dart and dart again from the four pulpy folds charged with infinity . . .

A spark which has turned into fire, the unending fire of a terrifying kiss. Would you like it?

With what sort of car?
At what speed?
I am at your disposal and I await orders.

Translated from the Italian by Graziella Olga Sidoli

LORD DUNSANY (Ireland, 1878–1957)

The Demagogue and the Demi-Monde

A demagogue and a demi-mondaine chanced to arrive together at the gate of Paradise. And the Saint looked sorrowfully at them both.

"Why were you a demagogue?" he said to the first.

"Because," said the demagogue, "I stood for those principles that have made us what we are and have endeared our Party to the great heart of the people. In a word I stood unflinchingly on the plank of popular representation."

"And you?" said the Saint to her of the demi-monde.

"I wanted money," said the demi-mondaine.

And after some moments' thought the Saint said: "Well, come in; though you don't deserve to."

But to the demagogue he said: "We genuinely regret that the limited space at our disposal and our unfortunate lack of interest in those Questions that you have gone so far to inculcate and have so ably upheld in the past, prevent us from giving you the support for which you seek."

And he shut the golden door.

EDWARD THOMAS (England, 1878–1917)

One Sail at Sea

This is a simple world. On either hand the shore sweeps out in a long curve and ends in a perpendicular, ash-coloured cliff, carving the misty air as with a hatchet-stroke. The shore is of tawny, terraced sand, like hammered metal from the prints of the retreating waves; and here and there a group of wildly carved and tragic stones—*unde homines nati, durum genus*—such as must have been those stones from which Deucalion made the stony race of men to arise. Up over the sand, and among these stones the water slides in tracery like May blossom or silver mail. A little way out, the long wave lifts itself up laboriously into a shadowy cliff, nods proudly and crumbles, vain and swift, into a thousand sparks of foam. Far out the desolate, ridgy leagues vibrate and murmur with an unintelligible voice, not less intelligible than when one man says, "I believe," or another man, "I love," or another, "I am your friend." Almost at the horizon a sharp white sail sways, invisibly controlled. In a minute it does not move; in half an hour it has moved. It fascinates and becomes the image of the watcher's hopes, as when in some tranquil grief we wait, with faint curiosity and sad foretelling, to see how our plans will travel, smiling a little even when they stray or stop, because we have foretold it. Will the sail sink? Will it take wing into the sky? Will it go straight and far, and overcome and celebrate its success? But it only fades away, and presently another is there unasked, yet not surprising, and it also fades away, and the night has come, and still the sea speaks with tongues. In the moonlight one strange flower glistens, white as a campanula, like a sweet-pea in shape—the bleached thigh-bone of a rat—and we forget the rest.

ROBERT WALSER (Switzerland, 1878–1956)

The Job Application

Esteemed gentlemen,

I am a poor, young, unemployed person in the business field, my name is Wenzel, I am seeking a suitable position, and I take the liberty of asking you, nicely and politely, if perhaps in your airy, bright, amiable rooms such a position might be free. I know that your good firm is large, proud, old, and rich, thus I may yield to the pleasing supposition that a nice, easy, pretty little place would be available, into which, as into a kind of warm cubbyhole, I can slip. I am excellently suited, you should know, to occupy just such a modest haven, for my nature is altogether delicate, and I am essentially a quiet, polite, and dreamy child, who is made to feel cheerful by people thinking of him that he does not ask for much, and allowing him to take possession of a very, very small patch of existence, where he can be useful in his own way and thus feel at ease. A quiet, sweet, small place in the shade has always been the tender substance of all my dreams, and if now the illusions I have about you grow so intense as to make me hope that my dream, young and old, might be transformed into delicious, vivid reality, then you have, in me, the most zealous and most loyal servitor, who will take it as a matter of conscience to discharge precisely and punctually all his duties. Large and difficult tasks I cannot perform, and obligations of a far-ranging sort are too strenuous for my mind. I am not particularly clever, and first and foremost I do not like to strain my intelligence overmuch. I am a dreamer rather than a thinker, a zero rather than a force, dim rather than sharp. Assuredly there exists in your extensive institution, which I imagine to be overflowing with main and subsidiary functions and offices, work of the kind that one can do as in a dream?—I am, to put it frankly, a Chinese; that is to say, a person who deems everything small and modest to be beautiful and pleasing, and to whom all that is big and exacting is fearsome and horrid. I know only the need to feel at my ease, so that each day I can thank God for life's boon, with all its blessings. The passion to go far in the world is unknown to me. Africa with its deserts is to me not more foreign. Well, so now you know what sort of a person I am.—I write, as you see, a graceful and fluent hand, and you need not imagine me to be entirely without intelligence. My mind is clear, but it refuses to grasp things that are many, or too many by far, shunning them. I am sincere and honest, and

I am aware that this signifies precious little in the world in which we live, so I shall be waiting, esteemed gentlemen, to see what it will be your pleasure to reply to your respectful servant, positively drowning in obedience.

WENZEL

Translated from the German by Christopher Middleton

A Little Ramble

I walked through the mountains today. The weather was damp, and the entire region was gray. But the road was soft and in places very clean. At first I had my coat on; soon, however, I pulled it off, folded it together, and laid it upon my arm. The walk on the wonderful road gave me more and ever more pleasure; first it went up and then descended again. The mountains were huge, they seemed to go around. The whole mountainous world appeared to me like an enormous theater. The road snuggled up splendidly to the mountainsides. Then I came down into a deep ravine, a river roared at my feet, a train rushed past me with magnificent white smoke. The road went through the ravine like a smooth white stream, and as I walked on, to me it was as if the narrow valley were bending and winding around itself. Gray clouds lay on the mountains as though that were their resting place. I met a young traveler with a rucksack on his back, who asked if I had seen two other young fellows. No, I said. Had I come here from very far? Yes, I said, and went farther on my way. Not a long time, and I saw and heard the two young wanderers pass by with music. A village was especially beautiful with humble dwellings set thickly under the white cliffs. I encountered a few carts, otherwise nothing, and I had seen some children on the highway. We don't need to see anything out of the ordinary. We already see so much.

Translated from the German by Tom Whalen

GUILLAUME APOLLINAIRE (France, 1880–1918)

Little Recipes from Modern Magic

To Jean Mollet

The following manuscript was found in front of the omnibus office on the Place Pereire, the tenth of July this year.

I'm holding it at the owner's disposal if he can give me its exact description.

I have no idea of the real value of the recipes you're about to read. But they seemed to me sufficiently odd to arouse one's curiosity.

The magician's industry, which in our time is taking on the proportions of one of the most enjoyable arts—I'd almost say one of the most useful to high society—magic, had to undergo numerous transformations to get out of the ruts laid down by charlatanism and routine. The abuse seen in this last century, with table-turning, all kinds of mediums, hypnotism, cards, offhand palmistry, coffee grounds often harmful to the health, as in Turkey, for example, have given birth to troublesome and often exaggerated prejudices. The magician has been replaced by the fortune teller, if not by the clairvoyant.

But since the magician, refusing to compete with these absurd rivals, calls for surprising combinations from science and the fine arts, concerns himself above all with hygiene, studies the raw materials, arranges them in a rational manner, since finally magic has taken on new forms in perfect harmony with good taste and reason, these prejudices have greatly diminished. They will disappear completely when creations made for the theatre and costume parties are distinguished from those destined for good company. For the former, the recipes for fast results, but too violent to endure. For the salons, the simple and suave combinations, the serious methods, which, without appearing to do so, master destiny, and which, in short, confer power and talent.

Considered from this double point of view, the magician's art merits the esteem and the interest of sensible people. I hope to show one proof of this in these recipes chosen for use by society people.

Salve for avoiding car trouble

It's very easy to make. You take several fillets of sole—new shoes are not necessary, old ones being fine for this use: in fact the sole should be aged well. Take every precaution that the sole not take on your odor as you clean it—to do so, dredge your hands in flour beforehand. Cut the sole into pieces and put them in a basket in the oven. When they have lost all their moisture, grind them up in a mortar and pass the dust through a very fine sieve. Finally, mix it with a solution of horse fat. You'll be delighted with it.

Poetry meters

It sometimes happens that such-and-such a young man—nearly a child—becomes highly successful in the salons with his metrics or with others' metrics, and one would wish to do the same.

Go to work for the gas company and you'll learn all about meters; if the recipe doesn't succeed, go to a gymnasium and learn about isometrics; and if that fails, study the metric system.

Another recipe for poetry

You should always carry an umbrella you never open. Revealed by M. André B., this recipe is supposed to have been entrusted to him by our dear M. P.F., prince of poets.

N.B. This most effective recipe is not easily used.

Vinegar for pennies from heaven

Take three pounds of freshly picked ice leaves. Peel them and spread them to dry somewhat; do not forget to stir from time to time so they won't warm up. Next let them marinate in twelve quarts of good Orléans vinegar. Then distill in a double boiler, over a medium heat at the start. You will easily obtain eight quarts from this operation and pennies will rain down in abundance.

Antihygienic powder for having lots of children

Powdered beans from last season	3 kg
Sifted sugar	1 kg
Magnesium	11 cc

Season it all with dried rose petals. Sprinkle it on your bed-sheets and do not get up until you have succeeded.

Eau de vie for speaking well

Para cress (spilanthus oleiacenus) in flower	
and with stems removed	125 g
Alcohol at 33 degrees	500 g
Macaroni	10g

Shake well before using, then wash your feet thoroughly with it.

Incantation for beating the stock market

Every morning you will eat a red herring while uttering forty times before and after: "Bucks and plug, clink and drink." And after ten days your dead stock will become live stock.

Recipe for glory

Carry with you four fountain pens, drink clear water, have a great man's mirror, and often look at yourself in it without smiling.

Remedy for arthritis

Drink gin and water and you'll see its effects before two months.

END OF THE LITTLE METHOD

~

It should be added that trustworthy people, among whom M. René Dalize, have used some of these recipes and have acknowledged their complete effectiveness.

Translated from the French by Ron Padgett

ROBERT MUSIL (Austria, 1880–1942)

Fishermen on the Baltic

On the beach they've dug out a little pit with their hands, and from a sack of black earth they're pouring in fat earthworms; the loose black earth and the mass of worms make for an obscure, moldy, enticing ugliness in the clean white sand. Beside this a very tidy looking wooden chest is placed. It looks like a long, not particularly wide drawer or counting board, and is full of clean yarn; and on the other side of the pit another such, but empty, drawer is placed.

The hundred hooks attached to the yarn in the one drawer are neatly arranged on the end of a small iron pole and are now being unfastened one after the other and laid in the empty drawer, the bottom of which is filled with nothing but clean wet sand. A very tidy operation. In the meantime, however, four long, lean and strong hands oversee the process as carefully as nurses to make sure that each hook gets a worm.

The men who do this crouch two by two on knees and heels, with mighty, bony backs, long, kindly faces, and pipes in their mouths. They exchange incomprehensible words that flow forth as softly as the motion of their hands. One of them takes up a fat earthworm with two fingers, tears it into three pieces with the same two fingers of the other hand, as easily and exactly as a shoemaker snips off the paper band after he's taken the measurement; the other one then presses these squirming pieces calmly and carefully onto each hook. This having been accomplished, the worms are then doused with water and laid in neat little beds, one next to the other, in the drawer with the soft sand, where they can die without immediately losing their freshness.

It is a quiet, delicate activity, whereby the coarse fishermen's fingers step softly as on tiptoes. You have to pay close attention. In fair weather the dark blue sky arches above and the seagulls circle high over the land like white swallows.

Clearhearing

I went to bed earlier than usual, feeling a slight cold, I might even have a fever. I am staring at the ceiling, or perhaps it's the reddish curtain over the balcony door of our hotel room that I see; it's hard to distinguish.

As soon as I'd finished with it, you too started to undress. I'm waiting. I can only hear you.

Incomprehensible, all the walking up and down; in this corner of the room, in that. You come over to lay something on your bed; I don't look up, but what could it be? In the meantime, you open your closet, put something in or take something out; I hear it close again. You lay hard, heavy objects on the table, others on the marble top of the commode. You are forever in motion. Then I recognize the familiar sounds of hair being undone and brushed. Then swirls of water in the sink. Even before that, clothes being shed; now, again; it's just incomprehensible to me how many clothes you take off. Finally, you've slipped out of your shoes. But now your stockings slide as constantly back and forth over the soft carpet as your shoes did before. You pour water into glasses; three, four times without stopping, I can't even guess why. In my imagination I have long since given up on anything imaginable, while you evidently keep finding new things to do in the realm of reality. I hear you slip into your nightgown. But you aren't finished yet and won't be for a while. Again there are a hundred little actions. I know that you're rushing for my sake; so all this must be absolutely necessary, part of your most intimate I, and like the mute motion of animals from morning till evening, you reach out with countless gestures, of which you're unaware, into a region where you've never heard my step!

By coincidence I feel it all, because I have a fever and am waiting for you.

Translated from the German by Peter Wortsman

JUAN RAMÓN JIMÉNEZ (Spain / Puerto Rico, 1881–1958)

The Moon

New York, April 23
To Alfonso Reyes

Broadway. Evening. Signs in the sky that make one dizzy with color. New constellations: The Pig, all green, dancing and waving greetings to the left and right with his straw hat, the Bottle which pops its ruddy cork with a muted detonation against a sun with eyes and a mouth, the Electric Stocking which dances madly by itself like a tail separated from a salamander, the Scotchman who displays and pours his whiskey with its white reflections, the Fountain of mallow-pink and orange water through whose shower, like a snake, pass hills and valleys of wavering sun and shade, links of gold and iron (that braid a shower of light and another of darkness ...), the Book which illuminates and extinguishes the successive imbecilities of its owner, the Ship which every moment, as it lights up, sails pitching toward its prison, to run aground immediately in the darkness ... and ...

The moon! Let's see! Look at it between those two tall buildings over there, above the river, over the red octave beneath, don't you see it? Wait, let's see! No ... is it the moon or just an advertisement of the moon?

Translated from the Spanish by H. R. Hayes

Long Stories

Long stories! That long! One page long! When will the day come when people will learn to lengthen a spark all the way to the sun from a sun gathered within a spark given to them by a man; the day we all realize nothing has size and that, therefore, what is sufficient is enough; the day we understand that things do not gain their worth from their size—this would put an end to the ridiculous attitudes seen by Micromega and that I see daily—(the day) when a whole book may be reduced to the size of an ant's hand, for an idea may enlarge it and turn it into the universe!

Translated from the Spanish by Antonio de Nicolás

VIRGINIA WOOLF (England, 1882–1941)

A Haunted House

Whatever hour you woke there was a door shutting. From room to room they went, hand in hand, lifting here, opening there, making sure—a ghostly couple.

"Here we left it," she said. And he added, "Oh, but here too!" "It's upstairs," she murmured. "And in the garden," he whispered. "Quietly," they said, "or we shall wake them."

But it wasn't that you woke us. Oh, no. "They're looking for it; they're drawing the curtain," one might say, and so read on a page or two. "Now they've found it," one would be certain, stopping the pencil on the margin. And then, tired of reading, one might rise and see for oneself, the house all empty, the doors standing open, only the wood pigeons bubbling with content and the hum of the threshing machine sounding from the farm. "What did I come in here for? What did I want to find?" My hands were empty. "Perhaps its upstairs then?" The apples were in the loft. And so down again, the garden still as ever, only the book had slipped into the grass.

But they had found it in the drawing-room. Not that one could ever see them. The windowpanes reflected apples, reflected roses; all the leaves were green in the glass. If they moved in the drawing-room, the apple only turned its yellow side. Yet, the moment after, if the door was opened, spread about the floor, hung upon the walls, pendant from the ceiling—what? My hands were empty. The shadow of a thrush crossed the carpet; from the deepest wells of silence the wood pigeon drew its bubble of sound. "Safe, safe, safe," the pulse of the house beat softly. "The treasure buried; the room . . ." the pulse stopped short. Oh, was that the buried treasure?

A moment later the light had faded. Out in the garden then? But the trees spun darkness for a wandering beam of sun. So fine, so rare, coolly sunk beneath the surface the beam I sought always burnt behind the glass. Death was the glass; death was between us; coming to the woman first, hundreds of years ago, leaving the house, sealing all the windows; the rooms were darkened. He left it, left her, went North, went East, saw the stars turned in the Southern sky; sought the house, found it dropped beneath the Downs. "Safe, safe, safe," the pulse of the house beat gladly. "The Treasure yours."

The wind roars up the avenue. Trees stoop and bend this way and that. Moonbeams splash and spill wildly in the rain. But the beam of the lamp falls straight from the window. The candle burns stiff and still. Wandering through the house, opening the windows, whispering not to wake us, the ghostly couple seek their joy.

"Here we slept," she says. And he adds, "Kisses without number." "Waking in the morning—" "Silver between the trees—" "Upstairs—" 'In the garden—" "When summer came—" 'In winter snowtime—" "The doors go shutting far in the distance, gently knocking like the pulse of a heart.

Nearer they come; cease at the doorway. The wind falls, the rain slides silver down the glass. Our eyes darken; we hear no steps beside us; we see no lady spread her ghostly cloak. His hands shield the lantern. "Look," he breathes. "Sound asleep. Love upon their lips."

Stooping, holding their silver lamp above us, long they look and deeply. Long they pause. The wind drives straightly; the flame stoops slightly. Wild beams of moonlight cross both floor and wall, and, meeting, stain the faces bent; the faces pondering; the faces that search the sleepers and seek their hidden joy.

"Safe, safe, safe," the heart of the house beats proudly. "Long years—" he sighs. "Again you found me." "Here," she murmurs, "sleeping; in the garden reading; laughing, rolling apples in the loft. Here we left our treasure—" Stooping, their light lifts the lids upon my eyes. "Safe! safe! safe!" the pulse of the house beats wildly. Waking, I cry "Oh, is this *your* buried treasure? The light in the heart."

FRANZ KAFKA (Austria-Hungary, 1883–1924)

Poseidon

Poseidon sat at his desk, going over the accounts. The administration of all the waters gave him endless work. He could have had as many assistants as he wanted, and indeed he had quite a number, but since he took his job very seriously he insisted on going through all the accounts again himself, and so his assistants were of little help to him. It cannot be said that he enjoyed the work; he carried it out simply because it was assigned to him; indeed he had frequently applied for what he called more cheerful work, but whenever various suggestions were put to him it turned out that nothing suited him so well as his present employment. Needless to say, it was very difficult to find him another job. After all, he could not possibly be put in charge of one particular ocean. Quite apart from the fact that in this case the work involved would not be less, only more petty, the great Poseidon could hold only a superior position. And when he was offered a post unrelated to the waters, the very idea made him feel sick, his divine breath came short and his brazen chest began to heave. As a matter of fact, no one took his troubles very seriously; when a mighty man complains one must pretend to yield, however hopeless the case may seem. No one ever really considered relieving Poseidon of his position; he had been destined to be God of the Seas since time immemorial, and that was how it had to remain.

What annoyed him most—and this was the chief cause of discontent with his job—was to learn of the rumors that were circulating about him; for instance, that he was constantly cruising through the waves with his trident. Instead of which here he was sitting in the depths of the world's ocean endlessly going over the accounts, an occasional journey to Jupiter being the only interruption of the monotony, a journey moreover from which he invariably returned in a furious temper. As a result he had hardly seen the oceans, save fleetingly during his hasty ascent to Olympus, and had never really sailed upon them. He used to say that he was postponing this until the end of the world, for then there might come a quiet moment when, just before the end and having gone through the last account, he could still make a quick little tour.

Translated from the German by Tania and James Stern

ERNST BLOCH (Germany, 1885–1977)

Disappointment with Amusement

One expected something different, and usually more. When it's less, that's annoying, but not always; it still offers something when it doesn't really matter. Or when it's really harmless, like a joke, which after all can also amuse when it falls flat—when it sets mountains in motion, as it were, only to bear a mouse.

As happened, for example, with that scene at the circus, lots of big words, expectations ever rising. The ring was cleared and nothing less was announced than the battle steed Bucephalos. That was also the name of Alexander the Great's personal horse. The mighty steel cable was already auspicious by which the ringmaster tried to drag the stallion into the ring. Only tried, of course; the stubborn, unseen something on the other end dragged him forward by the cable, outside, from where one could hear only stamping and angry whinnying. One, two, then three particularly brawny men came to the ringmaster's aid, pulled expertly at the cable, in vain, could only bring the cable to a standstill. Until a fourth came along and grabbed the cable, a very heavy boxer, come to help them from the next number, and now he finally moved the cable from a standstill and pulled it ever more back.

A final tug, all together, one could hear the clatter of mighty hoofs outside, triumph—and a wooden horse was visible at the end of the cable, rolled into the ring on its four wheels. The audience now laughed with relief at this great sight gag, laughed wholeheartedly, as we like to say. And not at all so disappointed at such a Bucephalos at the end of the tether. Even objectively, it was rather relieved by the humor, perhaps also because anticipation is not only joyful, but much more often fearful—and look, there was nothing to it! At least not in fairy tales; or even when something less childish comes, does not come out like a wooden horse, nevertheless fairy tales, the circus, all the way up to farce, all mean that the soup is always cooler when you eat it than when it was boiling. Whereas in the life as we still have it, the cooks in charge expect us to eat the soup even hotter.

Translated from the German by Anthony A. Nassar

T. S. ELIOT (United States / England, 1888–1965)

Hysteria

As she laughed I was aware of becoming involved in her laughter and being part of it, until her teeth were only accidental stars with a talent for squad-drill. I was drawn in by short gasps, inhaled at each momentary recovery, lost finally in the dark caverns of her throat, bruised by the ripple of unseen muscles. An elderly waiter with trembling hands was hurriedly spreading a pink and white checked cloth over the rusty green iron table, saying: "If the lady and gentleman wish to take their tea in the garden, if the lady and gentleman wish to take their tea in the garden . . ." I decided that if the shaking of her breasts could be stopped, some of the fragments of the afternoon might be collected, and I concentrated my attention with careful subtlety to this end.

FERNANDO PESSOA (Portugal, 1888–1935)

I went into the barbershop as usual, with the pleasant sensation of entering a familiar place, easily and naturally. New things are distressing to my sensibility; I'm only at ease in places where I've already been.

After I'd sat down in the chair, I happened to ask the young barber, occupied in fastening a clean, cool cloth around my neck, about his older colleague from the chair to the right, a spry fellow who had been sick. I didn't ask this because I felt obliged to ask something; it was the place and my memory that sparked the question. "He passed away yesterday," flatly answered the barber's voice behind me and the linen cloth as his fingers withdrew from the final tuck of the cloth in between my shirt collar and my neck. The whole of my irrational good mood abruptly died, like the eternally missing barber from the adjacent chair. A chill swept over all my thoughts. I said nothing.

Nostalgia! I even feel it for people and things that were nothing to me, because time's fleeing is for me an anguish, and life's mystery is a torture. Faces I habitually see on my habitual streets—if I stop seeing them I become sad. And they were nothing to me, except perhaps the symbol of all of life.

The nondescript old man with dirty gaiters who often crossed my path at nine-thirty in the morning... The crippled seller of lottery tickets who would pester me in vain... The round and ruddy old man smoking a cigar at the door of the tobacco shop... The pale tobacco shop owner... What has happened to them all, who because I regularly saw them were a part of my life? Tomorrow I too will vanish from the Rua da Prata, the Rua dos Douradores, the Rua dos Fanqueiros. Tomorrow I too—I this soul that feels and thinks, this universe I am for myself—yes, tomorrow I too will be the one who no longer walks these streets, whom others will vaguely evoke with a "What's become of him?" And everything I've done, everything I've felt and everything I've lived will amount merely to one less passer-by on the everyday streets of some city or other.

Translated from the Portuguese by Richard Zenith

RAMÓN GÓMEZ DE LA SERNA
(Spain / Argentina, 1888–1963)

He has the eyes of a tightly-sewn button.

*

Up among the stars there isn't a single nightingale.

*

The q is the p coming back from a walk.

*

The peacock is a retired myth.

*

The silk scarf is the goodbye of a caress.

*

The girl with a hoop in her hand goes off to the flower garden as if to school, to play with circumferences and tangents.

*

At night on a lonely train we travel with two women: the one with us and the one reflected in the glass.

*

In mineral water invisible fish bubble up, the souls of aquatic silence, the breathing of frogs, extinct fish, and last gasps.

*

When we go by a jail we feel as if our shadow—one of our shadows—is in one of the cells of an inner courtyard.

*

What a tragedy! Her hands grew old and her rings didn't.

*

The hardest fish to catch is soap in water.

Translated from the Spanish by Bill Zavatsky

WALTER BENJAMIN (Germany, 1892–1940)

Chinese Curios

These are days when no one should rely unduly on his "competence." Strength lies in improvisation. All the decisive blows are struck left-handed.

At the beginning of the long downhill lane that leads to the house of———, whom I visited each evening, is a gate. After she moved, the opening of its archway henceforth stood before me like an ear that has lost the power of hearing.

A child in his nightshirt cannot be prevailed upon to greet an arriving visitor. Those present, invoking a higher moral standpoint, admonish him in vain to overcome his prudery. A few minutes later he reappears, now stark naked, before the visitor. In the meantime he has washed.

The power of a country road when one is walking along it is different from the power it has when one is flying over it by airplane. In the same way, the power of a text when it is read is different from the power it has when it is copied out. The airplane passenger sees only how the road pushes through the landscape, how it unfolds according to the same laws as the terrain surrounding it. Only he who walks the road on foot learns of the power it commands, and of how, from the very scenery that for the flier is only the unfurled plain, it calls forth distances, belvederes, clearings, prospects at each of its turns like a commander deploying soldiers at a front. Only the copied text thus commands the soul of him who is occupied with it, whereas the mere reader never discovers the new aspects of his inner self that are opened by the text, that road cut through the interior jungle forever closing behind it: because the reader follows the movement of his mind in the free flight of daydreaming, whereas the copier submits it to command. The Chinese practice of copying books was thus an incomparable guarantee of literary culture, and the transcript a key to China's enigmas.

Caution: Steps

Work on good prose has three steps: a musical stage when it is composed, an architectonic one when it is built, and a textile one when it is woven.

Translated from the German by Edmund Jephcott

JOSEPH ROTH (Austria, 1894–1939)

Rest While Watching the Demolition

Opposite the bistro where I've been sitting all day, an old building is being pulled down, a hotel I've lived in these past sixteen years—apart from such time as I was away on my travels.
Yesterday one wall, the back wall, was still standing, awaiting its
final night. The three other walls were already rubble, on the
half-fenced-off site. How oddly small the site seemed to me,
compared to the big hotel that had formerly occupied the same
space! You would have thought, too, that an empty site would
appear bigger than one that was built on. But probably it's the
sixteen years, now that they're over, seeming so precious to me,
so full of precious things, that I can't understand how they could
have elapsed in such a small space. And because the hotel is
shattered and the years I lived in it have gone, it seems bigger in
memory, much bigger than it can have been. On the one remaining wall I could still see the wallpaper in my room, which was sky
blue with a fine gold pattern. Then, yesterday, they put up a scaffolding against the wall, and two workers climbed up on it. With
pickax and sledgehammer they attacked my wallpaper, my wall;
and then, when it was reeling and decrepit, the men tied ropes
round the wall—the wall was to be put to death. The workers
climbed down, dismantling the scaffolding as they went. The
two ends of the rope hung down on either side of the wall. Each
man took hold of one end and pulled. And with a crash the wall
came down. Everything was obscured by a dense white cloud of
plaster dust and mortar. From it emerged, all coated in white
dust, like great millers who grind stones, the two men. They
made straight for me, as they had been doing twice each day.
They've known me since I've been sitting here. The younger one
gestures back over his shoulder with his thumb, and says: "It's
gone now, your wall!" I asked them both to stop and have a drink
with me, more as if they'd been building me a wall. We joked
about the wallpaper, the walls, my precious years. The workers
were demolition men; knocking things down was their job; they
would never think of building anything. "And quite right too!"

they said. "Everyone does the job they do, and gets paid the going rate! And this man here is the king of the demolition men," said the younger one. The older one smiled. That's how cheerful the destroyers were, and I with them.

Now I'm sitting facing the vacant lot, and hearing the hours go by. You lose one home after another, I say to myself. Here I am, sitting with my wanderer's staff. My feet are sore, my heart is tired, my eyes are dry. Misery crouches beside me, ever larger and ever gentler; pain takes an interest, becomes huge and kind; terror flutters up, and it doesn't even frighten me anymore. And that's the most desolate thing of all.

Unimaginable things happen, and the hand remains calm and doesn't clutch at the head. On my right is the little post office; the postman comes out and delivers my letters, bad letters mostly; when the hotel was still standing, he used to leave good letters on my table. A woman comes—one I used to love, and I smile, a shadow of an old smile I used to have, that I no longer miss. An old man shuffles by, wearing a pair of indoor slippers, and I envy him his shuffle and his being an old man. Boisterous customers stand around the bar, arguing. There is a series of unresolvable, albeit not-very-far-reaching differences of opinion between them on such matters as cigarette lighters, radios, racehorses, wives, makes of car, aperitifs, and other such weighty issues. A taxi driver walks in. The waiter brings him a glass of red wine. His taxi's waiting. The driver drinks his wine. Soon he's quite alone, facing the landlady across the bar. The waiter balances an empty can on a car tire. The guests laugh. They want me to laugh with them. Why not? I stand up, and I laugh. Who's that laughing in me? I've got misery waiting at my table, large, gentle misery. I won't be long, I'm just laughing!

Diagonally across from me is the barber, standing in front of his door, as white as a candle. Soon his customers will arrive, they will arrive at the end of their day's work, when the newspaper seller comes and brings me the evening papers, the ones that are full of heated skirmishes and cold blood, and that yet—one can't really believe it—flop rustling home on to the tables on the terrace like huge, exhausted peace doves at the end of their day.

All the terror of the world is in them, all the terror of the whole grisly day, that's what makes them so tired. When the first silvery streetlights glimmer on, a refugee, an exile, sometimes comes along, without a wanderer's staff, quite as if he were at home here, and—as if he wanted to prove to me in one breath that he felt at home, that he knew his way around, but also that where he felt at home wasn't home—he says: "I know somewhere you can get a good, cheap meal here." And I'm glad for him that he does. I'm glad that he walks off under the trail of silvery streetlights, and doesn't stop, now that night is falling, to take in the ever-ghostlier-looking dust on the empty lot opposite. Not everyone has to get used to rubble and to shattered walls.

The exile, the displaced person, has taken the newspapers away with him. He wants to read them in his good, cheap restaurant. In front of me the table is empty.

Das Neue Tage-Buch (Paris), June 25, 1938

Translated from the German by Michael Hoffman

JAMES THURBER (United States, 1894–1961)

Variations on the Theme

I

A fox, attracted by the scent of something, followed his nose to a tree in which sat a crow with a piece of cheese in his beak. "Oh, cheese," said the fox scornfully. "That's for mice."

The crow removed the cheese with his talons and said, "You always hate the thing you cannot have, as, for instance, grapes."

"Grapes are for the birds," said the fox haughtily. "I am an epicure, a gourmet, and a gastronome."

The embarrassed crow, ashamed to be seen eating mouse food by a great specialist in the art of dining, hastily dropped the cheese. The fox caught it deftly, swallowed it with relish, said "*Merci*," politely, and trotted away.

II

A fox had used all his blandishments in vain, for he could not flatter the crow in the tree and make him drop the cheese he held in his beak. Suddenly, the crow tossed the cheese to the astonished fox. Just then the farmer, from whose kitchen the loot had been stolen, appeared, carrying a rifle, looking for the robber. The fox turned and ran for the woods. "There goes the guilty son of a vixen now!" cried the crow, who, in case you do not happen to know it, can see the glint of sunlight on a gun barrel at a greater distance than anybody.

III

This time the fox, who was determined not to be outfoxed by a crow, stood his ground and did not run when the farmer appeared, carrying a rifle and looking for the robber.

"The teeth marks in this cheese are mine," said the fox, "but the beak marks were made by the true culprit up there in the tree. I submit this cheese in evidence, as Exhibit A, and bid you and the criminal a very good day." Whereupon he lit a cigarette and strolled away.

IV

In the great and ancient tradition, the crow in the tree with the cheese in his beak began singing, and the cheese fell into the fox's lap. "You sing like a shovel," said the fox, with a grin, but the crow pretended not to hear and cried out, "Quick, give me back the cheese! Here comes the farmer with his rifle!"

"Why should I give you back the cheese?" the wily fox demanded.

"Because the farmer has a gun, and I can fly faster than you can run."

So the frightened fox tossed the cheese back to the crow, who ate it, and said, "Dearie me, my eyes are playing tricks on me— or am I playing tricks on you? Which do you think?" But there was no reply, for the fox had slunk away into the woods.

JEAN TOOMER (United States, 1894–1967)

Karintha

> Her skin is like dusk on the eastern horizon,
> O cant you see it, O cant you see it,
> Her skin is like dusk on the eastern horizon
> . . . When the sun goes down.

Men had always wanted her, this Karintha, even as a child, Karintha carrying beauty, perfect as dusk when the sun goes down. Old men rode her hobby-horse upon their knees. Young men danced with her at frolics when they should have been dancing with their grown-up girls. God grant us youth, secretly prayed the old men. The young fellows counted the time to pass before she would be old enough to mate with them. This interest of the male, who wishes to ripen a growing thing too soon, could mean no good to her.

Karintha, at twelve, was a wild flash that told the other folks just what it was to live. At sunset, when there was no wind, and the pine-smoke from over by the sawmill hugged the earth, and you couldn't see more than a few feet in front, her sudden darting past you was a bit of vivid color, like a black bird that flashes in light. With the other children one could hear, some distance off, their feet flopping in the two-inch dust. Karintha's running was a whir. It had the sound of the red dust that sometimes makes a spiral in the road. At dusk, during the hush just after the sawmill had closed down, and before any of the women had started their supper-getting-ready songs, her voice, high-pitched, shrill, would put one's ears to itching. But no one ever thought to make her stop because of it. She stoned the cows, and beat her dog, and fought the other children . . . Even the preacher, who caught her at her mischief, told himself that she was as innocently lovely as a November cotton flower. Already, rumors were out about her. Homes in Georgia are most often built on the two-room plan. In one, you cook and eat, in the other you sleep, and there love goes on. Karintha had seen or heard, perhaps she had felt her parents loving. One could but imitate one's parents, for to follow them was the way of God. She played "home" with a small boy who was not afraid to do her bidding. That started the whole thing. Old men could no longer ride her hobby-horse upon their knees. But young men counted faster.

> Her skin is like dusk,
> O cant you see it,
> Her skin is like dusk,
> When the sun goes down.

Karintha is a woman. She who carries beauty, perfect as dusk when the sun goes down. She has been married many times. Old men remind her that a few years back they rode her hobby-horse upon their knees. Karintha smiles, and indulges them when she is in the mood for it. She has contempt for them. Karintha is a woman. Young men run stills to make her money. Young men go to the big cities and run on the road. Young men go away to college. They all want to bring her money. These are the young men who thought that all they had to was to count time. But Karintha is a woman, and she has had a child. A child fell out of her womb onto a bed of pine-needles in the forest. Pine-needles are smooth and sweet. They are elastic to the feet of rabbits . . . A sawmill was nearby. Its pyramidal sawdust pile smouldered. It is a year before one completely burns. Meanwhile, the smoke curls up and hangs in odd wraiths about the trees, curls up, and spreads itself out over the valley... Weeks after Karintha returned home the smoke was so heavy you tasted it in water. Some one made a song:

> Smoke is on the hills. Rise up.
> Smoke is on the hills, O rise
> And take my soul to Jesus.

Karintha is a woman. Men do not know that the soul of her was a growing thing ripened too soon. They will bring their money; they will die not having found it out...Karintha at twenty, carrying beauty, perfect as dusk when the sun goes down. Karintha...

> Her skin is like dusk on the eastern horizon,
> O cant you see it, O cant you see it,
> Her skin is like dusk on the eastern horizon
> ...When the sun goes down.

> Goes down...

PAUL ÉLUARD (France, 1895–1952) and
BENJAMIN PÉRET (France, 1899–1959)

Sleep that is singing makes the shadows tremble.

*

Dance rules over the white wood.

*

Whoever moves disappears.

*

You've read everything but drunk nothing.

*

I came, I sat down, I left.

*

When the road is done, do it again.

Translated from the French by Bill Zavatsky

MIKHAIL ZOSHCHENKO (Russia, 1895–1958)

Fantasy Shirt

Last Saturday after work I dropped by the shops. I had to buy a shirt.

On Sunday there was going to be a party at our place. I felt like dressing up a bit. I fancied buying some kind of a shirt that was a bit special. Some kind of fantasy shirt.

I chose one. A sort of sky-blue colour, with two detachable collars. Well, it was every bit as good as imported goods.

I headed off home as fast as I could. Tried it on. Luxury. A lovely sight. A joy to behold!

At the party I thought, the ladies would be throwing themselves at me.

I should admit, I'm fanatical about cleanliness. There I was trying on the shirt, and somehow I felt uncomfortable. God only knows, I thought. You never know how many people have had their hands all over it. Wouldn't be a bad idea to get it laundered. We're only talking about twenty kopecks. Then I could wear it with pleasure.

I ran over to the laundry woman. She lives in the same yard as me. Lukerya Petrovna.

"My dear Lukerya Petrovna," I said, "please do your best. The party's tomorrow. I've got to have it for tomorrow. Can I rely on you?"

"You can rely on me," she said. "Come round," she said, "just before the party and you can put your shirt on. It will be washed and pressed, with the two detachable collars."

The next day, before the party, I popped round to the laundry woman.

I took the shirt from her. I ran off to get changed.

I put the shirt on. But what on earth was this? Some kind of tiny shirt: the collar wouldn't fit and the cuffs were where the elbows had been. What the hell was going on?

I quickly hurried back to the laundry woman.

The laundry woman said:

"That's nothing unusual. It's only to be expected. New shirts these days always shrink. Either it's the material they're made from or the manufacturers don't wash the fabric. That's nothing."

"What do you mean nothing! It won't fit round my neck. It used to be," I said, "size 38, and now it's probably a 32."

The laundry woman said:

"And you can thank your lucky stars for that," she said. "The other day I washed one for the accountant, started off size 40 and now he'll be lucky if it's a five. The accountant threatened to smash my face in for that, but it's not my fault."

Damn it! What, I thought, can I do?

And I didn't have much time. It was time to go to the party.

I put the shirt on, and over it, to hide it, I squeezed on my old shirt, so as not to cause offence, and hurried off to the party.

It went well. No one noticed. It was OK.

Translated from the Russian by Jeremy Hicks

PAUL COLINET (Belgium, 1898–1957)

The Lobster

The lobster is a bird on stilts, in the species of nighthawks. He drinks cranially, is well developed, has been pointed out by Linné under the name of Forge Roussel. Its body shows 4/5 generally animal. The hindquarters are composed of a cluster of 17 metal spools, on divergent axles. The lobster is the only carnivorous bird that flies backwards.

His characteristic song, which resembles, but is harsher than, the civet-cat's, is produced by a spur's vibration in the cranial box, called the sub-machine-gun. The lobster's calcified eye is used, in shoemaking, to fasten half-boots.

Translated from the French by Rochelle Ratner

JORGE LUIS BORGES (Argentina, 1899–1986)

Dreamtigers

In my childhood I was a fervent worshiper of the tiger: not the jaguar, the spotted "tiger" of the Amazonian tangles and the isles of vegetation that float down the Paraná, but that striped, Asiatic, royal tiger, that can be faced only by a man of war, on a castle atop an elephant. I used to linger endlessly before one of the cages at the zoo; I judged vast encyclopedias and books of natural history by the splendor of their tigers. (I still remember those illustrations: I who cannot rightly recall the brow or the smile of a woman.) Childhood passed away, and the tigers and my passion for them grew old, but still they are in my dreams. At that submerged or chaotic level they keep prevailing. And so, as I sleep, some dream beguiles me, and suddenly I know I am dreaming. Then I think: This is a dream, a pure diversion of my will; and now that I have unlimited power, I am going to cause a tiger.

Oh, incompetence! Never can my dreams engender the wild beast I long for. The tiger indeed appears, but stuffed or flimsy, or with impure variations of shape, or of an implausible size, or all too fleeting, or with a touch of the dog or the bird.

Borges and I

It's the other one, it's Borges, that things happen to. I stroll about Buenos Aires and stop, perhaps mechanically now, to look at the arch of an entrance or an iron gate. News of Borges reaches me through the mail and I see his name on an academic ballot or in a biographical dictionary. I like hourglasses, maps, eighteenth-century typography, the taste of coffee, and Stevenson's prose. The other one shares these preferences with me, but in a vain way that converts them into the attributes of an actor. It would be too much to say that our relations are hostile; I live, I allow myself to live, so that Borges may contrive his literature and that literature justifies my existence. I do not mind confessing that he has managed to write some worthwhile pages, but those pages cannot save me, perhaps because the good part no longer belongs to anyone, not even to the other one, but rather to the Spanish language or to tradition. Otherwise, I am destined to be lost, definitively, and only a few instants of me will be able to survive in the other one. Little by little I am yielding him everything, although I am well aware of his perverse habit of falsifying and exaggerating. Spinoza held that all things long to preserve their own nature: the rock wants to be rock forever and the tiger, a tiger. But I must live on in Borges, not in myself—if indeed I am anyone—though I recognize myself less in his books than in many others, or than in the laborious strumming of a guitar. Years ago I tried to free myself from him and I passed from lower-middle-class myths to playing games with time and infinity, but those games are Borges' now, and I will have to conceive something else. Thus my life is running away, and I lose everything and everything belongs to oblivion, or to the other one.

I do not know which of us two is writing this page.

Translated from the Spanish by Mildred Boyer

HENRI MICHAUX (Belgium, 1899–1984)

Insects

As I went farther west, I saw nine-segmented insects with huge eyes like graters and latticework corselets like miners' lamps, others with murmuring antennae; some with twenty-odd pairs of legs that looked more like staples; others of black lacquer and mother-of-pearl that crunched underfoot like shells; still others high legged like daddy longlegs with little pin-eyes as red as the eyes of albino mice, veritable glowing coals on stems with an expression of ineffable panic; still others with an ivory head— surprisingly bald, so that suddenly one had the most fraternal feelings for them—so close, their legs kicking forward like piston rods zigzagging in the air.

Finally, there were transparent ones, bottles with hairy spots, perhaps: they came forward by the thousands—glassware, a display of light and sun so bright that afterward everything seemed ash and product of dark night.

Translated from the French by David Ball

My Pastimes

It's the rare person I meet whom I don't want to beat up. Others favor the interior monologue, stream-of-consciousness, art and dreams. Not me. I like to beat people up.

Now some people, unaware of my purposes, play right into my hands, sit opposite me in a grease joint, stay a while, pick their teeth, they want to eat.

Here's one now.

Notice how swiftly I grab him by the collar. Pow! Then I do it again. Bam! Pow!

Then I hang him on the coat rack. Unhang him. Hang him. Unhang him.

Then I toss him on the table, hit him, kick him, choke him. I mean, I beat the shit out of him.

Then I spit on him. I flood him with my spit.

He revives.

I rinse him off, I stretch him out (by now I'm losing interest, this is going on too long), I crumple him up, squeeze him dry, roll him into a ball, which I drop into my glass. Then I lift it in the air and spill it on the floor. "Waiter, get me a clean glass, will you?"

But I'm too fagged out, I pay the bill in a hurry and leave without another word.

Translated from the French by David Lehman

FRANCIS PONGE (France, 1899–1988)

The Pleasures of the Door

Kings do not touch doors.

They know nothing of this pleasure: pushing before one gently or brusquely one of those large familiar panels, then turning back to replace it—holding a door in one's arms.

The pleasure of grabbing the midriff of one of these tall obstacles to a room by its porcelain node; that short clinch during which movement stops, the eye widens, and the whole body adjusts to its new surrounding.

With a friendly hand one still holds on to it, before closing it decisively and shutting oneself in—which the click of the tight but well-oiled spring pleasantly confirms.

The Frog

When little matchsticks of rain bounce off drenched fields, an amphibian dwarf, a maimed Ophelia, barely the size of a fist, sometimes hops under the poet's feet and flings herself into the next pond.

Let the nervous little thing run away. She has lovely legs. Her whole body is sheathed in waterproof skin. Hardly meat, her long muscles have an elegance neither fish nor fowl. But to escape one's fingers, the virtue of fluidity joins forces with her struggle for life. Goitrous, she starts panting . . . And that pounding heart, those wrinkled eyelids, that drooping mouth, move me to let her go.

Translated from the French by Beth Archer Brombert

During his very well attended lectures at the Collège de France, he amused himself with all that.

He enjoyed prying, with the dignity of professional gestures, with relentless, expert hands, into the secret places of Proust or Rimbaud, then, exposing their so-called miracles, their mysteries, to the gaze of his very attentive audience, he would explain their "case."

With his sharp, mischievous little eyes, his ready-tied necktie and his square-trimmed beard, he looked enormously like the gentleman in the advertisements who, with one finger in the air, smilingly recommends Saponite, the best of soap powders, or the model Salamander: economy, security, comfort.

"There is nothing," he said, "you see I went to look for myself, because I won't be bluffed; nothing that I myself have not already studied clinically countless times, that I have not catalogued and explained.

"They should not upset you. Look, in my hands they are like trembling, nude little children, and I am holding them up to you in the hollow of my hand, as though I were their creator, their father, I have emptied them for you of their power and their mystery. I have tracked down, harried what was miraculous about them.

"Now they hardly differ from the intelligent, curious and amusing eccentrics who come and tell me their interminable stories, to get me to help them, appreciate them, and reassure them.

"You can no more be affected than my daughters are when they entertain their girl friends in their mother's parlor, and chatter and laugh gaily without being concerned with what I am saying to my patients in the next room."

This was what he taught at the Collège de France. And in the entire neighborhood, in all the nearby Faculties, in the literature, law, history and philosophy courses, at the Institute and at the Palais de Justice, in the buses, the *métros*, in all the government offices, sensible men, normal men, active men, worthy, wholesome, strong men, triumphed.

Avoiding the shops filled with pretty things, the women trotting briskly along, the café waiters, the medical students, the traffic policemen, the clerks from notary offices, Rimbaud or Proust, having been torn from life, cast out from life and deprived of support, were probably wandering aimlessly through the streets, or dozing away, their heads resting on their chests, in some dusty public square.

Translated from the French by Maria Jolas

ANDREAS EMBIRIKOS (Greece, 1901–1975)

Completion of Freighter Steamboat

Like the waters of a sworn jury her eyes' calmness was troubled yet her recovered sight finally prevailed and flew to the clear sky of her domed dream as does a fly from a sleeping child's nose to the tumult of brilliant silence. Then the law-observers' assembly decided to kill silence once and for all and erect on that very point the statue of her eyes' calmness for the young woman was holding her recovered sight inside her hands like a miraculous snake.

Translated from the Greek by Nikos Stabakis

LAURA (RIDING) JACKSON
(United States, 1901–1991)

How Came It About?

How came it about that Mrs. Paradise the dressmaker is here to dress me, and Mr. Babcock the bootmaker to boot me and a whole science of service to serve me, and that I am precisely here to be served? Do not speak to me of economics: that is merely a question of how we arrange matters between us. And do not speak to me of genesis: I am discussing the question of Mrs. Paradise and Mr. Babcock and myself and the others as immediate causes of one another, I am not discussing creation. Personally, I do not believe in creation. Creation is stealing one thing to turn it into another. What I *am* discussing is existence, uncorrupted by art—how came it about, and so forth. Do not speak to me of love: Mrs. Paradise and Mr. Babcock and myself and all the others do not like each other, in fact, we dislike each other because each of us is most certainly the cause of the other. I am the reason for Mrs. Paradise's making frocks and Mrs. Paradise is the reason for my wearing frocks. If it were not for each other we should be occupied only with ourselves; we should not exist. How then came we to exist? I ask this question. Mrs. Paradise asks this question. I am Mrs. Paradise's answer. Mrs. Paradise is my answer. As for Mr. Babcock, he has hair on his nose and I never look at him. As for all the others, I must put up a notice asking them to ring the bell gently.

~

There is a woman in this city who loathes me. There are people everywhere who loathe me. I could name them; if they were in a book I could turn to the exact page. People who loathe me do so for one of two reasons: because I have frightened them because I have loathed them (that is, made my death-face at them, which I shall not describe as it might in this way lose some of its virtue) or because they are interested in me and there seems no practical way of (or excuse for) satisfying their interest. As to love, that is another matter—it has nothing to do with either interest or fear. Love is simply a matter of history, beginning like cancer from small incidents. There is nothing further to be said about it.

But as to loathing: I feel an intense intimacy with those who have this loathing interest in me. Further than this, I know what they mean, I sympathize with them, I understand them. There should be a name (as poetic as love) for this relationship between loather and loathed; it is of the closest and more full of passion than incest.

To continue about this woman. What is to her irritation is to me myself. She has therefore a very direct sense of me, as I have a very direct sense of her, from being a kind of focus of her nervous system. There is no sentiment, no irony between us, nothing but feeling: it is an utterly serious relationship.

> For if one eat my meat, though it be known
> The meat was mine, the excrement is his own.

I forget in what context these words were used by Donne—but they express very accurately how organic I feel this relationship to be. The tie between us is as positive as the tie between twins is negative. I think of her often. She is a painter—not a very good painter. I understand this too: it is difficult to explain, but quite clear to myself that one of the reasons I am attached to her is that she is not a good painter. Also her clothes, which do not fit her well: this again makes me even more attached to her. If she knew this she would be exasperated against me all the more, and I should like it; not because I want to annoy her but because this would make our relationship still more intense. It would be terrible to me if we ever became friends; like a divorce.

LUIS CERNUDA (Spain, 1902–1963)

The Teacher

I had him for a class in rhetoric, and he was short, chubby, with glasses like the ones Schubert wears in his portraits, walking through the cloisters in small slow strides, breviary in hand or with his hands resting in his cloak pockets, cap pushed well back on his large head with its thick gray hair. Nearly always quiet, or when paired with another professor speaking in measured tones, his voice strong and resonant, but most of the time alone in his cell, where he kept a few secular books mixed in with the religious ones, and from which I could see in springtime the green leaves and dark fruit of a mulberry tree climbing the wall and covering the gloomy little patio his window opened on.

One day in class he tried to read us some verses, his voice aglow with heartfelt enthusiasm, and it must have been hard for him to understand the mockery, veiled at first, then open and hostile, of the students—because he admired poetry and its art, in a pedantic way, naturally. It was he who tried to get me to recite sometimes, although a shyness stronger than pleasure froze my delivery; he who encouraged me to write my first poems, critiquing them then and giving me as an esthetic precept what in my literary papers would always be a graceful hold on the material.

He put me at the head of the class, a distinction for which I soon paid with a certain unpopularity among my schoolmates, and before final exams, as if understanding my diffidence and lack of confidence, he told me: "Go to the chapel and pray. That will give you courage."

Once I got to the university, in my self-absorption I stopped going to see him. One deep gold morning in fall, on my way to my early first class, I saw a poor little funeral turning the corner, the red brick wall of the school, which I'd forgotten; it was his. It was my heart, without hearing from anyone else, that told me so. He must have died alone. I don't know how he held up through those last days of his life.

The Shops

Those little shops were on the Plaza del Pan, behind the Church of the Savior, where the Galicians parked, seated on the ground or leaning against the wall, their empty sacks on their shoulders and a handful of cords in their fist, waiting for a trunk or a piece of furniture to move. The shops were tucked into the church's wall, some defended by a little glass door, others with their shutters wide open on the plaza, and closed only at night. Inside, behind the counter, silent and solitary, a neat little old man, dressed in black, stood weighing something in a tiny scale with intense concentration, or a woman in lunar white, her hair pulled into a knot with a comb stuck in it, was slowly fanning herself. What were those merchants selling? In the dark rear of the shop you might just catch a glimpse of something gleaming in a display case, a vase with complex patterns of gems and filigree and the purplish teardrops of some long coral ear-rings. In others the merchandise was lace: delicate strips of spun spray, hanging the length of the wall on a background of yellow or sky-blue paper.

On the plaza, the Galicians (a designation by trade not geog-raphy, as some of them were from Santander or León) were hunched over, soft and tired-looking, more from the weight of years than the thankless loads their work condemned them to. They were the ones who, during Holy Week, at the height of the brotherhoods, could be seen with their clenched faces peer-ing out from behind the velvet platforms, shouldering the gold mass of statues and candelabras and bouquets, lined up like slaves along the benches of a galley. Beside their painful super-human labor with no shelter but the pavement where they were parked, the aristocratic merchants seemed to belong to another world. But they also subtly belonged together, like vestiges of a vanished day and age. In the little shops the silks and precious gems no longer sparkled, and the shoppers scarcely stopped there anymore. But in their seclusion, in their stillness, shop-keeper and porter alike were descended from the merchants and artisans of the East, and as the day wound down outside their door, the customer, in order to take home the amphora or the tapestry they'd just bought, had to seek out amid the bustle of the square the person big and strong enough to haul the merchandise.

In those little shops on the Plaza del Pan every one of the objects on display was still something unique, and therefore precious, crafted with care, sometimes right there in the back room, in accordance with a tradition passed from generation to generation, from master to apprentice, and it expressed or strove to express in an ingenuous way something fine and dis-tinctive. Their drowsy atmosphere still seemed at times to flare up with the pure fire of the metals, and an aroma of sandalwood or faint perfume to float there vaguely like a trace of something someone had left behind.

Translated from the Spanish by Stephen Kessler

MALCOLM DE CHAZAL (Mauritius, 1902–1981)

Every flower is a Mona Lisa following our glance whenever we look at it.

*

There is far north, *yonder*, far south, and *here* is the equator of words.

*

The mouth is the kind of fruit that must be eaten skin and all. Kisses you have to peel go down hard.

*

The emptied container of a sick man's voice.

*

Sudden strong feeling thins the lips. Petals become tissue-fine blown by the wind.

*

Denial is born in the eyes. It begins to grow and then stops growing in the fixed expression of the mouth. For all final leave-takings and absolute goodbyes, "sentimentality" clamps its hold on the lips. The lips turn their back on us last of all.

Translated from the French by Irving Weiss

RAYMOND QUENEAU (France, 1903–1976)

A Story of Your Own

1—Would you like to know the story of the three lively little peas?

    if yes, go to 4

    if no, go to 2.

2—Would you prefer that of the three tall slender beanpoles?

    if yes, go to 16

    if no, go to 3.

3—Would you prefer that of the three medium-sized mediocre bushes?

if yes, go to 17

if no, go to 21.

4—Once upon a time there were three little peas dressed in green who were sleeping soundly in their pod. Their oh so chubby faces were breathing through the holes of their nostrils and one could hear their sweet, harmonious snoring.

if you prefer another description, go to 9

if this one suits you, go to 5.

5—They were not dreaming. In fact, these little beings never dream.

if you prefer that they dream, go to 6

otherwise, go to 7.

6—They were dreaming. In fact, these little beings always dream and their nights secrete charming visions.

if you want to know these dreams, go to 11

if you're not particularly keen to, then go to 7.

7—Their dainty feet were dipped in warm socks and they wore black velvet gloves to bed.

if you prefer gloves of a different color go to 8

if this color suits you, go to 10.

8—They wore blue velvet gloves to bed.

if you prefer gloves of a different color, go to 7

if this color suits you, go to 10.

9—Once upon a time there were three little peas knocking about on the highways. When evening came, they quickly fell asleep, tired and weary.

if you want to know the rest, go to 5

if not, go to 21.

10—All three had the same dream, for they loved each other tenderly and, like good and proud thrins, always had similar dreams.

if you want to know their dream, go to 11

if not, go to 12.

11—They dreamed that they were getting their soup at the soup kitchen and that on opening their billies they discovered that it was vetch soup. They woke up, horrified.

if you want to know why they woke up horrified,

look up the word "vetch" in Webster's and let's not mention it again

if you don't think it's worth going deeper into the
matter, go to 12.

12—Opopoï! they cried as they opened their eyes. Opopoï! what sort of dream did we give birth to! Bad omen, said the first. Yah, said the second, you said it, I'm all sad now. Don't get in a tizzy, said the third, who was the craftiest of the three, this isn't something to get upset over, but something to understand, to cut a long story short, I'm going to analyze it for you.

if you want to know the interpretation of this dream
right away, go to 15

if, on the contrary, you wish to know the reactions
of the other two, go to 13.

13—That's a lot of hooey, said the first. Since when do you know how to analyze dreams. Yeah, since when? added the second.

if you too would like to know since when, go to 14

if not, go to 14 anyway, because you still won't know
why.

14—Since when? cried the third. How should I know! The fact is I analyze them. You'll see!

if you too want to see, go to 15

if not, go to 15 anyway, because you'll see nothing.

15—Well, let's see, then, said his brothers. I don't like your irony, he replied, and you won't know anything. Anyway, hasn't your feeling of horror dimmed during this rather lively conversation? Vanished, even? So what's the point of stirring up the quagmire of your papilionaceous unconscious? Let's go wash up at the fountain instead and greet this happy morning with hygiene and sacred euphoria! No sooner said than done: there they are slipping out of their pod, letting themselves gently roll along the ground and then, jogging, they merrily reach the theater of their ablutions.

if you want to know what happens at the theater of
their ablutions, go to 16

if you would rather not, you go to 21.

16—Three big beanpoles were watching them.

if the three tall beanpoles displease you, go to 21

if they suit you, go to 18.

17—Three medium-sized mediocre bushes were watching them.

if the three medium-sized mediocre bushes displease you, go to 21

if they suit you, go to 18.

18—Finding themselves eyeballed in this way, the three nimble
little peas who were very modest ran off.

if you want to know what they did next, go to 19

if you don't want to know, you go to 21.

19—They ran speedily to get back to their pod and, shutting it
again behind them, went back to sleep.

if you would like to know the rest, go to 20

if you do not want to know, you go to 21.

20—There is no rest the story is over.

21—In that case, the story is also over.

Translated from the French by Marc Lowenthal

F I L L Ì A   (Italy, 1904–1936)

New Year's Eve Dinner

Nowadays habit has killed the joy in big dinners on New Year's
Eve: for many years the same elements have conspired to produce a happiness which has been enjoyed too often. Everyone
knows in advance the precise mechanism of events.

Family memories, felicitations and forecasts roll out like
newspapers from presses. Old habits must be cast off to escape
this monotony.

There are a thousand ways to revitalize this occasion: here
is one which we put to the test with the Futursimultaneists in
Rome: Mattia, Belli, D'Avila, Pandolfo, Battistella, Vignazia, etc.

At midnight after the endless chit-chat of waiting it is
announced that dinner is served. In the dining room the tables
have been removed and the guests are seated on chairs placed in
a row, Indian file, one behind the other.

The inevitable turkey arrives, served by the waiters on metal plates: the turkey is stuffed with mandarins and salami.

Everyone eats in compulsory silence: the desire for noise and jollity is suppressed.

Then suddenly a live turkey is let loose in the room, and it flounders about in terror, to the surprise of the men and the squeals of the women who can't understand this resurrection of the food they've just eaten. Order is reestablished and everyone puts away his momentarily uncontained joy.

Beaten by the silence, in an attempt to start any sort of conversation one of those present says:

"I haven't yet expressed my good wishes for the New Year."

Then as if following an order they all jump up and hurl themselves against the unwary conservator of tradition, whom they pummel repeatedly. Finally, happiness, exasperated by too much inaction, explodes and the guests disperse about the house, the most daring invading the kitchen.

The cook and two waiters are removed by force and everyone sets to thinking up a way of varying the meal. A fierce competition between the hot ovens, while frying pans and saucepans pass from hand to hand amidst laughter, shouts and a rain of ingredients.

Meanwhile others have discovered the wine cellar and thus an exceptional banquet is put together, which goes from kitchen to bedroom, from entrance hall to bathroom, to cellar. The dishes, put together almost by magic, follow one upon the other in the spirit of speed and harmony that animates the new cooks.

A guest tells the owner of the house:

"Fifteen years ago, on this same date . . ."

But that same moment he is presented with a bowl full of spumante with cauliflowers, slices of lemon and roast beef floating in it: the memory of the past is shipwrecked in a stunning present.

The youngest guests shout:

"Bury your memories! We must start the year in a quite different way from the pre-war banquets!"

Three gramophones function as tables and from on top of the records, which have become rotating plates, people pluck little sugar-coated candies, cylinders of Parmesan cheese and hard-boiled eggs, while three different rhythms of Japanese music accompany the dynamic service.

The owner of the house suddenly turns out the lights. Stupefaction. In the darkness the voice of one of the guests is heard:

"This year we will succeed in breaking through the envelope of the atmosphere and reach the planets. I invite you all to a banquet next New Year's Eve on the moon, where we will finally taste foods of a flavour unknown to our palates and unimaginable drinks!"

Formula by the Futurist Aeropainter
FILLÌA

Translated from the Italian by Suzanne Brill

DANIIL KHARMS (Russia, 1905–1942)

At two o'clock on Nevsky Prospect, or rather on the Avenue of October 25th, nothing of note occurred. No, no, that man who stopped nearby the "Coliseum" was there purely by accident. Maybe his boot came untied, or maybe he wanted to light a cigarette. Or something else entirely! He's just a visitor and doesn't know where to go. But where are his things? Wait, he's lifting his head for some reason, as if to look into the third floor, or even the fourth, maybe even the fifth. No, look, he simply sneezed and now he's on his way again. He slouches a little and his shoulders are raised. His green overcoat flaps in the wind. Just now he turned onto Nadezhdenskaya and disappeared around the corner.

A shoeshine man of eastern features stared after him and smoothed down his fluffy mustache with his hand.

His overcoat was long and thick, of a purple hue, either plaid or maybe striped, or maybe, damn it all, polka-dot.

Translated from the Russian by Matvei Yankelevich

STANLEY KUNITZ (United States, 1905–2006)

The Old Darned Man

Back in the thirties, in the midst of the Depression, I fled the city and moved to a Connecticut farm. It was the period of my first marriage. We lived in an old gambrel house, built about 1740, on top of a ridge called Wormwood Hill. I had bought the house, together with more than 100 acres of woodland and pasture, for $500 down. It had no electricity, no heat, no running water, and it was in bad repair, but it was a great, beautiful house. I spent most of three years, working with my hands, making it habitable. At that time early American art and furniture were practically being given away. Poor as we were, we managed to fill the house with priceless stuff. We were so far from the city and from all signs of progress that we might as well have been living in another age.

One spring there appeared on the road, climbing up the hill, a man in a patchwork suit, with a battered silk hat on his head. His trousers and swallow-tail coat had been mended so many times, with varicolored swatches, that when he approached us, over the brow of the hill, he looked like a crazyquilt on stilts.

He was an itinerant tinker, dried-out and old, thin as a scarecrow, with a high, cracked voice. He asked for pots and pans to repair, scissors and knives to sharpen. In the shade of the sugar maples, that a colonel in Washington's army was said to have planted, he set up his shop and silently went to work on the articles I handed to him.

When he was done, I offered him lunch in the kitchen. He would not sit down to eat, but accepted some food in a bag. "I have been here before," he said to me quietly. On our way out, while we were standing in the front hall at the foot of the staircase, he suddenly cried, "I hear the worms tumbling in this house." "What do you mean?" I asked. He did not answer, but cupped his hands over his eyes. I took it as a bad omen, a fateful prophecy, about my house, my marriage. And so it turned out to be.

Some time later I learned that my visitor was a legendary figure, known throughout the countryside as the Old Darned

Man. He had been a brilliant divinity student at Yale, engaged to a childhood sweetheart, with the wedding set for the day after graduation. But on that very day, while he waited at the church, the news was brought to him that she had run off with his dearest friend. Ever since then he had been wandering distractedly from village to village in his wedding clothes.

As for the worms, they belonged to a forgotten page in local history. Late in the nineteenth century the housewives of the region, dreaming of a fortune to be made, had started a cottage industry in silkworm culture, importing the worms from China. The parlors of every farmhouse were lined with stacks of silkworm trays, in which the worms munched on mulberry leaves, making clicking and whispering noises. That was the sound heard in my hall.

It's a story without a happy ending. The worms died; the dreams of riches faded; abandoned plows rusted in the farmyards; one breathless summer day a black-funneled twister wheeled up Wormwood Hill from the stricken valley, dismantling my house, my barn, my grove of sugar maples; the face of my bride darkened and broke into a wild laughter; I never saw the Old Darned Man again.

SAMUEL BECKETT (Ireland / France, 1906–1989)

One Evening

He was found lying on the ground. No one had missed him. No one was looking for him. An old woman found him. To put it vaguely. It happened so long ago. She was straying in search of wild flowers. Yellow only. With no eyes but for these she stumbled on him lying there. He lay face downward and arms outspread. He wore a greatcoat in spite of the time of year. Hidden by the body a long row of buttons fastened it all the way down. Buttons of all shapes and sizes. Worn upright the skirts swept the ground. That seems to hang together. Near the head a hat lay askew on the ground. At once on its brim and crown. He lay inconspicuous in the greenish coat. To catch an eye searching from afar there was only the white head. May she have seen him somewhere before? Somewhere on his feet before? Not too fast. She was all in black. The hem of her long black skirt trailed in the grass. It was close of day. Should she now move away into the east her shadow would go before. A long black shadow. It was lambing time. But there were no lambs. She could see none. Were a third party to chance that way theirs were the only bodies he would see. First that of the old woman standing. Then on drawing near it lying on the ground. That seems to hang together. The deserted fields. The old woman all in black stockstill. The body stockstill on the ground. Yellow at the end of the black arm. The white hair in the grass. The east foundering in night. Not too fast. The weather. Sky overcast all day till evening. In the west-north-west near the verge already the sun came out at last. Rain? A few drops if you will. A few drops in the morning if you will. In the present to conclude. It happened so long ago. Cooped indoors all day she comes out with the sun. She makes haste to gain the fields. Surprised to have seen no one on the way she strays feverishly in search of the wild flowers. Feverishly seeing the imminence of night. She remarks with surprise the absence of lambs in great numbers here at this time of year. She is wearing the black she took on when widowed young. It is to reflower the grave she strays in search of the flowers he had loved. But for the need of yellow at the end of the black arm there would be none. There are therefore only as few as possible. This is for her the third surprise since she came out. For they grow in plenty here at this time of year. Her old friend her shadow irks her. So much so that she turns to face the sun. Any flower wide of her course she reaches sidelong. She craves for sundown to end and to stray freely again in the long afterglow. Further to her distress the familiar rustle of her long black skirt in the grass. She moves with half-closed eyes as if drawn on into the glare. She may say to herself it is too much strangeness for a single March or April evening. No one abroad. Not a single lamb. Scarcely a flower. Shadow and rustle irksome. And to crown all the shock of her foot against a body. Chance. No one had missed him. No one was looking for him. Black and green

of the garments touching now. Near the white head the yellow
of the few plucked flowers. The old sunlit face. Tableau vivant if
you will. In its way. All is silent from now on. For as long as she
cannot move. The sun disappears at last and with it all shadow.
All shadow here. Slow fade of afterglow. Night without moon
or stars. All that seems to hang together. But no more about it

Translated from the French by the Author

RENÉ CHAR (France, 1907–1988)

Van Gogh's Haunts

I've always felt like a nothing, having in my final resting place
such a neighbor as van Gogh, who, I have been assured by several inhabitants of St. Rémy, was an impassioned painter, if a
little unreliable. He would take long walks at night, disappear-
ing among thick cypresses, which, however, could be easily
approached by the swift stars. Or he would stir up a mistral
with the cumbersome presence of his easel, his palette and his
wild bundles of canvases. Thus saddled, he packed himself off
to the vicinity of Montmajour, a ruin known for its perils. Arles
and Les Baux, the country threading toward the Rhone, were
also the settings for meanderings and sudden spurts of work by
a vaguely suspicious artist, if you judged by his eyes and his red
bristle without grasping the truth.

It was only later that a smokescreen of explanations was
hurled forth about him: This frequenter of the brothel of Arles
was in fact a decent man, who was taken in a demented state to
the asylum of Saint-Paul-de-Mausole just a few hundred yards
from Glanum, then still a buried city, but hinted at by a cradle-
shaped arc, which van Gogh had painted with the utmost skill in
one of his works. I understood, in looking at his drawings, that he
had up to that time *worked*, and only for us. And why not add to
this story something which occurred in another space and time?

This countryside, down to the belly of its grasshoppers, was
fully communicated to us by a hand and a wrist. From what

cauldron and from what paradise did Vincent van Gogh surge? From what great suffering did he produce those pebbles, those irises and those marshes, those narrow roads, those farms, that wheat, those vines, that river? Sublime work! In another century, locked behind the iron bars of several misfortunes, my own life tracked me down in a similar terrain! I realized this and tried to barter with Vincent's profound vision, but while his eyes were enriched by their truth, their novel flowers, mine were wounded, not gladdened, by melting snow. A dog I loved no longer seemed to feel obliged to respond to my call; in the same way the earth hung back, hesitant about man's approaching destiny.

Translated from the French by Susanne Dubroff

LEONARDO SINISGALLI (Italy, 1908–1981)

We're No Longer Punctual

We're no longer punctual in our meetings with nature. The world's gears seem to turn according to a law different from our own. Perhaps our blood simply takes a little longer to circulate through the body. We become aware of an event only after it's happened, of a voice when it's extinct.

Translated from the Italian by W. S. Di Piero

ENRIQUE ANDERSON IMBERT
(Argentina / United States, 1910–2000)

The Ring

Friday, at the fisherman's house. When they opened the fish they found a ring in its belly. The fish had swallowed it, at the bottom of the sea. The younger daughter put the ring on her finger. At school it surprised all her little friends: it was an undulating ring of water.

Dialogue with the Pursuer

In the mirrors Ramón caught a glimpse of someone watching him from behind. Also, behind him, he could hear a rustling, feel a breathing. If he turned around, nothing. But he began to talk to his pursuer, all the time. And he ended by walking sideways, like a crab. This is how we knew him, curved to the right, his head twisted, his mouth murmuring to one side, streaming blue from one strangely enlarged eye, in dialogue with the invisible demon who was always treading on his heels.

Translated from the Spanish by Isabel Reade

E. M. CIORAN (Romania / France, 1911–1995)

Almost all works are made with flashes of imitation, with studied shudders and stolen ecstasies.

*

That uncertain feeling when we try to imagine the daily life of great minds... Whatever could it be that Socrates was doing around two in the afternoon?

*

A philosophical vogue is as irresistible as a gastronomic one: an idea is no better refuted than a sauce.

*

I knew nothing about her; our encounter nonetheless took the most macabre turn: I spoke to her of the sea, of a certain commentary on Ecclesiastes. And imagine my stupefaction when, after my tirade on the hysteria of the waves, she produced this remark: "Self-pity is not a good thing."

*

The secret of my adaptation to life?—I've changed despairs the way I've changed shirts.

Translated from the French by Richard Howard

MAX FRISCH (Switzerland, 1911–1991)

Catalogue

Chestnuts as they burst gleaming from their green burrs / snow-flakes beneath the microscope / rock gardens Japanese style / book printing / desert caravans with camels on the yellow horizon / rain on railroad coach windows at night / an art nouveau vase in an antique shop / the mirage in the Anatolian desert, when one seems to see pools of blue water, the desert in general / turbines / sunrise through green Venetian blinds / manuscripts / coal heaps in the rain / the hair and skin of children / building sites / seagulls on the black mud flats at low tide / the blue sparkling of blow lamps / Goya / things seen through a telescope / wood shavings under a carpenter's bench / lava at night / photographs from the beginning of this century / horses on the misty Jura mountains / maps, old and new / the legs of a mulatto girl beneath her coat / bird tracks on the snow / inns in the suburbs / granite / a face the day after death / thistles between marbles in Greece / eyes, mouths / the inside of shells / the reflection of one skyscraper in the windows of another / pearlfisher girls / kaleidoscopes / ferns, faded and bleached / the hands of beloved old people / pebbles in a mountain stream / a Mayan relief in its original site / mushrooms / a crane in motion / walls with outdated posters / snakes gliding with raised heads through the water / a theater once viewed from the gridiron / fish in the market, fishing nets drying on the pavement, fish of all kinds / summer lightning / flight of the black Alpine chough, seeing it take off over the precipice as one stands on the ridge / a pair of lovers in a quiet museum / the feel of the hide on a living cow / sunlight reflected in a glass of red wine (Merlot) / a prairie fire / the amber light inside circus tents on a sunny afternoon / X-ray pictures one cannot decipher, one's own skeleton seemingly wrapped in fog or cotton wool / breakers at sea, a freighter on the horizon / blast furnaces / a red curtain seen from the dark street outside, the shadow of an unknown person on it / a glass, glasses, glass of all kinds / spider's webs in the woods against the sun / etchings on yellow-stained paper / a lot of people with umbrellas, headlights gleaming on the asphalt / oil portrait of one's own mother as a girl, painted by her father / the robes of religious orders to which I do not belong / the olive-green leather of an English writing desk / the look of a revered man, when he takes his glasses off to clean them / the network of gleaming rails outside a large railroad station at night / cats / milky moonlight over the jungle as one lies in a hammock drinking beer from a can, sweating and unable to sleep, thinking of nothing / libraries / a yellow bulldozer, moving mountains / vines, for example in Valais / films / a man's hat rolling down the Spanish Steps in Rome / a line of fresh paint applied to the wall with a broad brush / three branches before the window, winter sky above red brick houses in Manhattan, smoke rising from strangers' chimneys / the neck of a woman combing her hair / a Russian peasant before the icons in the Kremlin / Lake Zurich in March, the black fields, the blueness of snow in shadow...

Etc.

Etc.

Etc.

Joy (affirmation) through the mere act of seeing.

Translated from the German by Geoffrey Skelton

CZESLAW MILOSZ (Poland / United States, 1911–2004)

Road-Side Dog

I went on a journey in order to acquaint myself with my province, in a two-horse wagon with a lot of fodder and a tin bucket rattling in the back. The bucket was required for the horses to drink from. I traveled through a country of hills and pine groves that gave way to woodlands, where swirls of smoke hovered over the roofs of houses, as if they were on fire, for they were chimneyless cabins; I crossed districts of fields and lakes. It was so interesting to be moving, to give the horses their rein, and wait until, in the next valley, a village slowly appeared, or a park with the white spot of a manor in it. And always we were barked at by a dog, assiduous in its duty. That was the beginning of the century; this is its end. I have been thinking not only of the people who lived there once but also of the generations of dogs accompanying them in their everyday bustle, and one night—I don't know where it came from—in a pre-dawn sleep, that funny and tender phrase composed itself: a road-side dog.

O!

O objects of my desire, for whose sake I was able to practice asceticism, to be ardent, heroic, what pity I feel any time I think of your lips and hands and breasts and bellies consigned to bitter earth!

Christopher Robin

In April of 1996 the international press carried the news of the death, at age seventy-five, of Christopher Robin Milne, immortalized in a book by his father, A. A. Milne, Winnie-the-Pooh, *as Christopher Robin.*

I must think suddenly of matters too difficult for a bear of little brain. I have never asked myself what lies beyond the place where we live, I and Rabbit, Piglet and Eeyore, with our friend Christopher Robin. That is, we continued to live here, and nothing changed, and I just ate my little something. Only Christopher Robin left for a moment.

Owl says that immediately beyond our garden Time begins, and that it is an awfully deep well. If you fall in it, you go down and down, very quickly, and no one knows what happens to you next. I was a bit worried about Christopher Robin falling in, but he came back and then I asked him about the well. "Old bear," he answered. "I was in it and I was falling and I was changing as I fell. My legs became long, I was a big person, I wore trousers down to the ground, I had a gray beard, then I grew old, hunched, and I walked with a cane, and then I died. It was probably just a dream, it was quite unreal. The only real thing was you, old bear, and our shared fun. Now I won't go anywhere, even if I'm called for an afternoon snack."

Translated from the Polish by the Author and Robert Hass

KENNETH PATCHEN (United States, 1911–1972)

In Order To

Apply for the position (I've forgotten now for what) I had to marry the Second Mayor's daughter by twelve noon. The order arrived three minutes of.

I already had a wife; the Second Mayor was childless: but I did it.

Next they told me to shave off my father's beard. All right. No matter that he'd been a eunuch, and had succumbed in early childhood: I did it, I shaved him.

Then they told me to burn a village; next, a fair-sized town; then, a city; a bigger city; a small, down-at-heels country; then one of "the great powers"; then another (another, another)— In fact, they went right on until they'd told me to burn up every man-made thing on the face of the earth! And I did it, I burned away every last trace, I left nothing, nothing of any kind whatever.

Then they told me to blow it all to hell and gone! And I blew it all to hell and gone (oh, didn't I) . . .

Now, they said, put it back together again; put it all back the way it was when you started.

Well . . . it was my turn to tell *them* something! Shucks, I didn't want any job that bad.

At This Moment

As I say this a flashing wheel of children spins across the sun-drenched lawn!

The Late Afternoon

A shadow falls across the table ... drinks slowly of a cup, nibbles the roseleaf ...

You're All Nuts

Boobs, scamps, frauds, and all you assorted blaugh-swilling drearies—oh, COME OFF IT!

JOHN CAGE (United States, 1912–1992)

One evening when I was still living at Grand Street and Monroe, Isamu Noguchi came to visit me. There was nothing in the room (no furniture, no paintings). The floor was covered, wall to wall, with cocoa matting. The windows had no curtains, no drapes. Isamu Noguchi said, "An old shoe would look beautiful in this room."

*

Morris Graves used to have an old Ford in Seattle. He had removed all the seats and put in a table and chairs so that the car was like a small furnished room with books, a vase with flowers and so forth. One day he drove up to a luncheonette, parked, opened the door on the street side, unrolled a red carpet across the sidewalk. Then he walked on the carpet, went in, and ordered a hamburger. Meanwhile a crowd gathered, expecting something strange to happen. However, all Graves did was eat the hamburger, pay his bill, get back in the car, roll up the carpet, and drive off.

*

On Yap Island phosphorescent fungi are used as hair ornaments for moonlight dances.

AIMÉ CÉSAIRE (Martinique, 1913–2008)

It Is the Courage of Men Which Is Dislocated

The extraordinary telephony from the central fire to galaxies installed in one second and by what orders! The rain, it's the testy way here and now to strike out everything that exists, everything that's been created, cried out, said, lied about, soiled. Where on earth did you hear that rain falls?

It is the courage of men which is dislocated. Rain is always wholehearted. Rain exults. It is a levy en masse of inspiration, a jolt of tropical sleep; a forward of lympths; a frenzy of caterpillars and faculae; a tumultuous assault against everything that burrows in warrens; the thrust counter-current to gravity of a thousand crazed rounds of ammunition and the tur-ra-mas that jump as they advance—sea horses toward the finallys and the suburbs.

Finally! The tree bursts with grenade. The rock explodes. Tenderness: now and then this great repose. Tenderness: now and then this orchestra playing and intertwining steps like plaited wicker.

Tenderness, but that of adorable tortures: the setting in motion of a fire of bit-braces which drill and force the void to scream star. It is blood. Moreover it is hard to understand how it is enough to feed the extraordinary devolution of horses which from ridge to ridge turn back on the momentum of the ravines.

No more monarchy. And it is perpetual this invention of ecstatic chants, of abbreviated prayers, of meticulous spider ceremonials, of saws which splash about, of unknotted hair, of enameled glass mosque lamps which collide, of seas which flow and ebb, of an alembic, of worms which at full steam trumpet unforgettable condensations.

Unforgettable indeed. An assagai dance the likes of which has never been seen and ten thousand victory flags torn from the cetaceans and waved by the earth.

The vineyard of wrath has peddled to the very sky the alcohol of its repose and its salvation.

Translated from the French by Clayton Eshleman and Annette Smith

DAVID IGNATOW (United States, 1914–1997)

The Diner

For Sartre

If I order a sandwich and get a plate of ham and eggs instead, has communication broken down? Is there a chef in the house? There's no chef. I get only silence. Who brought me the ham and eggs? I was sitting at the counter when it arrived. I don't remember anyone bringing it. I'm leaving right now to find another place to eat in, a bit more congenial than this silence, with no one to witness that I ordered exactly what I say I did. But now the door is closed and I can't leave.

Will someone please open the door, the one who gave me the ham and eggs instead of a sandwich? If I'm dissatisfied and want to leave why must I stay? Can the proprietor do as he pleases with anyone on his property? Am I his property too? What do you know! I have to eat what's given me or go hungry. I have to be nice about it too and say thank you to the silence. But I want to know why I can't have what I want that's such an innocent wish as between a sandwich and a plate of ham and eggs? What have I said or did I say what I thought I did or am I in my own country where my language is spoken? Where am I? Why can't I leave this diner? This is not my country. I don't belong here. I never even got a passport to come. I don't remember leaving. I don't remember crossing the border and I'm the only guy here at the counter. Something phony is going on. Somebody is trying to drive me nuts or rob me or kill me. I want to go back where I came from. I was on the road hungry, driving. It was dark and I hadn't eaten my dinner.

You know, it's quite possible I made these ham and eggs myself instead of a sandwich. It may be I'm the owner because no one else is here and I have the key to open the door, exactly like my car key. I must have arranged it that way. Now when in hell did I buy this diner and who needs it!

OCTAVIO PAZ (Mexico, 1914–1998)

Marvels of Will

At precisely three o'clock don Pedro would arrive at our table, greet each customer, mumble to himself some indecipherable sentences, and silently take a seat. He would order a cup of coffee, light a cigarette, listen to the chatter, sip his coffee, pay the waiter, take his hat, grab his case, say good afternoon, and leave. And so it was every day.

What did don Pedro say upon sitting and rising, with serious face and hard eyes? He said:

"I hope you die."

Don Pedro repeated the phrase many times each day. Upon rising, upon completing his morning preparations, upon entering and leaving his house—at eight o'clock, at one, at two-thirty, at seven-forty—in the café, in the office, before and after every meal, when going to bed each night. He repeated it between his teeth or in a loud voice, alone or with others. Sometimes with only his eyes. Always with all his soul.

No one knew to whom he addressed these words. Everyone ignored the origin of his hate. When someone wanted to dig deeper into the story, don Pedro would turn his head with disdain and fall silent, modest. Perhaps it was a causeless hate, a pure hate. But the feeling nourished him, gave seriousness to his life, majesty to his years. Dressed in black, he seemed to be prematurely mourning for his victim.

One afternoon don Pedro arrived graver than usual. He sat down heavily, and, in the center of the silence that was created by his presence, he simply dropped these words:

"I killed him."

Who and how? Some smiled, wanting to the take the thing as a joke. Don Pedro's look stopped them. All of us felt uncomfortable. That sense of the void of death was certain. Slowly the group dispersed. Don Pedro remained alone, more serious than ever, a little withered, like a burnt-out star, but tranquil, without remorse.

He did not return the next day. He never returned. Did he die? Maybe he needed that life-giving hate. Maybe he still lives and now hates another. I examine my actions, and advise you to do the same. Perhaps you too have incurred the same obstinate, patient anger of those small myopic eyes. Have you ever thought how many—perhaps very close to you—watch you with the same eyes as don Pedro?

Translated from the Spanish by Eliot Weinberger

ALEKSANDR SOLZHENITSYN (Russia, 1918–2008)

Lake Segden

No one writes about this lake and it is spoken of only in whispers. As though to an enchanted castle, all roads to it are barred and over each one hangs a forbidding sign—a plain, blunt straight line.

Man or beast, faced by that sign, must turn back. Some earthly power has put that sign there; past it none may ride, none may walk, crawl, or even fly.

Guards with swords and pistols lurk beside the path in the nearby pine grove.

You may circle and circle the silent wood searching for a way through to the lake, but you will find none and there will be no one to ask, for no one goes into this wood. They have all been frightened away. Your only chance to venture through will be one afternoon in the rain along a cattle track, in the wake of the dull clink of a cowbell. And from your first glimpse of it, vast and shimmering between the tree trunks, you know before you reach its banks that you will be in thrall to this place for the rest of your life.

Segden Lake is as round as though traced out with a pair of compasses. If you were to shout from one side (but you must not shout, or you will be heard), only a fading echo would reach the other bank. It is a long way across. Woods immure the lakeside entirely, a dense forest of row upon unbroken row of trees. As you come out of the wood to the water's edge, you can see the whole of the forbidden shore: here a strip of yellow sand, there a grey stubble of reeds, there a lush swathe of grass. The water is smooth, calm, and unruffled, and apart from some patches of weed by the shore, the white lake bed gleams through the translucent water.

A secret lake in a secret forest. The water looks up and the sky gazes down upon it. If there is a world beyond the forest, it is unknown, invisible; if it exists, it has no place here.

Here is somewhere to settle forever, a place where a man could live in harmony with the elements and be inspired.

But it cannot be. An evil prince, a squint-eyed villain, has claimed the lake for his own: there is his house, there is his bathing place. His evil brood goes fishing here, shoots duck from his boat. First a wisp of blue smoke above the lake, then a moment later the shot.

Away beyond the woods, the people sweat and heave, whilst all the roads leading here are closed lest they intrude. Fish and game are bred for the villain's pleasure. Here there are traces where someone lit a fire but it was put out and he was driven away.

Beloved, deserted lake.

My native land . . .

Translated from the Russian by Michael Glenny

PAUL CELAN (Romania / France, 1920–1970)

The next day the deportations about to begin, at night Rafael showed up, mantled in a vast hopelessness of black silk, with hood, his burning gazes were crossing on my forehead, torrents of wine began streaming on my cheeks, they scattered on the floor, men sipped it in their sleep.—Come, said Rafael, placing over my too shiny shoulders a hopelessness not unlike the one he was wearing. I was leaning towards mother, I was kissing her, incestuously, and then, out of the house. A huge swarm of large black butterflies, in from the tropics, thwarted my advance. Rafael dragged me after him and we descended in the direction of the railway tracks. Under foot I felt the tracks, heard the whistle of a locomotive, very near, my heart tightened. The train rattled over our heads.

I opened my eyes. In front of me, across a huge expanse, stood a vast candelabra with thousands of arms.—Is it gold?! I whispered to Rafael.—Gold. You'll crawl up one of the arms, so that, then, when I have lifted it up into the heavens, you'll hook it up to the sky. Before the break of dawn, people will be able to save themselves, flying there. I'll show them the way, and you'll welcome them.

I crawled up one of the arms, Rafael was shifting from one arm to the other, was touching them one after the other, the candelabra began to lift. A leaf fell on my forehead, on the very spot my friend had touched with his gaze, a maple leaf. I look all around: this cannot be the sky. Hours pass and I haven't found anything. I know: down there the people gathered, Rafael touched them with his thin fingers, and they lifted off, and me, I'm still rising.

Where is the sky? Where?

Translated from the Romanian by Julian Semilian and Sanda Agalidi

CLARICE LISPECTOR (Brazil, 1920–1977)

The Fifth Story

This story could be called "The Statues." Another possible title would be "The Killing." Or even "How to Kill Cockroaches." So I shall tell at least three stories, all of them true, because none of the three will contradict the others. Although they constitute one story, they could become a thousand and one, were I to be granted a thousand and one nights.

The first story, "How To Kill Cockroaches," begins like this: I was complaining about the cockroaches. A woman heard me complain. She gave me a recipe for killing them. I was to mix together equal quantities of sugar, flour and gypsum. The flour and sugar would attract the cockroaches, the gypsum would dry up their insides. I followed her advice. The cockroaches died.

The next story is really the first, and it is called "The Killing." It begins like this: I was complaining about the cockroaches. A woman heard me complain. The recipe follows. And then the killing takes place. The truth is that I had only complained in abstract terms about the cockroaches, for they were not even mine: they belonged to the ground floor and climbed up the pipes in the building into our apartment. It was only when I prepared the mixture that they also became mine. On our behalf, therefore, I began to measure and weigh ingredients with greater concentration. A vague loathing had taken possession of me, a sense of outrage. By day, the cockroaches were invisible and no one would believe in the evil secret which eroded such a tranquil household. But if the cockroaches, like evil secrets, slept by day, there I was preparing their nightly poison. Meticulous, eager, I prepared the elixir of prolonged death. An angry fear and my own evil secret guided me. Now I coldly wanted one thing only: to kill every cockroach in existence. Cockroaches climb up the pipes while weary people sleep. And now the recipe was ready, looking so white. As if I were dealing with cockroaches as cunning as myself, I carefully spread the powder until it looked like part of the surface dust. From my bed, in the silence of the apartment, I imagined them climbing up one by one into the kitchen where darkness slept, a solitary towel alert on the clothes-line. I awoke hours later, startled at having overslept. It was beginning to grow light. I walked across the kitchen. There they lay on the floor of the scullery, huge and brittle. During the night I had killed them. On our behalf, it was beginning to grow light. On a nearby hill, a cockerel crowed.

The third story which now begins is called "The Statues." It begins by saying that I had been complaining about the cockroaches. Then the same woman appears on the scene. And so it goes on to the point where I awake as it is beginning to grow light, and I awake still feeling sleepy and I walk across the kitchen. Even more sleepy is the scullery floor with its tiled perspective. And in the shadows of dawn, there is a purplish hue which distances everything; at my feet, I perceive patches of light and shade, scores of rigid statues scattered everywhere. The cockroaches that have hardened from core to shell. Some are lying upside down. Others arrested in the midst of some movement that will never be completed. In the mouths of some of the cockroaches, there are traces of white powder. I am the first to observe the dawn breaking over Pompei. I know what this night has been, I know about the orgy in the dark. In some, the gypsum has hardened as slowly as in some organic process, and the cockroaches, with ever more tortuous movements, have greedily intensified the night's pleasures, trying to escape from their insides. Until they turn to stone, in innocent terror and with such, but such an expression of pained reproach. Others— suddenly assailed by their own core, without even having perceived that their inner form was turning to stone!—these are suddenly crystallized, just like a word arrested on someone's lips: I love . . . The cockroaches, invoking the name of love in vain, sang on a summer's night. While the cockroach over there, the one with the brown antennae smeared with white, must have realized too late that it had become mummified precisely because it did not know how to use things with the gratuitous grace of the *in vain*: "It is just that I looked too closely inside myself! it is just that I looked too closely inside . . ."—from my frigid height as a human being, I watch the destruction of a world. Dawn breaks. Here and there, the parched antennae of dead cockroaches quiver in the breeze. The cockerel from the previous story crows.

The fourth story opens a new era in the household. The story begins as usual: I was complaining about the cockroaches. It goes on up to the point when I see the statues in plaster of Paris. Inevitably dead. I look towards the pipes where this same night an infestation will reappear, swarming slowly upwards in Indian file. Should I renew the lethal sugar every night? like someone who no longer sleeps without the avidity of some rite. And should I take myself somnambulant out to the terrace early each morning? in my craving to encounter the statues which my perspiring night has erected. I trembled with depraved pleasure at the vision of my double existence as a witch. I also trembled at the sight of that hardening gypsum, the depravity of existence which would shatter my internal form.

The grim moment of choosing between two paths, which I thought would separate, convinced that any choice would mean sacrificing either myself or my soul. I chose. And today I secretly carry a plaque of virtue in my heart: "This house has been disinfected."

The fifth story is called "Leibnitz and The Transcendence of Love in Polynesia". . . It begins like this: I was complaining about the cockroaches.

The Future of Something Delicate

—Mummy, I have seen a tiny hurricane but still so tiny, that all it could do was to rustle three tiny leaves on the street-corner . . .

Translated from the Portuguese by Giovanni Pontiero

AUGUSTO MONTERROSO (Guatemala, 1921–2003)

The Dinosaur

When he awoke, the dinosaur was still there.

Errata and Final Notice

Somewhere on page 45 a comma is missing, omitted consciously or unconsciously by the typesetter who failed to include it on that day, at that time, on that machine; any imbalance this error may cause in the world is his responsibility.

Except for the table of contents, which for unknown reasons comes last in Spanish, the book ends on this page, number 152, which does not mean it could not also begin again here in a backward motion as useless and irrational as the one undertaken by the reader to reach this point.

Translated from the Spanish by Edith Grossman

GIORGIO MANGANELLI (Italy, 1922–1990)

This thoughtful and pointlessly melancholy man has been living for many years, by now, in the basement, because the house that rose above it has been destroyed or is uninhabitable. When the religious wars broke out, he had hoped it was a question—he was a foreigner in that country and practiced another religion—of the customary depravities to which that region's inhabitants were inclined, all of them sanguineous of dying in some noisy and exhibitionistic way, and of killing others with particular cruelty. He bore no love for that country, where he lived as the secretary to the ambassador of another country, where wars of religion were not waged. His country fought atheistic wars, scientifically based. At the moment when the wars of religion had broken out, the secretary had been unable to return to his native land, where a ferocious scientific war was then underway: a war concerned, at least in origin, with hexagons and acids, but which bit by bit had then expanded to the inclusion of nearly all the disciplines, with the sole exclusion of ancient history. Now, the secretary, whom you see in sober dress, has been said, in generic terms, to practice another religion, but there is also the possibility that he practices none at all. What his country most respects is allegiance to ideals upon scientific bases; he himself, however, has no great love

of science, and if he had to choose a field in which to special-
ize, ancient history would be his choice. But since this is the only
non-controversial subject, choosing it would have been regarded
as suspect, and derided as cowardly. He would have been put
to death. Fortuitously, the outbreak of the religious war had
allowed him to give no response to requests for clarification that
had come from his homeland, but at the very same time he had
definitively exiled himself in the country of religious wars. For
years he had ventured no more than a few dozen yards from his
cellar; he was probably the only foreigner left in a country where
massacre was pandemic, and becoming pedantic; a country that
no longer had cities, but picturesque expanses of ruins awaiting
the death of the last combatant, so as then to grow ivy-covered
and be transported into History. Though he had never admitted
it in so many words, he liked to live in that territory precisely for
its being the theater of a war that was alien to him. So History
was none of his doing, but was something perceived as a rumble
to which he had grown accustomed; as a lover of ancient history and dead languages, he too looked forward to living—as had
always been his dream—in a country made only and entirely of
ruins among grasses that have no history.

Translated from the Italian by Henry Martin

ITALO CALVINO (Italy, 1923–1985)

Nero and Bertha

This particular Bertha was a poor woman who did nothing but
spin, being a skillful spinner.

One day as she was going along she met Nero, the Roman
emperor, to whom she said, "May God grant you health so good
you'll live a thousand years!"

Nero, whom not a soul could abide because he was so mean,
was astounded to hear someone wishing him a thousand years of
life, and he replied, "Why do you say that to me, my good woman?"

"Because a bad one is always followed by one still worse."

Nero then said, "Very well, bring to my palace all you spin between now and tomorrow morning." At that, he left her.

As she spun, Bertha said to herself, "What will he do with the thread I'm spinning? I wouldn't put it past him to hang me with it! That hangman is capable of everything!"

Next morning, right on time, here she was at Nero's palace. He invited her in, received the thread she had spun, and said, "Tie the end of the ball to the palace door and walk away as far as you can go with the thread." Then he called his chief steward and said, "For the length of the thread, the land on both sides of the road belongs to this woman."

Bertha thanked him and walked away very happy. From that day on she no longer needed to spin, for she had become a lady.

When word of the event got around Rome, all the poor women went to Nero in hopes of a present such as he had given Bertha.

But Nero replied, "The good old times when Bertha spun are no more."

Translated from the Italian by George Martin

ZBIGNIEW HERBERT (Poland, 1924–1998)

Hell

Counting from the top: a chimney, antennae, a warped tin roof. Through a round window you see a girl trapped in threads whom the moon forgot to draw in and left to the mercy of gossipmongers and spiders. Farther down a woman reads a letter, cools her face with powder, and goes on reading. On the first floor a young man is walking back and forth thinking: how can I go outdoors with these bitten lips and shoes falling apart? The café downstairs is empty; it's still morning.

Just one couple in a corner. They are holding hands. He says: "We will always be together. Waiter, a black coffee and a lemonade, please." The waiter goes behind the curtain and once there, bursts out laughing.

The History of the Minotaur

The true history of the prince Minotaur is told in the yet unde-ciphered script Linear A. He was—despite later rumors—the authentic son of King Minos and Pasiphaë. The little boy was born healthy, but with an abnormally large head—which for-tune-tellers read as a sign of his future wisdom. In fact with the years the Minotaur grew into a robust, slightly melancholy idiot. The king decided to give him up to be educated as a priest. But the priests explained that they couldn't accept the feeble-minded prince, for that might diminish the authority of reli-gion, already undermined by the invention of the wheel.

Minos then brought in the engineer Daedalus, who was fash-ionable in Greece at the time as the creator of a popular branch of pedagogical architecture. And so the labyrinth arose. Within its system of pathways, from elementary to more and more complicated, its variations in levels and rungs of abstraction, it was supposed to train the Minotaur prince in the principles of correct thinking.

So the unhappy prince wandered along the pathways of induction and deduction, prodded by his preceptors, gazing blankly at ideological frescos. He didn't get them at all.

Having exhausted all his resources, King Minos resolved to get rid of this disgrace to the royal line. He brought in (again from Greece, which was known for its able men) the ace assas-sin Theseus. And Theseus killed the Minotaur. On this point myth and history agree.

Through the labyrinth—now a useless primer—Theseus makes his way back carrying the big, bloody head of the Minotaur with its goggling eyes, in which for the first time wis-dom had begun to sprout—of a kind ordinarily attributed to experience.

Translated from the Polish by Alissa Valles

BOB KAUFMAN (United States, 1925–1986)

Picasso's Balcony

Pale morning light, dying in shadows, loving the earth in mid-day rays, casting blue to skies in rings, sowing powder trails across balconies. Hung in evening to swing gently, on shoulders of time, growing old, yet swallowing events of a thousand nights of dying and loving, all blue. Gone to that tomb, hidden in cubic air, breathing sounds of sorrow.

Crying love rising from the lips of wounded flowers, wailing, sobbing, breathing uneven sounds of sorrow, lying in wells of earth, throbbing, covered with desperate laughter, out of cool angels, spread over night. Dancing blue images, shades of blue pasts, all yesterdays, tomorrows, breaking on pebbled bodies, on sands of blue and coral, spent.

Life lying heaped in mounds, with volcano mouth tops, puckered, open, sucking in atoms of air, sprinkling in atoms of air, coloring space, with flecks of brilliance, opaline glistening, in eyes, in flames.

Blue flames burning, on rusty cliffs, overlooking blue seas, bluish. In sad times, hurt seabirds come to wail in ice white wind, alone, and wail in starlight wells, cold pits of evening, and endings, flinging rounds of flame sheeted balls of jagged bone, eaten, with remains of torn flowers, overwhelming afterthoughts, binding loves, classic pains, casting elongated shadows, of early blue.

Stringing hours together in thin melodic lines, wrapped around the pearl neck of morning, beneath the laughter, of sad sea birds.

KENNETH KOCH (United States, 1925–2002)

Venice

I dreamed last night that Marcello told me it was too complicated. I had this dream last night. I wrote the libretto this past
summer, in July.

Everything is a dream, said his friend. What's the difference
if Marcello sets the libretto or not?

None, he said. But *you* write a libretto and then let's just
see if you'd prefer to have it set or not. I'd like Marcello to set
it, and Ronconi to direct it, and for there to be simultaneous
performances outdoors above the Canal in Venice and at the
Metropolitan Opera. That's what I want.

When I heard my wife's voice on the telephone, calling me
in Venice from New York City, I knew that someone must have
died. We didn't phone each other now about ordinary things.

Venice. The cemetery. Walking around. Arm in arm, sometimes. Occasionally, hand in hand. Her eyes look up. His look
down. They look down together. A grave.

Evening. Later. The shine of plates. The smile of knives and
of forks.

Hotel. Stone balcony. Opposite church. Great big faces.
Almost in the room. Stone they stare at them with their own
face. And yet since it is Carnival he and she put on masks. One
red mask his. One black mask hers. This is happiness. There is
no other. Cold water faucet. A slight pain in the chest.

She takes. Opposite church. To miss what massive. Increasing
silence. Man at the desk. Woman at the desk.

Dream band. Marchers off the street. Canal-side restaurant.
No more eels! Isthmuses of islands.

I have. I have a reason. I have a reason to be sad. Here is a
reason to be joyful. A grass turf. A striped day. But, most of all,
this girl.

It became what it began to be: a cemetery. An island dedicated to the dead.

Black were the gondolas in the canals, and black the clothing that the gondoliers wore. Black were the buttons on the

coat that he did not put on, to go out, because it was spring. Black were the steps on the stairway when he first came to them, blinded by the sun. And then his body went off.

Again said Marcello, I said I won't set it and I won't. It's too complicated. A librettist in writing should seek only to inspire the writing of music. You haven't done that.

I have more friends than you, Marcello, I said.

Ah, but they don't set libretti, Marcello said. But if I don't set it, of course you are free to give it to someone else. But here. Let me look at it one last time.

At this point I woke up. The complicated dream was at an end. Actually, Morton had died, and I was walking around thinking, thinking, whether I wanted to or not. Thinking neither of Morton nor of the opera but of you.

ROBERT BLY (United States, 1926–)

The Dead Seal

1.

Walking north toward the point, I come on a dead seal. From a few feet away, he looks like a brown log. The body is on its back, dead only a few hours. I stand and look at him. There's a quiver in the dead flesh: My God, he's still alive. And a shock goes through me, as if a wall of my room had fallen away.

His head is arched back, the small eyes closed; the whiskers sometimes rise and fall. He is dying. This is the oil. Here on its back is the oil that heats our houses so efficiently. Wind blows fine sand back toward the ocean. The flipper near me lies folded over the stomach, looking like an unfinished arm, lightly glazed with sand at the edges. The other flipper lies half underneath. And the seal's skin looks like an old overcoat, scratched here and there—by sharp mussel shells maybe.

I reach out and touch him. Suddenly he rears up, turns over. He gives three cries: Awaark! Awaark! Awaark!—like the cries from Christmas toys. He lunges toward me; I am terrified and leap back, though I know there can be no teeth in that jaw. He starts flopping toward the sea. But he falls over, on his face. He does not want to go back to the sea. He looks up at the sky, and he looks like an old lady who has lost her hair. He puts his chin back down on the sand, rearranges his flippers, and waits for me to go. I go.

2.

The next day I go back to say good-bye. He's dead now. But he's not. He's a quarter mile farther up the shore. Today he is thinner, squatting on his stomach, head out. The ribs show much more: each vertebra on the back under the coat is visible, shiny. He breathes in and out.

A wave comes in, touches his nose. He turns and looks at me—the eyes slanted; the crown of his head looks like a boy's leather jacket bending over some bicycle bars. He is taking a long time to die. The whiskers white as porcupine quills, the forehead slopes. . . . Goodbye, brother, die in the sound of the waves. Forgive us if we have killed you. Long live your race, your inner-tube race, so uncomfortable on land, so comfortable in the ocean. Be comfortable in death then, when the sand will be out of your nostrils, and you can swim in long loops through the pure death, ducking under as assassinations break above you. You don't want to be touched by me. I climb the cliff and go home the other way.

CHRISTOPHER MIDDLETON (England, 1926–)

A Warm Place Revisited

Stendhal noticed at La Brède that there was no parquetry for the floor, that the fireplace, though baronial, was not dominated by a mirror, and that the right-hand jamb of it had been worn down by the slipper which Montesquieu placed there one hundred years before, to prop up the knee on which he chose to write *Le Grandeur des Romains*.

FRANK O'HARA (United States, 1926–1966)

Meditations in an Emergency

Am I to become profligate as if I were a blonde? Or religious as
if I were French?

Each time my heart is broken it makes me feel more adven-
turous (and how the same names keep recurring on that interminable list!), but one of these days there'll be nothing left with
which to venture forth.

Why should I share you? Why don't you get rid of someone
else for a change?

I am the least difficult of men. All I want is boundless love.

Even trees understand me! Good heavens, I lie under them,
too, don't I? I'm just like a pile of leaves.

However, I have never clogged myself with the praises of pas-
toral life, nor with nostalgia for an innocent past of perverted
acts in pastures. No. One need never leave the confines of New
York to get all the greenery one wishes—I can't even enjoy a
blade of grass unless I know there's a subway handy, or a record
store or some other sign that people do not totally *regret* life.
It is more important to affirm the least sincere; the clouds get
enough attention as it is and even they continue to pass. Do
they know what they're missing? Uh huh.

My eyes are vague blue, like the sky, and change all the time;
they are indiscriminate but fleeting, entirely specific and dis-
loyal, so that no one trusts me. I am always looking away. Or
again at something after it has given me up. It makes me restless and that makes me unhappy, but I cannot keep them still.
If only I had grey, green, black, brown, yellow eyes; I would
stay at home and do something. It's not that I'm curious. On
the contrary, I am bored but it's my duty to be attentive, I
am needed by things as the sky must be above the earth. And
lately, so great has *their* anxiety become, I can spare myself
little sleep.

Now there is only one man I love to kiss when he is unshaven. Heterosexuality! you are inexorably approaching. (How discourage her?)

St. Serapion, I wrap myself in the robes of your whiteness which is like midnight in Dostoevsky. How am I to become a legend, my dear? I've tried love, but that hides you in the bosom of another and I am always springing forth from it like the lotus—the ecstasy of always bursting forth! (but one must not be distracted by it!) or like a hyacinth, "to keep the filth of life away," yes, there, even in the heart, where the filth is pumped in and slanders and pollutes and determines. I will my will, though I may become famous for a mysterious vacancy in that department, that greenhouse.

Destroy yourself, if you don't know!
It is easy to be beautiful; it is difficult to appear so. I admire you, beloved, for the trap you've set. It's like a final chapter no one reads because the plot is over.
"Fanny Brown is run away—scampered off with a Cornet of Horse; I do love that little Minx, & hope She may be happy, tho' She has vexed me by this Exploit a little too.—Poor silly Cecchina! or F:B: as we used to call her.—I wish She had a good Whipping and 10,000 pounds."—Mrs. Thrale.

I've got to get out of here. I choose a piece of shawl and my dirtiest suntans. I'll be back, I'll re-emerge, defeated, from the valley; you don't want me to go where you go, so I go where you don't want me to. It's only afternoon, there's a lot ahead. There won't be any mail downstairs. Turning, I spit in the lock and the knob turns.

JOHN ASHBERY (United States, 1927–)

Vendanges

A tall building in the fifteenth arrondissement faded away slowly and then completely vanished. Toward November the weather grew very bitter. No one knew why or even noticed. I forgot to tell you your hat looked perky.

A new way of falling asleep has been discovered. Senior citizens snoop around to impose that sleep. You awake feeling refreshed but something has changed. Perhaps it's the children singing too much. Sophie shouldn't have taken them to the concert. I pleaded with her at the time, to no avail. Also, they have the run of the yard. Someone else might want to use it, or have it be empty. All the chairs were sat on in one night.

And I was pale and restless. The actors walked with me to the cabins. I knew that someone was about to lose or destroy my life's work, or invention. Yet something urged calm on me.

There is an occasional friend left, yes. Married men, hand to mouth. I went down to the exhibition. We came back and listened to some records. Strange, I hadn't noticed the lava pouring. But it's there, she said, every night of the year, like a river. I guess I notice things less now than I used to,

when I was young.

And the arbitrariness of so much of it, like sheep's wool from a carding comb. You can't afford to be vigilant, she said. You must stay this way, always, open and vulnerable. Like a body cavity. Then if you are noticed it will be too late to file the architectural pants. We must, as you say, keep in touch. Not to be noticed. If it was for this I was born, I murmured under my breath. What have I been doing around here, all this month? Waiting for the repairman, I suppose.

Where were you when the last droplets dribbled? Fastening my garter belt to my panty hose. The whole thing was over in less time than you could say Jack Robinson and we were back at base camp, one little thing after another gone wrong, yet on the whole life is spiritual. Still, it is time to pull up stakes. Probably we'll meet a hooded stranger on the path who will point out a direction for us to take, and that will be okay too, interesting even if it's boring.

I remember the world of cherry blossoms looking up at the sun and wondering, what have I done to deserve this or anything else?

W. S. MERWIN (United States, 1927–)

The Dachau Shoe

My cousin Gene (he's really only a second cousin) has a shoe he picked up at Dachau. It's a pretty worn-out shoe. It wasn't top quality in the first place, he explained. The sole is cracked clear across and has pulled loose from the upper on both sides, and the upper is split at the ball of the foot. There's no lace and there's no heel.

He explained he didn't steal it because it must have belonged to a Jew who was dead. He explained that he wanted some little thing. He explained that the Russians looted everything. They just took anything. He explained that it wasn't top quality to begin with. He explained that the guards or the kapos would have taken it if it had been any good. He explained that he was lucky to have got anything. He explained that it wasn't wrong because the Germans were defeated. He explained that everybody was picking up something. A lot of guys wanted flags or daggers or medals or things like that, but that kind of thing didn't appeal to him so much. He kept it on the mantelpiece for a while but he explained that it wasn't a trophy.

He explained that it's no use being vindictive. He explained that he wasn't. Nobody's perfect. Actually we share a German grandfather. But he explained that this was the reason why we had to fight that war. What happened at Dachau was a crime that could not be allowed to pass. But he explained that we could not really do anything to stop it while the war was going on because we had to win the war first. He explained that we couldn't always do just what we would have liked to do. He explained that the Russians killed a lot of Jews too. After a couple of years he put the shoe away in a drawer. He explained that the dust collected in it.

Now he has it down in the cellar in a box. He explains that the central heating makes it crack worse. He'll show it to you, though, any time you ask. He explains how it looks. He explains how it's hard to take it in, even for him. He explains how it was raining, and there weren't many things left when he got there. He explains how there wasn't anything of value and you didn't want to get caught taking anything of that kind, even if there had been. He explains how everything inside smelled. He explains how it was just lying out in the mud, probably right where it had come off. He explains that he ought to keep it. A thing like that.

You really ought to go and see it. He'll show it to you. All you have to do is ask. It's not that it's really a very interesting shoe when you come right down to it but you learn a lot from his explanations.

Make This Simple Test

Blindfold yourself with some suitable object. If time permits remain still for a moment. You may feel one or more of your senses begin to swim back toward you in the darkness, singly and without their names. Meanwhile have someone else arrange the products to be used in a row in front of you. It is preferable to have them in identical containers, though that is not necessary. Where possible, perform the test by having the other person feed you a portion—a spoonful—of each of the products in turn, without comment.

Guess what each one is, and have the other person write down what you say.

Then remove the blindfold. While arranging the products the other person should have detached part of the label or container from each and placed it in front of the product it belongs to, like a title. This bit of legend must not contain the product's trade name nor its generic name, nor any suggestion of the product's taste or desirability. Or price. It should be limited to that part of the label or container which enumerates the actual components of the product in question.

Thus, for instance:

"Contains dextrinized flours, cocoa processed with alkali, non-fat dry milk solids, yeast nutrients, vegetable proteins, agar, hydrogenated vegetable oil, dried egg yolk, GUAR, sodium cyclamate, soya lecithin, imitation lemon oil, acetyl tartaric esters of mono- and diglycerides as emulsifiers, polysorbate 60, 1/10 of 1% of sodium benzoate to retard spoilage."

Or:

"Contains anhydrated potatoes, powdered whey, vegetable gum, emulsifier (glycerol monostearate), invert syrup, shortening with freshness preserver, lactose, sorbic acid to retard mold growth, caramel color, natural and artificial flavors, sodium acid pyrophosphate, sodium bisulfate."

Or:

"Contains beef extract, wheat and soya derivatives, food starch-modified, dry sweet whey, calcium carageenan, vegetable oil, sodium phosphates to preserve freshness, BHA, BHT, prophylene glycol, pectin, niacinamide, artificial flavor, U.S. certified color."

There should be not less than three separate products.

Taste again, without the blindfold. Guess again and have the other person record the answers. Replace the blindfold. Have the other person change the order of the products and again feed you a spoonful of each.

Guess again what you are eating or drinking in each case (if you can make the distinction). But this time do not stop there. Guess why you are eating or drinking it. Guess what it may do for you. Guess what it was meant to do for you. By whom. When.

Where. Why. Guess where in the course of evolution you took the first step toward it. Guess which of your organs recognize it. Guess whether it is welcomed to their temples. Guess how it figures in their prayers. Guess how completely you become what you eat. Guess how soon. Guess at the taste of locusts and wild honey. Guess at the taste of water. Guess what the rivers see as they die. Guess why the babies are burning. Guess why there is silence in heaven. Guess why you were ever born.

CHARLES TOMLINSON (England, 1927–)

Poem

The muscles which move the eyeballs, we are told, derive from a musculature which once occupied the body end to end ... Sunblaze as day goes, and the light blots back the scene to iris the half-shut lashes. A look can no longer extricate the centre of the skyline copse. But the last greys, the departing glows caught by the creepers bearding its mass, prevail on the half-blinded retina. Branches deal with the air, vibrating the beams that thread into one's eye. So that 'over there' and 'in here' compound a truce neither signed—a truce that, insensibly and categorically, grows to a decree, and what one hoped for and what one is, must measure themselves against those demands which the eye receives, delivering its writ on us through a musculature which occupies the body end to end.

JAMES WRIGHT (United States, 1927–1980)

Old Bud

Old Bud Romick weighed three hundred pounds if he weighed an ounce, and he weighed an ounce. He used to sit on his front porch swing, enraged and helpless, while his two tiny grandchildren, hilarious and hellish little boys, scampered just out of his reach and yelled hideously, "Hell on you, Grandpa." His unbelievable Adam's apple purpled and shone like the burl on the root of a white oak, and he sang his God Damns in despair.

Old Bud Romick has fallen asleep as the twilight comes down Pearl Street in Martins Ferry, Ohio. The window shutters close here and there, and the flowing streetcars glow past into silence, their wicker seats empty, for the factory whistles have all blown down, and the widows all gone home. Empty, too, are the cinder alleys, smelling of warm summer asphalt. The streetlight columns, faintly golden, fill with the cracked mirrors of June bugs' wings. Old Bud Romick sags still on the porch swing. The rusty chains do their best for his body in the dark.

The dark turns around him, a stain like the bruise on a plum somebody somehow missed and left under a leaf. His two hellions have long since giggled their way upstairs. Old Bud Romick is talking lightly in his sleep, and an evening shower brings him a sticky new sycamore leaf in his sleep.

Whether or not he is aware of leaves, I don't know. I don't know whether or not he is aware of anything touching his face. Whether or not he dreams of how slender sycamores are, how slender young women are when they walk beneath the trees without caring how green they are, how lucky a plum might be if it dies without being eaten, I don't know.

GAEL TURNBULL (Scotland, 1928–2004)

In the corner of a railway station he notices a young couple sleeping, their heads on their rucksacks, while the commuters hurry past and the taxis sound nearby. They appear to be students and he remembers his own youth: the hitch-hiking, the overnight buses, the post war cafés, his digs, the girls for whom he yearned, his incoherence, his shame, even the occasional moments of camaraderie or happiness, piercing him even yet by their intensity and brevity.

Search though he may, he can find nothing durable for which he might have nostalgia, until it comes to him: their ability to sleep, curled up oblivious, while the world crashes forward about their ears.

*

A man stands waving goodbye to his grandson as a train pulls out of a station, the same from which he left when he had come to visit his own grandfather at the same age, now a lifetime away. Indeed, he has no articulate memory of his grandfather who died shortly after, and certainly none of that last goodbye. This had always been a sorrow, that so poignant a moment should be gone for ever.

But as he walks up into the town, he feels no loss at the realisation that his own grandson might scarcely remember, perhaps not at all, and so becomes aware of his grandfather in another way, more intense than any memory, more intense even than the image of that little boy waving to him through the still receding window.

*

A woman has devoted her life to her family. One evening at the table as her husband talks of his day at work and the children of their friends at school, she picks up her half finished meal and turns it over on its face, carefully pressing it down onto the tablecloth.

The children stare open mouthed. Her husband finally gasps, "What are you doing?" She smiles at him sadly, shaking her head. "You understand nothing. It wasn't me who did that. The woman who did that, by doing it, no longer exists."

Double Vision—*The Rewrite*

A fat man in a plaid suit walked west on 23rd Street, passing the quiet bar where Ritter sat, drink in hand.

"I saw him on the bus to work. This morning," the bartender said, her eyes intent. "72nd Street, Central Park West."

Ritter turned, looked out the window. The fat man wasn't there.

"This morning," Ritter said, "a guy in a gray suit and vest passed my building."

"This afternoon," he continued, in restaurant scent of garlic, ketchup, french fries and sizzling chops, "I saw him again, walking west, on 20th Street."

Blue skies.

Fingertips on glass.

In muted outside auto traffic, icy vodka.

Daffodil yellow.

DONALD BARTHELME (United States, 1931–1989)

The King of Jazz

Well I'm the king of jazz now, thought Hokie Mokie to himself as he oiled the slide on his trombone. Hasn't been a 'bone man been king of jazz for many years. But now that Spicy MacLammermoor, the old king, is dead, I guess I'm it. Maybe I better play a few notes out of this window here, to reassure myself.

"Wow!" said somebody standing on the sidewalk. "Did you hear that?"

"I did," said his companion.

"Can you distinguish our great homemade American jazz performers, each from the other?"

"Used to could."

"Then who was that playing?"

"Sounds like Hokie Mokie to me. Those few but perfectly selected notes have the real epiphanic glow."

"The what?"

"The real epiphanic glow, such as is obtained only by artists of the caliber of Hokie Mokie, who's from Pass Christian, Mississippi. He's the king of jazz, now that Spicy MacLammermoor is gone."

Hokie Mokie put his trombone in its trombone case and went to a gig. At the gig everyone fell back before him, bowing.

"Hi Bucky! Hi Zoot! Hi Freddie! Hi George! Hi Thad! Hi Roy! Hi Dexter! Hi Jo! Hi Willie! Hi Greens!"

"What we gonna play, Hokie? You the king of jazz now, you gotta decide."

"How 'bout 'Smoke'?"

"Wow!" everybody said. "Did you hear that? Hokie Mokie can just knock a fella out, just the way he pronounces a word. What a intonation on that boy! God Almighty!"

"I don't want to play 'Smoke,'" somebody said.

"Would you repeat that, stranger?"

"I don't want to play 'Smoke.' 'Smoke' is dull. I don't like the changes. I refuse to play 'Smoke.'"

"He refuses to play 'Smoke'! But Hokie Mokie is the king of jazz and he says 'Smoke'!"

"Man, you from outa town or something? What do you mean you refuse to play 'Smoke'? How'd you get on this gig anyhow? Who hired you?"

"I am Hideo Yamaguchi, from Tokyo, Japan."

"Oh, you're one of those Japanese cats, eh?"

"Yes I'm the top trombone man in all of Japan."

"Well you're welcome here until we hear you play. Tell me, is the Tennessee Tea Room still the top jazz place in Tokyo?"

"No, the top jazz place in Tokyo is the Square Box now."

"That's nice. OK, now we gonna play 'Smoke' just like Hokie said. You ready, Hokie? OK, give you four for nothin'. One! Two! Three! Four!"

The two men who had been standing under Hokie's window had followed him into the club. Now they said:

"Good God!"

"Yes, that's Hokie's famous 'English sunrise' way of playing. Playing with lots of rays coming out of it, some red rays, some blue rays, some green rays, some green stemming from a violet center, some olive stemming from a tan center—"

"That young Japanese fellow is pretty good, too."

"Yes, he is pretty good. And he holds his horn in a peculiar way. That's frequently the mark of a superior player."

"Bent over like that with his head between his knees—good God, he's sensational!"

He's sensational, Hokie thought. Maybe I ought to kill him.

But at that moment somebody came in the door pushing in front of him a four-and-one-half-octave marimba. Yes, it was Fat Man Jones, and he began to play even before he was fully in the door.

"What're we playing?"

" 'Billie's Bounce.'"

"That's what I thought it was. What're we in?"

"F."

"That's what I thought we were in. Didn't you use to play with Maynard?"

"Yeah I was in that band for a while until I was in the hospital."

"What for?"

"I was tired."

"What can we add to Hokie's fantastic playing?"

"How 'bout some rain or stars?"

"Maybe that's presumptuous?"

"Ask him if he'd mind."

"You ask him, I'm scared. You don't fool around with the king of jazz. That young Japanese guy's pretty good, too."

"He's sensational."

"You think he's playing in Japanese?"

"Well I don't think it's English."

This trombone's been makin' my neck green for thirty-five

years, Hokie thought. How come I got to stand up to yet another challenge, this late in life?

"Well, Hideo—"

"Yes, Mr. Mokie?"

"You did well on both 'Smoke' and 'Billie's Bounce.' You're just about as good as me, I regret to say. In fact, I've decided you're *better* than me. It's a hideous thing to contemplate, but there it is. I have only been the king of jazz for twenty-four hours, but the unforgiving logic of this art demands we bow to Truth, when we hear it."

"Maybe you're mistaken?"

"No, I got ears. I'm not mistaken. Hideo Yamaguchi is the new king of jazz."

"You want to be king emeritus?"

"No, I'm just going to fold up my horn and steal away. This gig is yours, Hideo. You can pick the next tune."

"How 'bout 'Cream'?"

"OK, you heard what Hideo said, it's 'Cream.' You ready, Hideo?"

"Hokie, you don't have to leave. You can play too. Just move a little over to the side there—"

"Thank you, Hideo, that's very gracious of you. I guess I will play a little, since I'm still here. Sotto voce, of course."

"Hideo is wonderful on 'Cream'!"

"Yes, I imagine it's his best tune."

"What's that sound coming in from the side there?"

"Which side?"

"The left."

"You mean that sound that sounds like the cutting edge of life? That sounds like polar bears crossing Arctic ice pans? That sounds like a herd of musk ox in full flight? That sounds like male walruses diving to the bottom of the sea? That sounds like fumaroles smoking on the slopes of Mt. Katmai? That sounds like the wild turkey walking through the deep, soft forest? That sounds like beavers chewing trees in an Appalachian marsh? That sounds like an oyster fungus growing on an aspen trunk? That sounds like a mule deer wandering a montane of the Sierra Nevada? That sounds like prairie dogs kissing? That sounds like witchgrass tumbling or a river meandering? That sounds like manatees munching seaweed at Cape Sable? That sounds like coatimundis moving in packs across the face of Arkansas? That sounds like—"

"Good God, it's Hokie! Even with a cup mute on, he's blowing Hideo right off the stand!"

"Hideo's playing on his knees now! Good God, he's reaching into his belt for a large steel sword—Stop him!"

"Wow! That was the most exciting 'Cream' ever played! Is Hideo all right?"

"Yes, somebody is getting him a glass of water."

"You're my man, Hokie! That was the dadblangedest thing I ever saw!"

"You're the king of jazz once again!"

"Hokie Mokie is the most happening thing there is!"

"Yes, Mr. Hokie sir, I have to admit it, you blew me right off the stand. I see I have many years of work and study before me still."

"That's OK, son. Don't think a thing about it. It happens to the best of us. Or it almost happens to the best of us. Now I want everybody to have a good time because we're gonna play 'Flats.' 'Flats' is next."

"With your permission, sir, I will return to my hotel and pack. I am most grateful for everything I have learned here."

"That's OK, Hideo. Have a nice day. He-he. Now, 'Flats.'"

THOMAS BERNHARD (Austria, 1931–1989)

Fourati

In Montreux, on Lake Geneva, we noticed a lady sitting on a park bench on the shore of the lake, who would, from time to time, on this same park bench, receive and then dismiss again the most diverse visitors, without moving a muscle. Twice a car stopped in front of her on the lake shore, and a young man in uniform got out, brought her the newspapers, and then drove off again; we thought it must be her private chauffeur. The lady was wrapped in several blankets, and we guessed her age to be well over seventy. Sometimes she would wave at a passerby. Probably, we thought, she is one of those rich and respectable Swiss ladies who live on Lake Geneva in the winter while their business is carried on in the rest of the world. The woman was, as we were soon informed, actually one of the richest and most respectable of the Swiss ladies who spend the winter on Lake Geneva; for twenty years she had been a paraplegic and had had her chauffeur drive her almost every day for those twenty years to the shore of Lake Geneva, had always had herself installed on the same bench, and had had the newspapers brought to her. For decades Montreux has owed fifty percent of its tax revenues to her. The famous hypnotist Fourati had hypnotized her twenty years ago and had been unable to bring her out of the hypnosis. In this way Fourati, as is well known, had ruined not only the lady's life but his own as well.

Pisa and Venice

The mayors of Pisa and Venice had agreed to scandalize visitors to their cities, who had for centuries been equally charmed by Venice and Pisa, by secretly and overnight having the tower of Pisa moved to Venice and the campanile of Venice moved to Pisa and set up there. They could not, however, keep their plan a secret, and on the very night on which they were going to have the tower of Pisa moved to Venice and the campanile of Venice moved to Pisa they were committed to the lunatic asylum, the mayor of Pisa in the nature of things to the lunatic asylum in Venice and the mayor of Venice to the lunatic asylum in Pisa. The Italian authorities were able to handle the affair in complete confidentiality.

Translated from the German by Kenneth J. Northcott

TOMAS TRANSTRÖMER (Sweden, 1931–)

The Bookcase

It was brought from the dead woman's apartment. It stood empty a few days, empty until I filled it with books, all the bound ones, those bulky tomes. With that act I had let in the underworld. Something swelled up from below, mounted slowly, inexorably, like mercury in a gigantic thermometer. You were not allowed to turn your head away.

The black volumes, their closed faces. They're like the Algerians who stood at the Friedrichstrasse border crossing, waiting for the *Volkspolizei* to check their passports. My own passport lay a long time in various glass cubicles. And the fog all over Berlin that day, it is also in this bookcase. An old despair lives in there, it tastes of Passchendaele and the Treaty of Versailles—the taste, in fact, is older than that. The black heavy tomes—I come back to them—they are themselves a sort of passport, and they are so fat because they have accumulated so many stamps through the centuries. There is one trip, apparently, for which your baggage can't be heavy enough, once you've embarked, when finally you . . .

All the old historians are there, and are invited to climb up and look into our family. Nothing can be heard, but the lips move all the time behind the glass ("Passchendaele". . .). One is reminded of a venerable government office—now follows a true ghost story—a grand building where portraits of long-dead men hang behind glass, and one morning there appeared a blur on the inside of the glass. They had begun breathing during the night.

The bookcase is even more powerful. Glares straight across the border zone! A shimmering membrane, the shimmering membrane of a dark river in which the room is forced to mirror itself. And you must not turn your head away.

Translated from the Swedish by May Swenson

VERN RUTSALA (United States, 1934–)

How We Get By

By hook or crook, by shoestring and bootstrap, by running and hiding, by mortice and tenon, by moving under cover of darkness, by wit and dumb luck, by spit and polish, by weights and measures, by love or money, by hurrying up and waiting, by word of mouth, by bread and board, by slice and dice, by not letting the left hand know, by bed and breakfast, by nuts and bolts, by nodding and smiling, by mortar and pestle, by hammer and tongs, by never crying over what we spill, by backing and filling, by surf and turf, by health and safety, by soup and sandwich, by bourbon and water, by offense and defense, by being as dumb as an ox is strong, by mind and body, by day for night, by sturm and drang, by fire and ice, by hit or miss—oh yes, by hit or miss.

SONIA SANCHEZ (United States, 1934–)

A Letter to Ezekiel Mphahlele

dear zeke,

i've just left your house where you and rebecca served a dinner of peace to me and my sons. the ride home is not as long as the way i came, two centuries of hunger brought me along many detours before i recognized your house. it is raining and as i watch the raindrops spin like colored beads on the windshield, i hear your voice calling out to your ancestors to prepare a place for you, for you were returning home leaving the skeleton rites of twenty years behind.

you and rebecca have been walking a long time. your feet have crossed the african continent to this western one where you moved amid leaden eyes and laughter that froze you in snow/capped memories. your journey began in 1957, when the ruling class could not understand your yawns of freedom, the motion of a million eyes to see for themselves what life was/is and could be, and you cut across the burial grounds of south africa where many of your comrades slept and you cut across those black africans smiling their long smiles from diplomatic teeth. now you are returning home. now your mother's womb cries out to you. now your history demands your heartbeat. and you turn your body toward the whirlwind of change, toward young black voices calling for a dignity speeding beyond control, on the right side of the road. but this nite full of whispering summer trees, this nite nodding with south african faces, heard you say, sonia. i must be buried in my country in my own homeland, my bones must replenish the black earth from whence they came, our bones must fertilize the ground on which we walk or we shall never walk as men and women in the 21st century.

i talked to my sons as the car chased the longlegged rain running before us. i told them that men and women are measured by their acts not by their swaggering speech or walk, or the money they have stashed between their legs. i talked to my sons about bravery outside of bruce lee grunts and jabs, outside of star wars' knights fertilizing america's green youth into continued fantasies while reality explodes underground in neutron boldness. i said you have just sat and eaten amid bravery. relish the taste. stir it around and around in your mouth until the quick sweetness of it becomes bitter, then swallow it slowly, letting this new astringent taste burn the throat. bravery is no easy taste to swallow. i said this man and woman we have just left this nite have decided to walk like panthers in their country, to breathe again their own breath suspended by twenty years of exile, to settle in the maternal space of their birth where there are men who "shake hands without hearts" waiting for them. they are a fixed portrait of courage.

it is 2 A.M., my children stretch themselves in dreams, kicking away the room's shadows. i stare at the night piling in little heaps near my bed. zeke. maybe you are a madman. i a mad woman to want to walk across the sea, to saddle time while singing a future note. we follow the new day's breath, we answer old bruises waiting to descend upon our heads, we answer screams creeping out of holes and shells buried by memories waiting to be cleansed. you invoking the ghosts lurking inside this child/ woman. you breaking my curtain of silence. i love the tom-tom days you are marching, your feet rooted in the sea. save a space for me and mine zeke and rebecca. this lost woman, who walks her own shadow for peace.

MARK STRAND (United States, 1934–)

The Mysterious Arrival of an Unusual Letter

It had been a long day at work and a long ride back to the small apartment where I lived. When I got there I flicked on the light and saw on the table an envelope with my name on it. Where was the clock? Where was the calendar? The handwriting was my father's, but he had been dead for forty years. As one might, I began to think that maybe, just maybe, he was alive, living a secret life somewhere nearby. How else to explain the envelope? To steady myself, I sat down, opened it, and pulled out the letter. "Dear Son" was the way it began. "Dear Son" and then nothing.

The Emergency Room at Dusk

The retired commander was upset. His room in the castle was cold, so was the room across the hall, and all the other rooms as well. He should never have bought this castle when there were so many other, cheaper, warmer castles for sale. But he liked the way this one looked—its stone turrets rising into the winter air, its main gate, even its frozen moat, on which he thought someday he might ice skate, had a silvery charm. He poured himself a brandy and lit a cigar, and tried to concentrate on other things—his many victories, the bravery of his men—but his thoughts swirled in tiny eddies, settling first here, then there, moving as the wind does from empty town to empty town.

Provisional Eternity

A man and a woman lay in bed. "Just one more time," said the man, "just one more time." "Why do you keep saying that?" said the woman. "Because I never want it to end," said the man. "What don't you want to end?" said the woman. "This," said the man, "this never wanting it to end."

JACK ANDERSON (United States, 1935–)

Phalaris and The Bull: A Story and an Examination

The Story:

The tyrant Phalaris locked his prisoners inside a magnificently wrought brazen bull and tortured them over a slow fire. So that nothing unseemly might spoil his feasting, he commanded the royal artisans to design the bull in such a way that its smoke rose in spicy clouds of incense. When the screams of the dying reached the tyrant's ears, they had the sound of sweet music. And when the bull was reopened, the victims' bones shone like jewels and were made into bracelets.

The Examination:

1. This story appears to be allegorical. Of what is it an allegory?
2. Which person or persons do you consider most vile: the tyrant Phalaris, the artisans who carried out his orders, or the court ladies who wore the bone bracelets?
3. Do you think it right that your sympathy extends almost automatically to the victims? But do you know who the victims were or why they were condemned? What if the victims had been Hitler and your twelve least favorite contemporary political figures—would this knowledge affect your sympathies?
4. Do you not sometimes wish that certain people might die, do you not long for the deaths of prime ministers or dictators, do you not envision presidents dying of heart attacks, generals shooting themselves while cleaning their rifles,

skinflint landlords pushed into wells by rebellious peasants, industrialists skidding on newly waxed floors and sailing through penthouse windows, War Department scientists exposed to radiation while goosing cute researchers in the lab, demagogues exploding with the leaky gas main, your mother-in-law scalded by a pot of boiling chicken soup— do you not wish any or all of these were dead?

5. If the death of one man could bring bliss to the world, would you order that one death? If the deaths of two men could do it, would you order those two deaths? Or five deaths? Or a hundred? Or twenty million? How many deaths would you order to bring bliss to the world?

6. If it required only one man's death, after all, to bring bliss to the world and you sanctioned such a death, how would you feel should you learn that that one man was to be you?

7. Do you think that the most monstrous thing about the story of Phalaris is not that a tyrant put prisoners to death—since that has happened throughout history—but the particularly gruesome way he went about it?

8. Yet do you never catch yourself wishing that once, only once, once only but definitely once, you could sit beside the tyrant just to satisfy your curiosity about what the bull looked like, what the music sounded like?

9. Would you consider Phalaris and his artisans more, or less, reprehensible if the screams of the dying had reached the ear undisguised? If you were one of the victims, would it make any difference to you?

10. Which do you consider the more truly good man: the victim who wishes his screams to be heard as screams, or he who wishes them to be heard as music? Do you think your answer is relevant to the problem of why at executions we praise the victim who meets his death with stoic calm and witty epigrams, rather than he who must be dragged to the scaffold pissing in his pants? In your opinion, is it or is it not a good thing that we do so?

11. Learning at this point in the examination that the first victim of the bull was the chief artisan who designed it, do you

(a) believe that the artisan deserved his fate?, and (b) feel vaguely uncomfortable about your own occupation, job, profession, or calling? Why or why not?

12. Based upon your interpretation of the story of Phalaris and the bull, do you view yourself in the light of your present situation in life as metaphorically equivalent to tyrant, artisan, victim, or wearer of bone jewelry?

13. And which am I?

Les Sylphides

Tonight there is to be a performance of *Les Sylphides*. But the ballet is not to be in the opera house, it is scheduled for somewhere in Central Park. At the entrance to the park, each of us is given a bicycle and told, "Now you must find *Les Sylphides* for yourself." So we all pedal off in every direction.

It is a warm spring evening. There is a full moon in the sky. The paths are lighted with electric moons. There are leaves on the trees, and on the benches sit kids, bums, retired stockbrokers, middle-aged matrons with sore feet and shopping bags. We circle the lagoon, coast down the roadways, or jounce over boulders and into the bushes. But still we find no *Les Sylphides* in the park.

As we cross the Sheep Meadow like a flock of sheep, we ring our bells and call to each other. "Hoo-hoo," we call, "have you found *Les Sylphides*?

"Hoo-hoo," go the echoes, "we've found no *Sylphides*."

Then someone—or, maybe, someone else—calls back, "I think they are dancing around Cleopatra's Needle . . . I think they are dancing in the Bethesda Fountain . . . I think they are dancing in the Children's Zoo . . . I know they are dancing *Les Sylphides* in the Ramble." We set out to look.

Nothing but water is dancing in the fountain. The baby animals in the zoo are huddled asleep. Only the wind goes round Cleopatra's Needle. And when we zoom through the Ramble, the flustered lovers pull up their pants in a rush and get caught in the zippers.

An hour or so later, we see something vague at the top of a tree. It never grows clear and is hence indefinable. Only its effects can be described: it rustles the branches and keeps on blurring, as though about to melt into air. Yet, possessing the inertia of generalized things, it doesn't melt completely, but stays as it is: indistinct, unformed, about to melt, and mushy. While we watch, a voice is whispering in our thoughts, "You are on the edge of finding *Les Sylphides*." Since it is not our voice, we assume it is genuine.

We burst into applause and kiss each other juicily. Once more we pedal off on our bikes, tossing bouquets of flowers on every side. The baskets on our handlebars fill up with the bouquets that everyone else is tossing to us. We are happy that we almost have found *Les Sylphides*. We are so happy that we ride around in circles—no hands—tossing flowers to each other and humming soft songs.

Then we stop for a picnic of cold chicken and white wine. Someone has brought potato salad and someone else has brought cole slaw. When we have eaten the chicken and finished the wine, it is time to go home.

MICHAEL BENEDIKT (United States, 1935–2007)

The Atmosphere of Amphitheatre

Whenever we turn on a faucet, the celebrated tube of water appears. We say "tube" because it appears not to be moving, it appears as likely to have been produced from the porcelain upwards as from the spigot downwards, as is the usual case. As for me, whenever I turn on any faucet, I satisfy my curiosity regarding its nature and character by simply telling myself that "a column is coming." This is why a person in a bathroom with both sink faucets running and the bathtub faucets dripping may be reminded of standing on a plantation veranda; and why it may be enough to walk through the laundryroom in the basement to experience a feeling reminiscent of standing among the ruins of Greek Temple architecture.

The Judgment

A man dresses up like a judge and stands before a mirror and sentences himself to loneliness for the rest of his life.

But, your Honor, you haven't heard my side of it . . .

You have no *side* of it; you have been found guilty of impersonating a judge and standing before a mirror admiring yourself.

I throw myself on the mercy of the court; I acted only out of loneliness . . .

Loneliness is no excuse for violating the law.

But, your Honor, please, I've been lonely all my life. Isn't the debt almost paid?—Not more loneliness!—I demand my sentence be shortened! I've already paid for my crime!

I make no deals with convicted criminals. If you think you can do better try another judge.

But, your Honor . . .

Clear the court and go to bed!

The Automobile

A man had just married an automobile.

But I mean to say, said his father, that the automobile is not a person because it is something different.

For instance, compare it to your mother. Do you see how it is different from your mother? Somehow it seems wider, doesn't it? And besides, your mother wears her hair differently.

You ought to try to find something in the world that looks like mother.

I have mother, isn't that enough of a thing that looks like mother? Do I have to gather more mothers?

They are all old ladies who do not in the least excite any wish to procreate, said the son.

But you cannot procreate with an automobile, said father.

The son shows father an ignition key. See, here is a special penis which does with the automobile as the man with the woman; and the automobile gives birth to a place far from this place, dropping its puppy miles as it goes.

Does that make me a grandfather? said the father.

That makes you where you are when I am far away, said the son.

Father and mother watch an automobile with a *just married* sign on it growing smaller in a road.

Antimatter

On the other side of a mirror there's an inverse world, where the insane go sane; where bones climb out of the earth and recede to the first slime of love.

And in the evening the sun is just rising.

Lovers cry because they are a day younger, and soon childhood robs them of their pleasure.

In such a world there is much sadness which, of course, is joy. . .

Headlights in the Night

As a man slept his car drove up the stairs into his bedroom, blinking its headlights.

Meanwhile the man dreams that the moon has a sister who has at last come back into home orbit, to circle around the parental earth.

The moon and her sister are like headlights of an unseen automobile coming out of space to the dark sleeping side of earth.

It is the Inspector General arriving in his touring car from the stars; one of those terrible automobiles that shrink and swell.

When the Inspector General wishes to go through the stars to visit the earth, he merely steps into his car and then steps out; his car has swollen the distance without moving.

The man's car, getting no response, shifts into reverse and backs out of his bedroom down the stairs.

HELGA NOVAK (Germany / Iceland, 1935–)

Eat a Good Meal

I am seldom in this city. I am here by chance.

I have an acquaintance in this city. She is a good friend. We carry on an intimate and extensive correspondence with one another.

I am here by chance. I don't want to run into my friend. I am stopping only for a day. I don't have any time. If I see her I'll have to devote myself to her. She always takes possession of me. She says, what are *you* doing here, or what *are* you doing here, or what are you doing *here*. I say, nothing at all. She pulls me. She drags me along with her. She says, and you didn't even give me a call. I say, I was just about to. She says, then it's perfectly splendid that we've run into each other. I say, yes. I ask, aren't you on your way to work. She says, nonsense, today's my housecleaning day. I say, then you probably have a lot of laundry. She says, I wouldn't think of washing now that you are here. I say, is there a movie around here. She says, movie. First a cafe.

She takes my arm. She says, when did you get here. I say, last evening. She says that isn't possible. And where did you sleep? I say, in a hotel. She says, come, come. We'll pack up your luggage immediately and take it to my house. I say, that won't be worth the trouble, I am continuing my trip this afternoon. She says, you are continuing your trip this afternoon, you can't do that to me. I say, don't be angry, I hardly have time. She says, well what are you up to. I say, nothing special. She says, incidentally how did the story turn out. I say, what story. She says, the story in your next to last letter. I say, in my next to last letter. She says, his name was Roland or Ronald. You know what I mean. I say, oh that one. She says, what do you mean that one. You wrote pages about him and that you didn't know up from down. I say, he's gone. She says, gone just like that. That is fantastic. I say, yes. Isn't there a movie here?

We go up Kaiserallee. We sit down in a coffee shop and smoke. She says, why do you keep talking about a movie. We haven't had a real good talk yet. I say, no. She says, have you already had breakfast? I say, no. She says, I'll get us something to eat. I say, I am not hungry. She says, but you must eat a good meal, do you want a sandwich or cake. I say, nothing.

She goes to the buffet. She takes two trays. She speaks with the help. I leave the coffee shop through the Königstrasse exit.

Translated from the German by Allen H. Chappel

STEVEN SCHRADER (United States, 1935–)

Xavier Cugat

Weekend nights my brother and his friends used to hang out at the corner candy store near the top of the stairs at Fort Washington Avenue and 187th Street. They wore leather jackets and smoked cigars, or at least pretended to, as they flirted with girls and made smart remarks. My brother boasted to me that he'd seen Xavier Cugat, the band leader, at the candy store many times. Cugat was courting Frances Lassman, later known as Abby Lane, who was in my brother's eighth grade class at P.S. 187. She was beautiful and wasn't allowed to go out with any of the boys in the neighborhood. According to my brother she was destined for more important things in life—a musical career and marriage to someone successful. Xavier Cugat was then in his thirties, at the height of his fame, and we all knew him from the movies and from photos in newspapers in which he stood in front of his orchestra, his Chihuahua cradled in one hand as he conducted with the other. Or else he'd be alone in the picture, smiling, his pencil-thin mustache curling upwards as he puffed a cigar. Cugat often stopped at the corner to buy himself a cigar. He'd pull up in his black Cadillac, walk briskly into the candy store, and nod to the boys on his way out. Then he'd drive up the hill to Cabrini Boulevard to the six-story apartment house where his future wife Frances lived.

DAVID YOUNG (United States, 1936–)

Four About Heavy Machinery

A huge cement truck turns the corner, and you get the full impact of its sensuality. Those ruts on the road and in the lawn! Even at night the cement plant has a strange energy, drawing adolescents to stare through its fences, causing the watchman to shine his light nervously among the parked and sleeping mixers. Still, from those fluid beginnings and slow revolutions, the cement itself forms the pale and stony squares of sidewalk. Reassuring. Roller skates, hopscotch, salted ice. Then the slow cracking from the tree roots below and we are back to sensuality again.

~

Cranes are not to be compared with trees, not with their almost Scandinavian sense of the importance of power and duty. Sometimes the face is very far from the heart, and the one thing you would like to do—lie down next to that beautiful passing stranger, for instance—is the thing that seems least possible. So you sway against the gray sky, pretending to a stiffness you do not feel. The building you helped create rises toward you, filled with the sounds of hammering and the strange shine of work lights.

~

To take some tutoring from pumps, I said. I was thinking about the windmill, that swaying, clanking lecturer. Slow cows come to drink from the tank. We filled it didn't we, harvesting water from weather, not by bringing it down from the sky like rain, but up from the earth like oil. Now, roll up your blue sleeve and plunge your arm into that tank. If you clench and unclench your fist regularly you can learn something about the submersible pump, beating down there where weather is a dream.

~

We have strong feelings about bulldozers, their buzzing and scraping, their clumsy abruptness, their way of tipping saplings into piles of burnable roots and brush. Our faces get vinegary when we think of it. But the bulldozer's point of view is remarkably different. The bulldozer thinks of itself as a lover. It considers that its loved one, from whom it is always separated, is wrapped in many short, soft, buttery strips of leather. It imagines itself removing these worn leather wrappings, one at a time and with great tenderness, to get at the body of the loved one. Perverse, you will say. But see, you have already entered the life of the bulldozer: your hands reach for the next piece of leather. Shrubs and young trees go under.

GIANNI CELATI (Italy / England, 1937–)

A Scholar's Idea of Happy Endings

The son of a chemist was studying abroad. On his father's death, he returned home to look after the dispensary, becoming the chemist of a small village on the outskirts of Viadana in the province of Mantua.

Word of his learning had spread in the country areas, fed by rumours about his huge library, about his prodigious cure for ear-ache, his ultra-modern method for irrigating the fields, and his fluency in twelve languages, not to mention rumours that he was translating the *Divine Comedy* into German.

The owner of a cheese-making factory in the area decided to pay a stipend to the scholar, who was by now middle-aged, in return for which he would help his daughter with her grammar school education. The girl, a sporting type, was not doing too well at school and, furthermore, she hated books, Latin, and good Italian prose. The chemist accepted—more from love of learning than for any financial motive—and every day for a whole summer he went to give lessons to the young athlete.

And one day it happened that the young athlete fell in love with him—so much so that she dropped all sport in favour of writing poetry, Latin verse and, of course, long letters.

There are still people who talk of the car the chemist bought to mark the occasion, the couple's long country trips, and even of nocturnal liaisons in a barn.

At any rate, evidence of their late-summer affair only came to light the following winter when a bundle of letters was confiscated by the nuns at the girl's convent school, and duly handed over to her parents. The contents of these letters seemed so disgusting in the eyes of the owner of the cheese-making factory that he decided to ruin the chemist, and drive him from the village forever.

The girl's brothers, who were active fascists at the time, ransacked his shop on the village square a number of times, and on one occasion gave its owner a savage beating.

However, all this does not seem to have unduly worried the chemist. For a while, he continued to receive customers in the ransacked pharmacy, surrounded by broken window panes, torn down shelves and smashed jars. Then, one fine day, he shut up shop and withdrew among his books, rarely venturing out.

All the village knew him to be deep in his studies, and every now and again they saw him smiling as he crossed the square and headed for the post office to pick up new books that had arrived for him.

Some time later, he was taken to hospital and then to a sanatorium. He remained for a number of years in the sanatorium, and no one heard any more about him.

On his return from the sanatorium, the ageing scholar was extremely thin. An old housemaid, who had gone back to taking care of him, complained to everyone that he never wanted to eat: he said he didn't care to eat, and spent the whole day immersed in his books.

Thinner by the day, the man seldom went out and evidently no longer recognized anyone in the village, including the daughter of the now deceased owner of the cheese-making factory who he occasionally met in the square. Yet he smiled at all and sundry, and it is said he used to greet dogs by raising his hat.

Apparently, he had given up eating altogether after his old housemaid died and persisted in fasting for weeks on end, so that when he was found dead in his library (by a plumber) he was a skeleton in all but name: all that remained of him was wrinkled skin clinging to bones.

He was bent over the last page of a book onto which he was sticking a strip of paper.

Years later, his large library was inherited by a niece. The niece, rummaging through the books, believed she had worked out how the old scholar had spent the last part of his life.

For this man, every story, novel, or epic poem had to end happily. He obviously couldn't bear tragic endings, nor for a story to end on a sad or melancholic note. So, over the years, he devoted himself to re-writing the endings of some hundred or so books in every conceivable language. By inserting small sheets or strips of paper over passages that had to be re-written, he utterly changed the outcome of the stories, bringing them unfailingly to a happy ending.

Many of the last days of his life must have been dedicated to re-writing the eighth chapter of the third part of Madame Bovary, which is where Emma dies. In the new version, Emma recovers and is reunited with her husband.

His very last piece of work, however, consisted of the strip of paper he had in his fingers and which, on the point of dying of starvation, he was sticking onto the last line of a French translation of a Russian novel. This was possibly his masterpiece; by changing just three words, he transformed a tragedy into a satisfactory resolution of life's problems.

Translated from the Italian by Robert Lumley

MOACYR SCLIAR (Brazil, 1937–2011)

Agenda of Executive Jorge T. Flacks for Judgment Day

SEVEN A.M.

Get up (earlier, today). Don't think. Don't lie motionless in an attempt to recapture fleeting images; let dreams trickle away, jump out of bed.

From the terrace: watch the Sunrise—with dry eyes, without thinking of the millions, billions of years throughout which this poignant light, and so on and so forth. Nothing of the kind. A bath, soon afterward.

SEVEN-THIRTY A.M.

Breakfast: orange juice, toast, eggs. Eat with appetite, chew vigorously and swiftly; don't ruminate, don't mix food with bitter thoughts. Don't! Coffee. Very strong, with sugar today, just today, never again (from now on, avoid expressions such as "never again"). Finish off the meal with a glass of ice-cold water, sipping it slowly. Pay special attention to the ice cubes tinkling against the glass. Joyful sound.

EIGHT A.M.

Wake up the wife. Make love. And why not? She's been the companion of so many years. Wife, mother. Make love, yes, a quick act of love, but with the utmost tenderness. Let her go back to sleep afterward. Let her roam through the country of dreams as much as she wants; let her say farewell to her monsters, to her demons, to her fairies, to her princesses, to her godparents.

EIGHT-THIRTY A.M.

Gymnastics. Brisk, fierce movements. Afterward, feel the arms tingling, the head throbbing, splitting, almost: life.

NINE A.M.

Take the car out of the garage. Drive downtown. Take advantage of the time spent driving to do some thinking. Try to clarify certain doubts once and for all; maybe stop off at the rabbi's place. Maybe talk to a priest as well. Maybe bring priest and rabbi together?

TEN A.M.
At the office. Render decisions on the latest documents. Tidy up the desk. Clean out the drawers, throw away gewgaws. Set pen to paper. Write a letter, a poem, anything. Write.

TWELVE-THIRTY P.M.
Luncheon. Friends. Salad, cold cuts. Wine. Gab away, talk drivel. Laugh. Observe the faces. Memorize the details of the faces. Hug the friends. Hug them deeply touched. But tearless. No tears at all.

THREE-THIRTY P.M.
Phone Dr. Francisco. Ask if there's anything that can be done (quite unlikely); but say no to tranquilizers.

SIX P.M.
Return home. Get the family together, including the baby of the family. Mention they'll be taken for a drive, and get the station wagon out of the garage. Head for the outskirts of the city. Find a spot on an elevation with a panoramic view. Park. Have everybody get out of the car. In a low, quiet voice, explain what is about to happen: the earth, which will open up (explain: as if it were parched), the bones, which will appear—the bones only, white, clean—bones that will then be covered with flesh, with hair, with eyes, with finger and toenails: men, women, laughing, crying.

Conclude with: It's about to begin, children. It's about to begin. Up to now, everything has been a lark.

Translated from the Portuguese by Eloah F. Giacomelli

CHARLES SIMIC (Serbia / United States, 1938–)

"Everybody knows the story about me and Dr. Freud," says my grandfather.

"We were in love with the same pair of black shoes in the window of the same shoe store. The store, unfortunately, was always closed. There'd be a sign: DEATH IN THE FAMILY or BACK AFTER LUNCH, but no matter how long I waited, no one would come to open.

"Once I caught Dr. Freud there shamelessly admiring the shoes. We glared at each other before going our separate ways, never to meet again."

*

It was the epoch of the masters of levitation. Some evenings we saw solitary men and women floating above the dark tree tops. Could they have been sleeping or thinking? They made no attempt to navigate. The wind nudged them ever so slightly. We were afraid to speak, to breathe. Even the nightbirds were quiet. Later, we'd mention the little book clasped in the hands of the young woman, and the way that old man lost his hat to the cypresses.

In the morning there were not even clouds in the sky. We saw a few crows preen themselves at the edge of the road; the shirts raise their empty sleeves on the blind woman's clothesline.

*

My guardian angel is afraid of the dark. He pretends he's not, sends me ahead, tells me he'll be along in a moment. Pretty soon I can't see a thing. "This must be the darkest corner of heaven," someone whispers behind my back. It turns out her guardian angel is missing too. "It's an outrage," I tell her. "The dirty little cowards leaving us all alone," she whispers. And of course, for all we know, I might be a hundred years old already, and she just a sleepy little girl with glasses.

*

I knew a woman who collected black buttons she found in the street. Some years there'd be only one or two. When I asked her what for and why only black buttons, she shrugged her shoulders. She kept them in a jar on the coffee table. They seduced the eye. One button even had some thread left as if it had been torn in a hurry. A violent scene took place, a burst of passion on some dark doorway, and then she came along the next day and found the button.

*

A narrow street with windows weakly lit at dinner time and self-absorbed men and women standing around and an occasional child who eats alone looking at nothing.

*

My aspiration is to create a kind of nongenre made up of fiction, autobiography, the essay, poetry, and of course, the joke!

*

A scene from French movies of the fifties that I still love: A fly gets shut in a room with three armed thugs and a woman, gagged and bound, who watches them with eyes popping. In front of each man on the table there is a sugar cube and a pile of large bills. No one stirs. A naked bulb hangs from the ceiling by a long wire so they can see the fly count its legs. It counts them on the table, tantalizingly close to a sugar cube, and then it counts them at the end of someone's nose.

I have no idea if this is the way it really was in the movie. I've worked on the scene over the years, making little adjustments in it as one does with a poem.

*

Descartes, I hear, did his best philosophizing by lazing in bed past noon. Not me! I'm on the way to the dump, tooting my horn and waving to the neighbors.

LUISA VALENZUELA (Argentina, 1938–)

The Best Shod

An invasion of beggars, but there's one consolation: no one lacks shoes, there are more than enough shoes to go around. Sometimes, it's true, a shoe has to be taken off some severed leg found in the underbrush, and it's of no use except to somebody with only one good leg. But this doesn't happen very often, usually corpses are found with both shoes intact. Their clothing on the other hand isn't usable. Ordinarily it has bullet holes, bloodstains, or is torn apart, or an electric cattle prod has left burns that are ugly and difficult to hide. So we don't count on the clothes, but the shoes are like new. Generally they're good, they haven't had much wear because their owners haven't been allowed to get very far in life. They poke out their heads, they start thinking (thinking doesn't wear out shoes), and after just a few steps their career is cut off.

That is to say, we find shoes, and since they're not always the size we need, we've set up a little exchange post in a vacant lot downtown. We charge only a few pesos for the service: you can't ask much from a beggar, but even so it does help to pay for maté and some biscuits. We earn real money only when we manage to have a real sale. Sometimes the families of the dead people, who've heard of us heaven knows how, ask us to sell them the dead man's shoes if we have them. The shoes are the only thing that they can bury, poor things, because naturally the authorities would never let them have the body.

It's too bad that a good pair of shoes drops out of circulation, but we have to live and we can't refuse to work for a good cause. Ours is a true apostolate and that's what the police think, too, so they never bother us as we search about in vacant lots, sewer conduits, fallow fields, thickets, and other nooks and crannies where a corpse may be hidden. The police are well aware that, thanks to us, this city can boast of being the one with the best-shod beggars in the world.

The Celery Munchers

I suppose I could ask them to stop munching celery at three o'clock in the morning, but that doesn't seem right. What with the price of celery these days. It's also possible that they munch celery as a sign of nonconformity and that they're joining housewives in protesting the price of vegetables. Or perhaps they're doing it out of a sense of superiority, to show that they can eat what others buy only as a luxury or to wear as boutonnieres.

There are three of them and they sometimes eat in unison or counterpoint. The noise in the basement where we live is almost terrifying. The greengrocer, our boss, sleeps with us too, he's a thrifty man, and the first night he woke up with a start, thinking that rats were eating the merchandise. It was all right for them to eat us, but the merchandise . . . The rats leave us in peace though—they prefer the chickpeas. Now and then we give them a handful and they look grateful. The grocer doesn't know it—any gesture of generosity or waste gets him down. But the Celery Munchers chew with relish in the knowledge that they're consuming perishable merchandise—and besides, after the latest hike in prices almost nobody eats celery anymore, and the vegetable man would have to throw out the unsold celery if it weren't for three of his helpers—I'm not one of them of course—who get paid partly in celery. There's going to be a problem though when the celery runs out. The only other vegetables I know that make noise when you chew them are carrots, which they don't like, and radishes, which aren't half as good for the blood as celery.

Our boss is a heavy sleeper and acquires new habits easily, so the crunch-crunch of the Celery Munchers doesn't wake him up anymore. He stretches out on a pile of potatoes, covered with dirt, and ignores the sound of the human crushing machine. The Celery Munchers don't sleep much, their resistance to sleep is surprising: maybe it's due to some unknown property of celery. In any event the boss doesn't wake up anymore and the rhythmical chewing of the Celery Munchers puts me to sleep. You might say that our life is lived amid the green peace of garden vegetables, except for the neighbors' anxieties hanging over our heads. The grocery store is in the basement of a thirteen-story building, and in some strange way vibrations of fear filter down to us from the thirteen stories above. If only we knew what caused them, we might be able to attend some secret tenants' meeting. But these meetings take place in the locked laundry room at the top of the building and we belong to the basement. We don't have access to the terraces and that's why we're pasty white, the color of a turnip; if we don't even have the luxury of a little jaunt in an elevator, how can we know what goes on in tenants' meetings? The boss doesn't worry about such petty details: the elevators give him claustrophobia, the tenants' meetings make him sick, and moreover he's afraid that the owner will raise the rent if he sees him (that's why the boss doesn't bathe, so as to make himself practically indistinguishable from the potatoes). The store is doing well and is open all day, Sundays and holidays included. We don't complain because the longer it stays open the better ventilated the basement is and the less time we spend smelling the boss, but the rumors that trickle down to us disturb our sleep.

A search warrant is only a piece of paper but here we are, hoping that they stumble upon the truth by themselves because our protestations of innocence aren't getting us anywhere. The police arrived with the warrant and right away turned everything topsy-turvy: they overturned crates of fruit, rummaged like madmen in the barrels of chickpeas, uncorked the few bottles of wine that were left and drank them, claiming that they had to see what was inside, stamped on the potatoes, the onions, the turnips, and the celery (the Celery Munchers wept). They broke open the pumpkins to see if they had been hollowed out inside, and shook the carrots hoping they were mikes or heaven knows what. And screaming "You've been turned in! You've been turned in!" they smashed everything in sight.

It's true that a number of bombs have gone off in the neighborhood, but what can they be searching for in the grocery store? Imagine: they started by cautiously picking up each piece of fruit, holding it up to the light, and examining it, listening to it with a stethoscope. Then their fury mounted till it finally found its natural form of expression, which is kicking. They kicked first the fruit and then us a few times, until they realized that we had no hidden arms there, no gunpowder cache, nor were we digging secret tunnels or hiding terrorists or maintaining a people's jail behind a mountain of potatoes.

There was nothing at all, but we're in jail nonetheless. The boss cried—more for the lost merchandise than his lost freedom. The police refused to pay damages and now claim that the boss has to pay for cleaning their sticky boots. The Celery Munchers wept too; they're already showing alarming symptoms because of the lack of celery in their bloodstream. This has been not only a moral disaster but an economic one as well and I demanded an explanation; finally the chief of police released us and that was how we found out about the neighbors' turning us in: they thought we were undermining the building. At three o'clock in the morning, every morning. A noise like a train moving that didn't stop even after we were hauled in. In short, the Celery Munchers had been replaced by rats who quickly polished off the damaged merchandise.

The building has now been shored up, and calm restored. The Celery Munchers are running around loose but are muzzled at night. The rats are in jail. Rumor has it that they're being used for strange experiments, to torture political prisoners; the experiments won't get very far, because they're macrobiotic pacifist rats. We miss them, but we're reluctant to ask to have them returned to us because we don't want them back contaminated.

Translated from the Spanish by Helen Lane

MARGARET ATWOOD (Canada, 1939–)

Instructions for the Third Eye

The eye is the organ of vision, and the third eye is no exception to that. Open it and it sees, close it and it doesn't.

Most people have a third eye but they don't trust it. That wasn't really F., standing on the corner, hands in his overcoat pockets, waiting for the light to change: F. died two months ago. It's a trick my eyes played on me, they say. A trick of the light.

I've got nothing against telepathy, said Jane; but the telephone is so much more dependable.

~

What's the difference between vision and a vision? The former relates to something it's assumed you've seen, the latter to something it's assumed you haven't. Language is not always dependable either.

~

If you want to use the third eye you must close the other two. Then breathe evenly; then wait. This sometimes works; on the other hand, sometimes you merely go to sleep. That sometimes works also.

~

When you've had enough practice you don't have to bother with these preliminary steps. You find too that what you see depends partly on what you want to look at and partly on how. As I said, the third eye is only an eye.

~

There are some who resent the third eye. They would have it removed, if they could. They feel it as a parasite, squatting in the centre of the forehead, feeding on the brain.

To them the third eye shows only the worst scenery: the gassed and scorched corpses at the cave-mouth, the gutted babies, the spoor left by generals, and, closer to home, the hearts gone bubonic with jealousy and greed, glinting through the vests and sweaters of anyone at all. Torment, they say and see. The third eye can be merciless, especially when wounded.

~

But someone has to see these things. They exist. Try not to resist the third eye: it knows what it's doing. Leave it alone and it will show you that this truth is not the only truth. One day you will wake up and everything, the stones by the driveway, the brick houses, each brick, each leaf of each tree, your own body, will be glowing from within, lit up, so bright you can hardly look. You will reach out in any direction and you will touch the light itself.

~

After that there are no more instructions because there is no more choice. You see. You see.

SEAMUS HEANEY (Ireland, 1939–2013)

Cloistered

Light was calloused in the leaded panes of the college chapel and shafted into the terrazzo rink of the sanctuary. The duty priest tested his diction against pillar and plaster, we tested our elbows on the hard bevel of the benches or split the gold-barred thickness of our missals.

I could make a book of hours of those six years, a Flemish calendar of rite and pastime set on a walled hill. Look: there is a hillside cemetery behind us and across the river the plough going in a field and in between, the gated town. Here, an obedient clerk kissing a bishop's ring, here a frieze of seasonal games, and here the assiduous illuminator himself, bowed to his desk in a corner.

In the study hall my hand was cold as a scribe's in winter. The supervisor rustled past, sibilant, vapouring into his breviary, his welted brogues unexpectedly secular under the soutane. Now I bisected the line AB, now found my foothold in a main verb in Livy. From my dormer after lights out I revised the constellations and in the morning broke the ice on an enamelled water-jug with exhilarated self-regard.

ALEX KUO (United States, 1939–)

Growing Tomatoes

In 1944 when I was very young, my family lived in a huge house outside Chongqing, just a stone's throw from the river that flooded every spring. We had goats, ducks and geese that chased after me, and a vegetable garden. I remember my father gathering giant tomatoes from his garden and juicing them into a large porcelain bowl on the square dining room table. I still remember the glassfuls tasting dank and dark. To this day I still cannot stand its rawness, but drink it camouflaged in a Bloody Mary.

Since I've moved to Idaho and live in my own house, I've been raising vegetable gardens in the backyard every season. Among the corn, squash, eggplant, spinach and beet I've always saved room for a few tomato plants, even though I never eat them but give them away to friends at harvest time.

In the middle of the summer I sometimes walk out of the house and listen to these plants grow, often flicking tiny black aphids from off their stems and leaves. In these moments the tangy odor of their leaves draw childhood recollections of a father dead nineteen years, images of his hands immersed in the white porcelain bowl of tomato juice from his garden, him saying *Drink it, drink it, it's only good for you, it's vitamin C.*

Tonight, at exactly my father's age in 1944 and nearly five thousand miles and fifty years from my past, I wake to hear the tomato leaves brushing gently against the backdoor of my house in the breeze, and soon after, the fruit bursting like blood in the burgeoning quarter moon.

ROBERT HASS (United States, 1941–)

Novella

A woman who, as a thirteen-year-old girl, develops a friend-
ship with a blind painter, a painter who is going blind. She is
Catholic, lives in the country. He rents a cabin from her father,
and she walks through the woods—redwood, sword fern, sor-
rel—to visit him. He speaks to her as an equal and shows her
his work. He has begun to sculpt but still paints, relying on
color and the memory of line. He also keeps English biscuits in
a tin and gives her one each visit. She would like more but he
never gives her more. When he undresses her, she sometimes
watches him, watches his hands which are thick and square, or
his left eye with a small cloud like gray phlegm on the retina.
But usually not. Usually she thinks of the path to his house,
whether deer had eaten the tops of the fiddleheads, why they
don't eat the peppermint saprophytes sprouting along the
creek; or she visualizes the approach to the cabin, its large windows, the fuchsias in front of it where Anna's hummingbirds
always hover with dirty green plumage and jeweled throats.
Sometimes she thinks about her dream, the one in which her
mother wakes up with no hands. The cabin smells of oil paint,
but also of pine. The painter's touch is sexual and not sexual,
as she herself is. From time to time she remembers this interval
in the fall and winter of ninth grade. By spring the painter had
moved. By summer her period had started. And after that her
memory blurred, speeding up. One of her girlfriends French-
kissed a boy on a Friday night in the third row from the back at
the Tamalpais theater. The other betrayed her and the universe
by beginning to hang out with the popular girls whose fathers
bought them cars. When the memory of that time came to her,
it was touched by strangeness because it formed no pattern with
the other events in her life. It lay in her memory like one piece
of broken tile, salmon-colored or the deep green of wet leaves,
beautiful in itself but unusable in the design she was making.
Just the other day she remembered it. Her friends were coming
up from the beach with a bucket full of something, smiling and

waving to her, shouting something funny she couldn't make out, and suddenly she was there—the light flooding through the big windows, the litter of canvases, a white half-finished torso on the worktable, the sweet, wheaty odor of biscuits rising from the just-opened tin.

LYN HEJINIAN (United States, 1941–)

Once there was a girl and she went for a walk by herself and came upon a hole in the ground no bigger than her finger. She sat down beside it to wait and watch so that she might see what went into it or came out.

Overhead large white clouds floated in the blue but they never obscured the sun and a spider crawled over her ankle. The clouds changed shape but didn't depart though a breeze was blowing, it carried a round brown leaf past the hole, then brought it back, and dropped it.

Why is that a round brown leaf instead of a brown round one, the girl wondered, just as she had wondered earlier why the large white clouds weren't white large ones.

Dissatisfaction with how one shapes one's thoughts is not the same as dissatisfaction with the shape of things, she said aloud and irritably, yanking at the nearest stalks of grass and pulling them out of the ground. Sulkily tossing them into the breeze, feeling sorry for herself but also thinking herself grandly or at least subtly intelligent, she failed to notice the shifting of the leaf over the hole and the . . .

But whether it was a return or a departure, and of what, will be something we'll learn only tomorrow night, or some night not long after it.

First you must learn where the spider went.

Stories

A man walking in the rain eating a banana. Where is he coming from. Where is he going. Why is he eating a banana. How hard is the rain falling. Where did he get the banana. What is the banana's name. How fast is the man walking. Does he mind the rain. What does he have on his mind. Who is asking all these questions. Who is supposed to answer them. Why. Does it matter. How many questions about a man walking in the rain eating a banana are there. Is the previous question one of them or is it another kind of question, not about the man or the walking or the rain. If not, what's it a question about. Does each question raise another question. If so, what's the point. If not, what will the final question be. Does the man know any of the answers. Does he enjoy bananas. Walking in the rain. Can the man feel the weight of eyes on him, the weight of questions. Why does the banana's bright yellow seem the only color, the last possible color remaining in a gray world with a gray scrim of rain turning everything grayer. I know question after question after question. The only answer I know is this: all the stories I could make from this man walking in the rain eating a banana would be sad, unless I'm behind a window with you looking out at him.

ANTÓNIO LOBO ANTUNES (Portugal, 1942–)

Paradise

When I was little, there were two bakeries in Benfica. One right by the church, frequented by the bagaço-swigging proletariat, the floor was always strewn with sawdust and flattened cigarette butts, and that was called the Adega dos Ossos, where I was advised not to go for fear I might become fatally addicted to cherry brandy and cheap cigarettes and end my days playing dominoes, losing at cards and coughing into my handkerchief. It was a dark place, with lots of bottles on the walls, and in the window were more flies than custard tarts. Beyond the shelves and the spines of the bottles, a library of delirium tremens, I remember the squint-eyed bartender, his right eye furious and his left benevolently tender, and Senhor Manuel, the sacristan, who dropped by in his red surplice between masses and downed a few glasses with eucharistic unctuousness, hiding behind the fridge, afraid he might be spotted by the prior, who was all sternness and buttons from his neck to his shoes, and for whom wine, when not taken with wafers, had the devilish quality of leading the flock astray and causing them to postpone the six o'clock rosary in favor of the abominable vice of cards.

The other bakery, the Benfica Paradise, almost opposite the first, was frequented after mass by ladies whose devotion was rustproof, antimagnetic and bulletproof—for example, my grandmothers and my aunts whose intimate knowledge of the saints amazed me and who hastened to teach me the catechism after I asked, pointing my finger at the Holy Spirit

—What's that sparrow doing there?

explaining to me that God was not a sparrow, he was a dove, and I immediately imagined him in Praça de Camões eating out of the hands of pensioners, which hardly seemed to me an activity compatible with the creation of the universe.

Paradise was filled by ladies after mass and by men during it.

(When a cousin of mine indignantly asked her husband why he wasn't going to church, he replied with a small smug smile

—I don't need to: I'm in Paradise already. It's cooler and they serve beer.)

Unlike the Adega dos Ossos it smelled good, none of the employees had a squint, and dominoes was banned. Senhor Manuel's surplice did not flutter furtively behind the fridge and, most important of all, my brothers and I had an open account there for cake and ice cream. At first I was so touched by the generosity of that open account I almost wept with gratitude. I realize later that it was not really an act of generosity: it was because on Sundays we had lunch at my grandmother's house and the gift of ice cream and doughnuts was intended to distract me from the firm posterior of the cook whose charms I had recently discovered. Torn between two equally celestial Paradises, I hesitated for months on end between coconut fancies and the four rings of the stove.

I finally opted for the stove. When, sometime later, the cook married a policeman

(all the cooks married policemen)

and I tried to go back to the doughnuts, my grandmother, disillusioned with my sinful ways, had canceled the account. In desperation, I accompanied her on an excursion for widows to Fátima in an attempt to win back both her affection and the cakes: not even this heroic sacrifice moved her. And I went on to live in a painful state of double orphanhood from which no cheese pastry and no apron has yet shown any interest in rescuing me.

Translated from the Portuguese by Margaret Jull Costa

RON PADGETT (United States, 1942–)

The Salt and Pepper Shakers

My wife and I have been meaning to buy a set of salt and pepper shakers for the past several years. We have one set, which we carry back and forth between kitchen and table. For some reason, we have never gotten around to buying the second set. Apparently it isn't quite important enough for us to do but is important enough to make us think we ought to buy them at some point. "Where's the salt and pepper?" I am heard frequently to ask.

"Oh, they're in the kitchen," my wife answers wearily.

At which point our son says, "O.K., I know," and goes to get the salt and pepper.

And so we do not remember to buy the second set. If someone were to come up to us on the street and offer to give us a set right there on the spot, we would exclaim, "It's exactly what we need, it's amazing!" But no one does. I went outside a few minutes ago to check. Instead the streets were occupied by very bland "people" with no interest in giving me some salt and pepper shakers.

Perhaps our *mañana* attitude is caused by the satisfying beauty of the ones we do have. They are of the plain old diner variety, glass in vertical facets, with aluminum caps—transparent identical twins, except one is labeled "moi" and the other "tu." We bought them for twenty-nine cents in Arkansas in 1967. They evoke home fries and coffee, and I have no doubt that there is someone who just by looking at them can describe the society that produced them, just as you can read this and know me.

RIKKI DUCORNET (United States, 1943–)

Fydor's Bears

Fydor was a small man and he hunted bears. He knew everything there was to know about them: by the shape and size of a footprint read the age, weight, and speed of an animal; he knew their seasons of amorous encounters and the wild gardens they haunted for honey. And the bears knew Fydor: his tics, his tenacity, and his peculiar smell—rancid as old fat forgotten at the bottom of a can.

Still, Fydor was the more cunning. By the roots of windblown trees he dug deep traps and made them secret beneath weavings of bracken and leaves. Many times in the passing of the year would a bear sink with a nauseating thud to be stung by Fydor's arrows, enfevered with sleep, and hauled off to one of the many stout cages he kept in a cellar called home.

~

Fydor hated his bears yet could not live without them. Their intimate habits, their torments and hungers excited him, sickened him, obsessed him. He thrived in the stench of their fur, their urine, and their tears.

And in time the bears became obsessed with Fydor. Locked into their cages like flies in amber, they turned to him—for he was the only thing they could turn to. They watched him, memorized his habits: the way he shuffled across the littered floors, or held a pan of water beneath a tap. In time the bears knew Fydor better than a woman knows her man after sharing a half century of boredom and bed. And as alchemists fool with foul matter changing colors and structures, the bears—woolly and immense—entered into Fydor's dreams, and changed Fydor.

Night after night they lumbered down the narrow passages of Fydor's mind to browse its rag stalls, its cut-rate china shops, leaving droppings, making drafts, causing sunset changes. They brought burdens of flowers, of fire; as at a shrine, they drugged the air.

And vines grew inside Fydor's mind, and halls of green shadow; lean hills, red earth, and places of perpetual picnic. Fydor's skull—barren before—sprouted grass. His dim, fly-ridden eyes grew luminous. Bears were now coursing through his blood, inhabiting his heart, his liver, his testicles.

His nerves writhed bears. His skin crawled bears. His bowels groaned: *Bears!* His cock yearned: *Bears!* He ate, slept, dreamed, fucked, and defecated bears until waking in a frenzy of longing, his eyes wild and circling the room like bears on bicycles, he ran to them, his pants bulging with longing and with keys. Fingers trembling, he found the locks and set them free to lumber off into the night.

And Fydor followed them. With a gruff expression of joy half human, half brute, followed his makers into the forest. Another beast among beasts; perhaps less agile, less ferocious perhaps....

PHILLIP LOPATE (United States, 1943–)

The Tender Stranger

I was running to school in fourth grade to get to class before the bell and as I rounded a busy corner I banged into a tall man rushing from the other direction and I was thrown into the air.

He weighed so much more than I that I sailed for quite a ways before landing on the sidewalk.

"Are you all right?" The man bent over me. His overcoat was a fine camel's hair, such as I had seen only in the movies. He had on a soft beige scarf and brown woolen gloves and a brown fedora. "I'm so sorry, it was my fault completely. Are you all right?"

I nodded, laughing now at the comic spill I had taken, like a cartoon character. How could I explain to him that it had been a pleasure to fly through the air, that there was something even comforting about a collision with such a manly, yet considerate, adult as this stranger.

I pulled my sticky palms off the sidewalk. The skin was torn up, and bleeding.

"Here, I think I've got a Kleenex," he said. He reached into his pocket, felt around, and came up with a monogrammed handkerchief. I stared at the sharp crease in his pants as he crouched alongside me, brushing off the dirt; I was so in love with him that I felt too embarrassed to look at his face. "Does that hurt much?"

"No, it doesn't hurt at all," I lied.

"I just didn't see you. I was in too big of a hurry, I guess."

"I was also in a hurry."

"This corner is very tricky. People always seem to have accidents here."

I wondered how he knew that.

As though he could read my mind, he went on to explain: "I have a law office nearby, and I see these accident cases all the time."

Suddenly the words *Notary Public* popped into my mind. I had read them on golden decals in store windows and wondered often what they meant. "Are you a Notary Public?" I asked.

"No, just a lawyer," he laughed gently. "My name's Tony, Tony Bauer" (it sounded like). "My office is right across Roebling Street, on the second floor. Why don't you come visit me sometime?"

"Okay."

"Do you think you'll be able to walk now? Maybe we should take you to a drugstore first and get them to put some iodine on your hand."

"I'm all right. Honest."

"You sure now?"

"I'm all right," I said, letting him help me up. He handed me my blue-and-red bookbag. Only now did I realize I felt dizzy from the blow. Everything was whirling with black outlines in the winter snow. I was going to have another of my headaches.

"Well—goodbye for now. It was a pleasure meeting you," he said, and I felt he really meant it. "Too bad it had to come about this way." Then the stranger took off one glove, and was careful not to hurt my bruise in his handshake. I had never seen an adult show a child such tact. As his back turned and he walked away, I had the peculiar urge to yell out, "Daddy!"

Afterward I often tried rounding that same corner at full speed, but no one ever banged into me again.

STEPHEN MITCHELL (United States, 1943–)

Jonah

After the first few hours he came to feel quite at ease inside the belly of the whale. He found himself a dry, mildly fluorescent corner near one of the ribs, and settled down there on some huge organ (it was springy as a waterbed). Everything—the warmth, the darkness, the odor of the sea—stirred in him memories of an earlier comfort. His mother's womb? Or was it even before that, at the beginning of the circle which death would, perhaps soon, complete? He had known of God's mercy, but he had never suspected God's sense of humor. With nothing to do now until the next installment, he leaned back against the rib and let his mind rock back and forth. And often, for hours on end, during which he would lose track of Ninevah and Tarshish, his mission, his plight, himself, resonating through the vault: the strange, gurgling, long-breathed-out, beautiful song.

MICHAEL ONDAATJE (Ceylon / Canada, 1943–)

Harbour

I arrived in a plane but love the harbour. Dusk. And the turning on of electricity in ships, portholes of moon, the blue glide of a tug, the harbour road and its ship chandlers, soap makers, ice on bicycles, the hidden anonymous barber shops behind the pink dirt walls of Reclamation Street.

One frail memory dragged up out of the past—going to the harbour to say goodbye to a sister or mother, dusk. For years I loved the song, "Harbour Lights," and later in my teens danced disgracefully with girls, humming "Sea of Heartbreak."

There is nothing wise about a harbour, but it is real life. It is as sincere as a Singapore cassette. Infinite waters cohabit with flotsam on this side of the breakwater and the luxury liners and Maldive fishing vessels steam out to erase calm sea. Who was I saying goodbye to? Automatically as I travel on the tug with my brother-in-law, a pilot in the harbour, I sing "the lights in the harbour don't shine for me . . ." but I love it here, skimming out into the night anonymous among the lazy commerce, my nieces dancing on the breakwater as they wait, the lovely swallowing of thick night air as it carves around my brain, blunt, cleaning itself with nothing but this anonymity, with the magic words. *Harbour. Lost ship. Chandler. Estuary.*

How I Was Bathed

We are having a formal dinner. String hoppers, meat curry, egg rulang, papadams, potato curry. Alice's date chutney, seeni sambol, mallung and brinjals and iced water. All the dishes are on the table and a good part of the meal is spent passing them around to each other. It is my favourite meal—anything that has string hoppers and egg rulang I eat with a lascivious hunger. For dessert there is buffalo curd and jaggery sauce—a sweet honey made from the coconut, like maple syrup but with a smoky taste.

In this formal setting Gillian begins to describe to everyone present how I used to be bathed when I was five. She had heard the story in detail from Yasmine Gooneratne, who was a prefect with her at Bishop's College for Girls. I listen intently, making sure I get a good portion of the egg rulang.

The first school I went to was a girls' school in Colombo which accepted young boys of five or six for a couple of years. The nurse or ayah in charge of our cleanliness was a small, muscular and vicious woman named Maratina. I roamed with my pack of school friends, usually filthy from morning to night, and every second evening we were given a bath. The bathroom was a sparse empty stone room with open drains in the floor and a tap to one side. We were marched in by Maratina and ordered to strip. She collected our clothes, threw them out of the room, and locked the door. The eight of us were herded terrified into one corner.

Maratina filled a bucket with water and flung the contents towards our cowering screaming bodies. Another bucket was filled and hurled towards us hard as a police hose. Then she strode forward, grabbed a child by the hair, pulled him over to the centre, scrubbed him violently with carbolic soap and threw him towards the opposite side of the room. She plucked another and repeated the soaping. Totally in control of the squirming bodies she eventually scrubbed us all, then returned to the bucket and thrashed water over our soapy nakedness. Bleary-eyed, our bodies tingling and reeling, our hair curved back from the force of the throw, we stood there shining. She approached with a towel, dried us fast and brutally, and threw us out one by one to get into our sarongs and go to bed.

The guests, the children, everyone is laughing and Gillian is no doubt exaggerating Yasmine's account in her usual style, her long arms miming the capture and scrub of five-year-olds. I am dreaming and wondering why this was never to be traumatically remembered. It is the kind of event that should have surfaced as the first chapter of an anguished autobiographical novel. I am thinking also of Yasmine Gooneratne, now teaching at a university in Australia, whom I met just last year at an International Writers' Conference in New Delhi. We talked then mostly about Gillian who had also been at university with her. Why did *she* not tell me the story—this demure woman in a sari who was once "bath prefect" at Bishop's College Girl's School, who officiated over the cleansing of my lean five-year-old nakedness?

JAMES TATE (United States, 1943–)

Goodtime Jesus

Jesus got up one day a little later than usual. He had been dreaming so deep there was nothing left in his head. What was it? A nightmare, dead bodies walking all around him, eyes rolled back, skin falling off. But he wasn't afraid of that. It was a beautiful day. How 'bout some coffee? Don't mind if I do. Take a little ride on my donkey, I love that donkey. Hell, I love everybody.

What It Is

I was going to cry so I left the room and hid myself. A butterfly had let itself into the house and was breathing all the air fit to breathe. Janis was knitting me a sweater so I wouldn't freeze. Polly had just dismembered her anatomically correct doll. The dog was thinking about last summer, alternately bitter and amused.

I said to myself, *So what have you got to be happy about?* I was in the attic with a 3000 year old Etruscan coin. *At least you didn't wholly reveal yourself*, I said. I didn't have the slightest idea what I meant when I said that. So I repeated it in a slightly revised version: *At least you didn't totally reveal yourself,* I said, still perplexed, but also fascinated. I was arriving at a language that was really my own; that is, it no longer concerned others, it no longer sought common ground. I was cutting the anchor.

Polly walked in without knocking: "There's a package from UPS," she announced.

"Well, I'm not expecting anything," I replied.

She stood there frowning. And then, uninvited, she sat down

on a little rug. That rug had always been a mystery to me. No one knew where it came from and yet it had always been there. We never talked of moving it or throwing it out. I don't think it had ever been washed. Someone should at least shake it from time to time, expose it to some air.

"You're not even curious," she said

"About what?" The coin was burning a hole in my hand. And the rug was beginning to move, imperceptibly, but I was fairly sure it was beginning to move, or at least thinking of moving.

"The package," she said. "You probably ordered something late at night like you always do and now you've forgotten. It'll be a surprise. I like it when you do that because you always order the most useless things."

"Your pigtails are starting to crumble," I said. "Is there anywhere in the world you would rather live?" I inquired. It was a sincere question, the last one I had in stock.

"What's wrong with this?" she replied, and looked around the attic as if we might make do.

"I guess there are shortages everywhere," I said. "People find ways. I don't know how they do it but they do. Either that or . . ." and I stopped. "Children deserve better," I said. "But they're always getting by with less. I only pity the rich. They're dying faster than the rest of us."

When I get in these moods, Polly's the one I don't have to explain myself to, she just glides with me along the bottom, papa sting-ray and his daughter, sad, loving, beautiful—whatever it is, she just glides with me.

"Are you ever coming down again?" she asked, without petulance or pressure, just a point of information.

"Not until I'm very, very old. I have to get wise before I can come down, and I'm afraid that is going to take a very long time. It will be worth it," I said, "you'll see."

"Daddy," she said, "I think you know something already."

LYNNE TILLMAN (United States, 1944–)

Lunacies

The first astronaut to reach the Moon proclaimed: "One small step for man, one giant leap for mankind." Neil Armstrong, his head entombed in a white bubble, his eyes obliterated by Moon-resilient plastic, gravity-less in a bloated space suit, planted the U.S. flag right where he stood.

Later, Armstrong realized his mistake. He was supposed to have said: "One small step for *a* man, one giant leap for mankind."

"As you read this, the Moon is moving away from the Earth. Each year the Moon steals some of Earth's rotational energy and uses it to propel itself about 3.8 centimeters higher in its orbit."

He had never encountered a parasite he didn't, in some way, envy for a kind of perverse talent.

"The tidal forces of the Moon—and the Sun—don't act only on the oceans, they act on the land too. Stand on the equator, and the land beneath you will rise and fall as much as twenty-one inches over the course of twenty-four hours."

Vertigo restrained her from standing near expansive plate-glass windows on the upper floors of top-heavy skyscrapers. She teetered on high heels, the foundation undulating beneath her feet, or maybe she was moonstruck again.

"The Moon is about the same age as Earth. When the Moon was created, it was much closer to Earth and appeared ten times larger in the sky."

In Sunday school, he asked his teacher, "Why did God make the Moon without people?" His father told him the moon was too cold for people, it was the dark side of God's work; then his mother broke in, "Your father's being funny. Look at the TV. Michael Jackson, honey, he's moon-walking."

·

"The Moon is full when the Earth is between the Sun and Moon, it is a New Moon when the Moon is between the Sun and the Earth."

Nocturnal creatures, cats nightly play and prance, hunting mice, hearing their faint movements behind plaster walls, while their owners beseech moon gods for love and power.

"The Moon is not a planet, but a satellite of the Earth."

Being an identical twin was way cooler than being a virtual one—adopted at the same time, same age, but studies showed virtuals were very different people. He and his brother were unique, even if they looked the same, and he didn't moon about his lost individuality, the way his twin did.

"An afterglow—also called post-luminescence—is a wide arc of glowing light that can sometimes be seen high in the western sky at twilight; it is caused by fine particles of dust scattering light in the upper atmosphere."

She loved the line, "When a pickpocket meets a saint, he sees only his pockets." She scratched his right arm and nudged him. "Naked, you don't have pockets," he said, "unless you're a fuck-ing kangaroo." Moonlight did nothing for this guy.

"Alan Shepard, when he was on the Moon, hit a golf ball and drove it 2400 feet, nearly half a mile."

The moon is made of green cheese, and that crater on it, it's really a man in the moon. And I haven't drunk any moonshine.

"At the full Moon, the times of moonrise and moonset have advanced so that the Moon rises about the same time the Sun sets, and the Moon sets about the same time the sun rises."

Their honeymoon, after years of living together, still scared up traditional illusions, intimations of ecstasy, a time out from reality, and when the second night of connubial bliss yawned on, she quoted George Meredith, "Where may these lunatics have gone to spend the Moon."

"Ramadan begins with the sighting of the new crescent Moon in the ninth month of the lunar calendar. But whose sighting counts?"

She read the first sentence of the book: "A white dog bayed at the Moon, a true moon-dog, with moon-blindness, more blind sometimes than others." The writer must be a lunatic.

"Dr. Eugene Shoemaker, a geological surveyor who educated the Apollo mission astronauts about craters, never made it to the Moon . . . . He was rejected as an astronaut because of medical problems. After he died, his ashes were placed on board the Lunar Prospector spacecraft on January 6, 1999 . . . and fulfilled Dr. Shoemaker's last wish."

Once in a blue moon, the tides pull at us. They invoke humans to recall primitive ancestors who shouted at the sky, noise-makers who yowled in the dark, beckoning forces and spirits to aid their survival. Now, domesticated dogs guard their masters' lives, and house cats daydream about orangutans swinging happily from branch to branch. Human beings cannot stop being afraid of the dark or imagining complete freedom.

PAUL VIOLI (United States, 1944–2011)

Snorkeling with Captain Bravo

A belief in the perfectability of man boodle loop bloodle loop bloop bloop bloop can only lead to despair and needlessly heavy breathing bloodle loo loo bloop bloop bloop try not to laugh bloodoop just keep those flippers working close to the surface sputter sputter between worlds goolp goolp the fatal yawn of totalitarian bloodle loop boodle loop the violent die stupid deaths bloop bloop avoid cults goolp no theory no bloop system no book will save you doodle oop doop doop be a true seeker and fall forever upward like an angel bloop bloop bloop

Acknowledgments

The author wishes to express his profound gratitude to the following publications in which some of these works previously appeared: *Architectural Digest:* "This Lime-Tree Bower My Prison"; *Teen Life:* "On the Death of Chatterton"; *Cosmopolitan:* "Constancy to an Ideal Object"; *Bon Appetit:* "Drinking versus Thinking"; "The Eagle and the Tortoise"; *La Cucina Italiana:* "Fire, Famine and Slaughter"; *House Beautiful:* "Kublai Khan," "This Lime Tree Bower My Prison"; *Better Homes and Gardens:* "This Lime-Tree Bower My Prison," "Reflections on Having Left a Place of Retirement," "Fears in Solitude," "Dejection: an Ode"; *Modern Bride:* "The Rime of the Ancient Mariner"; *American Bride:* "A Lover's Complaint to His Mistress Who Deserted Him In Quest of a More Wealthy Husband in the East Indies"; *Mechanics Illustrated:* "Work Without Hope"; *Popular Mechanics:* "Work Without Hope"; *Interiors:* "Kublai Khan"; *Sports Illustrated:* "Dejection: an Ode"; *Hustler:* "Christabel."

SCOTT RUSSELL SANDERS (United States, 1945–)

Aurora Means Dawn

When Mr. and Mrs. Job Sheldon reached Ohio in 1800, with seven children, two oxen, and a bulging wagon, they were greeted by a bone-rattling thunderstorm. The children wailed. Mrs. Sheldon spoke of returning to Connecticut. The oxen pretended to be stone outcroppings, and would budge neither forward nor backward for all of Mr. Sheldon's thwacking.

Lightning toppled so many oaks and elms across the wagon track, in any case, that even a dozen agreeable oxen would have done them no good.

They camped. More precisely, they spent the night squatting in mud beneath the wagon, trying to keep dry. Mrs. Sheldon kept saying there had never been any storms even remotely like this one back in Connecticut. "Nor any cheap land," her husband added. "No land's cheap if you perish before setting eyes on it," she said. And that ended talk for the night. Every few minutes, Mrs. Sheldon would count the children, touching each head in turn, to make sure none of the seven had vanished in the deluge.

Next morning it was hard to tell just where the wagon track had been, there were so many trees down. Husband and wife tried cutting their way forward. After chopping up and dragging aside only a few felled trees, and with half the morning gone, they decided Mr. Sheldon should go fetch help from Aurora, their destination. On the land-company map they had carried from the East, Aurora was advertised as a village, with mill and store and clustered cabins. But the actual place turned out to consist of a surveyor's post, topped by a red streamer. So Mr. Sheldon walked to the next village shown on the map— Hudson—which fortunately did exist, and there he found eight men who agreed to help him clear the road.

Their axes flashed for hours in the sunlight before they reached the wagon. The children huddled in shirts while their outer garments dried on nearby bushes. Mrs. Sheldon sat fully dressed and shivering. With the track cleared, the oxen still could not move the wagon through the mud until all nine men and one woman and every child except the toddler and the baby put their shoulders to the wheels. Even though they reached Aurora after nightfall, making out the surveyor's post in lantern light, the eight ax men insisted on returning immediately to their own homes. The blades glinted on their shoulders as they disappeared from the circle of the campfire.

Dry at last, Mr. and Mrs. Sheldon carried the lantern through this forest that would become their farm. Aurora meant dawn;

they knew that. And their family was the dawn of dawn, the first glimmering in this new place. The next settlers did not come for three years.

DIANE WILLIAMS (United States, 1946–)

Glass of Fashion

My mother touched the doctor's hair—"Your hair—" she said. I was looking at the doctor's eyes—black and as sad as any eyes I had ever looked at—doleful, mournful—but I thought she is hard-hearted too, this doctor. She must be hard-hearted. Hard-hearted is part of her job. It has to be.

The doctor's hair was full and long and kinky and wavy and black. My mother's hair is short and white and kinky and wavy and I could see why my mother was admiring the doctor's hair. I was admiring the doctor's body in her jeans. She had what I thought was a girlish and perfect form in her jeans, an enviable form.

There were four of us backed up to the large window at the end of the hall, because I had said, "Let's go over to the window to talk"—my mother, my sister, and me, and this very young woman doctor with black hair, black eyes, and jeans on.

We were at the window at the hospital, at the end of a hall, down from what was left of my father. We were getting the report on my father, because I had said to the doctor, "Tell us."

Maybe the doctor was a little ashamed too, or belligerent, when she was telling us. Her eyes had such a film over them, so that they sparkled when she spoke of his cerebellum, about his brain stem, about the size of his cortical function. She said, "He doesn't know who he is. He does not know who he once was. He does not feel grief or frustration. He does not know who you are." What I was envying then were the doctor's legs in her jeans. "Maybe—" I said, "you know, maybe—he had such a big brain before—it is just possible," I said, "that even if his brain has been ravaged, he is still a smart enough person."

The doctor did not say anything about that. No one did.

Chrissy, one of Dad's day-shift nurses, was coming along then toward us. Her glasses are the kind my sister will not wear. She will not get glasses like that. My mother will not either. A serious person's glasses—even if Chrissy is only just a nurse, even if she cannot explain very much about the brain, because she explained to me she has been out of school for too long— I can tell she is serious, that she is serious about me too. If she were a man, I would call what we have shared romantic love—we have shared so much, so often here—talking about my father with feeling. If she were a man—even if she couldn't remember half of what she had learned about the brain—even if she had forgotten it all—*no*—if she had forgotten it all, totally, I don't think I'd want to spend the time of day in her presence. She would disgust me if she were a man like that. So when she called us, when she said, "Your father—" and then when I called "Dad! Dad!" from the—and it sounded even to me as if I expected he would rise up—then I was ready for what I was feeling when I touched his forehead—which was still warm. His mouth was open. The front of the lower row of his teeth was showing. The teeth had never looked, each of them, so terribly small. Some of his teeth were the last things on my father that I ever touched.

RAE ARMANTROUT (United States, 1947–)

Imaginary Places

Reading, we are allowed to follow someone else's train of thought as it starts off for an imaginary place. This train has been produced for us—or rather materialized and extended until it is almost nothing like the ephemeral realizations with which we're familiar. To see words pulled one by one into existence is to intrude on a privacy of sorts. But we *are* familiar with the contract between spectator and performer. Now the text isn't a train but an actress/model who takes off her school uniform piece by piece alone with the cameraman. She's a good girl playing at being bad, all the time knowing better. She invites us to join her in that knowledge. But this is getting us nowhere.

LOU BEACH (United States, 1947–)

The storm came over the ridge, a rocket, dropped rain like bees, filled the corral with water and noise. I watched lightning hit the apple tree and thought: "Fritters!" as we packed sandbags against the flood. There was nowhere to go that wasn't wet, the squall had punched a hole in the cabin roof and the barn was knee-high in mud. We'll bury Jess later, when the river recedes, before the ground turns hard again.

*

Shot by a monkey, Elsa leaned against the banyan, held a bandage to the wound. They'd entered camp just before dawn, made off with a pistol, some candy bars, and a Desmond Morris book. We counted as six shots rang out, one of them finding poor Elsa's arm. Relieved that the simian was out of ammunition, we packed up. On the way out of camp we noticed a monkey on the riverbank, hammering at a snake with the gun.

LYDIA DAVIS (United States, 1947–)

The Cedar Trees

When our women had all turned into cedar trees they would group together in a corner of the graveyard and moan in the high wind. At first, with our wives gone, our spirits rose and we all thought the sound was beautiful. But then we ceased to be aware of it, grew uneasy, and quarreled more often among ourselves.

That was during the year of high winds. Never before had such tumult raged in our village. Sparrows could not fly, but swerved and dropped into calm corners; clay tiles tumbled from the roofs and shattered on the pavement. Shrubbery whipped our low windows. Night after night we drank insanely and fell asleep in one another's arms.

When spring came, the winds died down and the sun was bright. At evening, long shadows fell across our floors, and only the glint of a knife blade could survive the darkness. And the darkness fell across our spirits, too. We no longer had a kind word for anyone. We went to our fields grudgingly. Silently we stared at the strangers who came to see our fountain and our church: we leaned against the lip of the fountain, our boots crossed, our maimed dogs shying away from us.

Then the road fell into disrepair. No strangers came. Even the traveling priest no longer dared enter the village, though the sun blazed in the water of the fountain, the valley far below was white with flowering fruit and nut trees, and the heat seeped into the pink stones of the church at noon and ebbed out at dusk. Cats paced silently over the beaten dirt, from doorway to doorway. Birds sang in the woods behind us. We waited in vain for visitors, hunger gnawing at our stomachs.

At last, somewhere deep in the heart of the cedar trees, our wives stirred and thought of us. And lazily, it seemed to us, carelessly, returned home. We looked on their mean lips, their hard eyes, and our hearts melted. We drank in the sound of their harsh voices like men coming out of the desert.

The Fish Tank

I stare at four fish in a tank in the supermarket. They are swimming in parallel formation against a small current created by a jet of water, and they are opening and closing their mouths and staring off into the distance with the one eye, each, that I can see. As I watch them through the glass, thinking how fresh they would be to eat, still alive now, and calculating whether I might buy one to cook for dinner, I also see, as though behind or through them, a larger, shadowy form darkening their tank, what there is of me on the glass, their predator.

Companion

We are sitting here together, my digestion and I. I am reading a book and it is working away at the lunch I ate a little while ago.

YUSEF KOMUNYAKAA (United States, 1947–)

The Deck

I have almost nailed my left thumb to the 2 x 4 brace that holds the deck together. This Saturday morning in June, I have sawed 2 x 6s, T-squared and levelled everything with three bubbles sealed in green glass, and now the sweat on my tongue tastes like what I am. I know I'm alone, using leverage to swing the long boards into place, but at times it seems as if there are two of us working side by side like old lovers guessing each other's moves.

This hammer is the only thing I own of yours, and it makes me feel I have carpentered for years. Even the crooked nails are going in straight. The handsaw glides through grease. The toe-nailed stubs hold. The deck has risen up around me, and now it's strong enough to support my weight, to not sway with this old, silly, wrong-footed dance I'm about to throw my whole body into.

Plumbed from sky to ground, this morning's work can take nearly anything! With so much uproar and punishment, foot-work and euphoria, I'm almost happy this Saturday.

I walk back inside and here you are. Plain and simple as the sun-light on the tools outside. Daddy, if you'd come back a week ago, or day before yesterday, I would have been ready to sit down and have a long talk with you. There were things I wanted to say. So many questions I wanted to ask, but now they've been answered with as much salt and truth as we can expect from the living.

GREGORY ORR (United States, 1947–)

Chateaubriand on the Niagara Frontier, 1791

He could be just one more erstwhile aristocrat lightfooting it from the guillotine who's crossed the Atlantic to research Rousseau's wonders of nature at first hand. And he is, but tonight, writing in his travel journal, he'll make his own contribution: the invention of the literary beauty of moonlight. It's a concept destined to fascinate and console the melancholic children and love-starved wives of the bourgeoisie he loathes.

It happens because he can't stand the smell of the frontier inn where he's stopped for the night: an earth-floored room with a fire in the middle. Everyone lies crowded together with their feet near the embers, their bodies radiating out, Indian and trapper alike. In a dream he can't share, they become greasy spokes of a great, breathing wheel. The wheel lifts itself upright, moves, then begins to roll along a rutted trail, deeper and deeper into the new world.

DAVID LEHMAN (United States, 1948–)

"But Only…"

I accompanied him to prison, taking the cell next to his, but only to make sure he wouldn't escape. That was the cover story, but only a credulous fool would believe it. We had taken a tour of chateau towers and church spires, disguising ourselves as clerics, but only to kill the time between assignments. One night as I slept a convention of architects and surveillance experts assembled a model prison in San Francisco but only because the California state legislature was throwing money at the problem of overcrowded correctional facilities. I slept fitfully, awakened by fears or loud neighbors, and decided to stay awake, but only because I had homework to do and now was as good a time as any to do it. A commotion outside caused me to go to the window but only for a few minutes. I opened the window and stuck my head out but only to see whether a revolution had commenced. I could see the eyes of the people in the street below, but only a few of them looked familiar. The people were looking up, but only because of a strong light flashing from the top of the building. There was misery in their eyes, but only because they had forgotten why they had gathered at four in the morning in this inauspicious part of the city.

CHRISTINE SCHUTT (United States, 1948–)

An Unseen Hand Passed Over Their Bodies

My son is coughing in his sleep next to me in my bed, where he has come to spend what is left of this night. My son's cough is red, noisy, and loose, a clattering wagon on its jagged way down, with me all ears to the racheting sound of my child-self in the bed next to Dad, who is tossing and threatening. "Stop coughing," Dad says. "You'll wake the dead." Bat flap and smoke in the dark of his voice make me hold back this need, hold back from Dad, whose fleshy skull clenches every raw cough I cough. I want to be still. I fix on the chafed, pitted folds at his neck with a promise to sleep, as if my quiet could ease and uncoil this turned-away man, but I can't and it's out, rude air through the pipes, a dry sound full of rust. Dad says, "I'm too old for this." He says, "Oblige me," and I watch the words turn in this room he calls his own, Dad's porch, sleeping headquarters, off-limits. How did I get here, close enough to smell him? That's what I want to know: How did I?

Rolled, damp toweling—the kind Dad sometimes swipes at me—he smells like that. He smells like shaving water, where he floats his brush and lets me blow apart the suds before he snaps a towel, says, "Out. That's enough; go get dressed." I only pretend to leave. He never shuts the door all the way, and I want to see, and I can, if I am careful, if I am clever. From where I am hiding, just outside the bathroom door, I can see him. I can see him oiling his back under the sunlamp. It makes me feel lazy just watching him: the way my father massages himself and rolls his shoulders in this heat. So much heat, so much white in wild refraction off the swivel mirror; I see he has to squint to see the parts of himself in the magnified side, where the black eye, lashless and fast, his eye, finds me.

I am almost sure of this—that my father only pretends I am not there.

Like he pretends in his bed this dopey snooze; says, "I give up"; says, "Let me just shut my eyes."

Am I not the woman he cannot keep out?

I want to wake him still.

I want to shrill in his ear: "Look, you!"

But the thought of him makes me close my eyes, try to sleep, a girl.

I hold to the edge of my bed and watch him sleep. I don't move. I let my son take up all the room he wants, knowing he will slip away before I am even awake, and even after I have been so quiet, so good.

LYNN EMANUEL (United States, 1949–)

April 18, the 21st Century

Cher Baudelaire,

Tonight as I boarded my train of thought and entered the first class compartment of my mind, I thought of Margaret Atwood who wrote, "I am in love with Raymond Chandler because of his interest in furniture." Baudelaire, I am no one but the insatiable identities that descend upon me and tonight it is you. I've thought, if Baudelaire were not Baudelaire, I would be Baudelaire, though in truth I have thought the same about Walter Benjamin when he says (I paraphrase), "I am in love with Baudelaire because of his interest in furniture. When writing about furniture Baudelaire is free from capitalism's philosophy and history and archaeology and is enthralled by upholstery, and this is a way of thinking and being that is wholly new in the world and was made so by Baudelaire."

No quotation is innocent. Every quotation is an act of ventriloquism. Every ventriloquism is an usurpation. As R. P. Blackmur said (and here I do not quote but paraphrase): "If you say there is no blackbird in a poem immediately a blackbird alights on the branch of a line." If you say, "I am only quoting," immediately your voice guiltily alights on the branches of the words.

In *Charles Baudelaire: A Lyric Poet in the Era of High Capitalism*, as Walter Benjamin carries forward the great cross of his love for you, as he is nailing himself to his love for you, at the height of his passion, he stops on page seventy-one to quote that gnat Maxime Du Camp:

Baudelaire had what is a great defect in a writer, a defect of which he was not aware: he was ignorant.... He remained unacquainted with history, physiology, archeology and philosophy.... He had little interest in the outside world; he may have been aware of it, but he certainly did not study it.

And in doing so, at the height of his love, Walter Benjamin enters and is entered, he becomes Maxime Du Camp. "Baudelaire knew nothing," says (sneers) Benjamin. Why, I have always wondered, does he do that?

Cher Baudelaire, I believe that behind or inside Benjamin's quotation from Maxime Du Camp, growing upon it as a vine grows on a trellis, there lives the envy and sorrow of a man cut off from the possibility of another's experience. There lives the envy of a man who knew history for another man who did not; there lives the love of a man (Benjamin) who loved philosophy for a man (you) who did not love it and by extension would not have loved him (Benjamin) or perhaps could not love him.

Would you have wasted an afternoon on Benjamin? No. Is there even one syllable in you to suggest that you care at all about Benjamin? No. Which must have hurt.

I, on the other hand, am perfectly aware that you adore me because we adore so many of the same things—furniture, women's dresses, recreational drugs. In every line and flourish I hear you calling out to me as I sit here in the furnishings of the future; I see you waving to me in the windows of my train of thought as though you were waving to yourself at some time in the future; as though I were you with my poems filled with dresses and drugs and unfaithful women, some of whom are me. How grateful you are that I have resurrected you, that you can live in the present with all its wonderful appurtenances, with its fantastic advances in perfumes, the advent of hair gel, the Alps of the four-inch stiletto. How lucky you are, cher Baudelaire, to have found me to shelter you, to have found the succulent hallways of my lines, and the shimmering windows of my tropes, and the sticky navels of the little hash pipes I have left lying about for you, the ease, the comfort, the respite my verse provides you. Or maybe not. I sit on my train and watch capitalism struggle in the windows. In the city of the mind the great alcove of night closes over us. Even over you, Baudelaire, who invented a world that had never before existed—a completely interior world of upholstery without philosophy—and in so doing gained the undying envy of the future Walter Benjamin, who was sentenced to live inside a world outside and who, therefore, had to save himself from that world and its history by committing suicide at Hotel de Francia in Port-Bou in September of 1940.

JAMAICA KINCAID (Antigua / United States, 1949–)

The Letter from Home

I milked the cows, I churned the butter, I stored the cheese, I baked the bread, I brewed the tea, I washed the clothes, I dressed the children; the cat meowed, the dog barked, the horse neighed, the mouse squeaked, the fly buzzed, the goldfish living in a bowl stretched its jaws; the door banged shut, the stairs creaked, the fridge hummed, the curtains billowed up, the pot boiled, the gas hissed through the stove, the tree branches heavy with snow crashed against the roof; my heart beat loudly *thud! thud!*, tiny beads of water gathered on my nose, my hair went limp, my waist grew folds, I shed my skin; lips have trembled, tears have flowed, cheeks have puffed, stomachs have twisted with pain; I went to the country, the car broke down, I walked back; the boat sailed, the waves broke, the horizon tipped, the jetty grew small, the air stung, some heads bobbed, some handkerchiefs fluttered; the drawers didn't close, the faucets dripped, the paint peeled, the walls cracked, the books tilted over, the rug no longer lay out flat; I ate my food, I chewed each mouthful thirty-two times, I swallowed carefully, my toe healed; there was a night, it was dark, there was a moon, it was full, there was a bed, it held sleep; there was movement, it was quick, there was a being, it stood still, there was a space, it was full, then there was nothing; a man came to the door and asked, "Are the children ready yet? Will they bear their mother's name? I suppose you have forgotten that my birthday falls on Monday after next? Will you come to visit me in hospital?"; I stood up, I sat down, I stood up again; the clock slowed down, the post came late, the afternoon turned cool; the cat licked his coat, tore the chair to shreds, slept in a drawer that didn't close; I entered a room, I felt my skin shiver, then dissolve, I lighted a candle, I saw something move, I recognized the shadow to be my own hand, I felt myself to be one thing; the wind was hard, the house swayed, the angiosperms prospered, the mammal-like reptiles vanished (Is the Heaven to be above? Is the Hell below? Does the Lamb still lie meek? Does the Lion roar? Will the streams all run clear?

Will we kiss each other deeply later?); in the peninsula some ancient ships are still anchored, in the field the ox stands still, in the village the leopard stalks its prey; the buildings are to be tall, the structures are to be sound, the stairs are to be winding, in the rooms sometimes there is to be a glow; the hats remain on the hat stand, the coats hang dead from the pegs, the hyacinths look as if they will bloom—I know their fragrance will be overpowering; the earth spins on its axis, the axis is imaginary, the valleys correspond to the mountains, the mountains correspond to the sea, the sea corresponds to the dry land, the dry land corresponds to the snake whose limbs are now reduced; I saw a man, He was in a shroud, I sat in a rowboat, He whistled sweetly to me, I narrowed my eyes, He beckoned to me, Come now; I turned and rowed away, as if I didn't know what I was doing.

BARRY YOURGRAU (South Africa / United States, 1949–)

Domestic Scene

I am turned into an animal: a weasel. I feel humiliated and small and stupid. Incredibly, my girlfriend doesn't notice when she wakes up beside me in the morning. I sit huddled on the edge of the bed, fixing on her my huge, mournful, brown weasel eyes. "This morning you put on the coffee water," she sighs, and she heads out to the shower.

Of course this simple request is quite beyond me, because of my size and because of my simple-minded digital capabilities. "Oh thanks," my girlfriend mutters with weary sarcasm, coming into the kitchen and finding the kettle on its side on the floor, where I had sent it tumbling with my hapless maneuverings. She slams the fridge door when she gets out the milk.

At the table, she eats her breakfast in silence dully ignoring me. I sit in my chair, feeling absurdly small and puny in it, with a bit of tail hanging down back. I have nothing to eat, so I fall to licking my paws. "For God's sake, can't you stop biting your damn nails?" my girlfriend murmurs.

I stop and stare at her. Something in me snaps. "You unfeeling brute!" I screech at her, all my woebegoneness flooding into rage. "Here I've been turned into some kind of rodent right under your nose—*and you haven't even noticed*!"

She stares back, dumbfounded. Her mouth is open. Then her eyes flash. She slams down her coffee mug so that it slops all over the table. "Look who's talking!" she bellows. She grabs handfuls of her large, loose ears. "What about what's happened to *me*?!" she rages.

ANNE CARSON (Canada, 1950–)

Short Talk On Sleep Stones

Camille Claudel lived the last thirty years of her life in an asylum wondering why, writing letters to her brother the poet, who had signed the papers. Come visit me, she says. Remember I am living here with madwomen, days are long. She did not smoke or stroll. She refused to sculpt. Although they gave her sleep stones—marble and granite and porphyry—she broke them then collected the pieces and buried these outside the walls at night. Night was when her hands grew, huger and huger until in the photograph they are like two parts of someone else loaded onto her knees.

CAROLYN FORCHÉ (United States, 1950–)

The Colonel

What you have heard is true. I was in his house. His wife carried a tray of coffee and sugar. His daughter filed her nails, his son went out for the night. There were daily papers, pet dogs, a pistol on the cushion beside him. The moon swung bare on its black cord over the house. On the television was a cop show. It was in English. Broken bottles were embedded in the walls around the house to scoop the kneecaps from a man's legs or cut his hands to lace. On the windows there were gratings like those in liquor stores. We had dinner, rack of lamb, good wine, a gold bell was on the table for calling the maid. The maid brought green mangoes, salt, a type of bread. I was asked how I enjoyed the country. There was a brief commercial in Spanish. His wife took everything away. There was some talk of how difficult it had become to govern. The parrot said hello on the terrace. The colonel told it to shut up, and pushed himself from the table. My friend said to me with his eyes: say nothing. The colonel returned with a sack used to bring groceries home. He spilled many human ears on the table. They were like dried peach halves. There is no other way to say this. He took one of them in his hands, shook it in our faces, dropped it into a water glass. It came alive there. I am tired of fooling around he said. As for the rights of anyone, tell your people they can go fuck themselves. He swept the ears to the floor with his arm and held the last of his wine in the air. Something for your poetry, no? he said. Some of the ears on the floor caught this scrap of his voice. Some of the ears on the floor were pressed to the ground.

May 1978

J O H N   Y A U   (United States, 1950–)

The Sleepless Night of Eugene Delacroix

In North Africa, Delacroix had seen a Jewish wedding which he described extensively in his journal:

> *She is silhouetted halfway against the door, halfway against the wall; nearer the foreground, an older woman, with a great deal of white, which conceals her almost entirely, the shadows full of reflections; white in the shadows.*

Nine years later, in the Salon of 1841, he exhibited a painting entitled, "Jewish Wedding."

After the wedding, the congratulations, the eating, drinking, and dancing, the bride and bridegroom walked out into the night; her white dress turned blue; it grew smaller; finally a speck of dust was blinked away.

On March 11, 1854, Eugene Delacroix sat down at his favorite desk (a gift—actually one of many he had received from a Pasha in Tangiers) and wrote in his journal:

> *A long interruption in these poor notes of daily happenings: I feel very badly about it; these trifling pages written down in such a fugitive way seem to me all that is left of my life, the more it flows away. My lack of memory makes them necessary for me; since the beginning of the year, the steady work needed for finishing at the Hôtel de Ville has been distracting me too much; since I finished it, and that will soon be a month since, my eyes are in a bad state, I am afraid to read and to write.*

He felt as he put down the pen and straightened his back that the rest of his evenings, his nights and days, would be filled with a new kind of darkness. At first he thought he could turn to his friends. But Mme Sand was on her way to Vienna, and Chopin had not received him twice in the last week. Most likely, he was in the throes of composition.

Delacroix felt his fears being heightened by the underlying silence of day becoming night. He wished he were sitting in the green brocade chair in Frederic's apartment, listening to him playing the piano. The evening's shadows, both inside and outside, were beginning to overlap, while he remained seated at his desk, his chin cupped between his hands, his eyes closed.

He remembered that twenty years ago M. Gros had told him that he had once lived a life devoted to excess. But now he, M. Gros, drank nothing but water with dinner. In fact, being deprived of a cigar after dinner was the greatest hardship of all the ones he had to face. Delacroix wondered what he had forgotten about that evening. What moments would never be retrieved?

It was well past midnight, yet restlessness permeated his movements. The moon slit the thick velvet drapes, but it couldn't reach him. Instead, on either side of his bed two strips of light wavered along the carpet. Outside, someone remarked on the sultry beauty of the night in a high silly voice. *I am afraid to read and to write.*

The lamp continued flickering; three dull concentric circles peered back from the ceiling. Delacroix rolled over on his side; he faced the night table, as he had done many times in the last few hours. Except for the table, everything had become a shadow; the chair in the corner was a blotch of darkness. He turned back to the table. A pile of books lay there, precariously balanced. They were a staircase rising in memory of the house that no longer surrounds them.

MEENA ALEXANDER (India / United States, 1951–)

Crossing the Indian Ocean

I was with my mother on the S.S. *Jehangir*, crossing the Indian Ocean. Midway on the journey I turned five. Bombay was far behind and Port Sudan still to come. It was my first sea voyage.

Until then I had lived on solid land, on the Indian subcontinent and all my journeys had been by train or car or on small wooden boats on the canals and waterways of the coastal region I come from.

The sea cast me loose.

The sea tore away from me all that I had. In doing so, it gave me an interior life far sooner than I would have had otherwise, but at great cost.

I was forced to enter another life, the life of the imagination. But it was not as yet the life of language.

I had few words at my disposal, and those I had came from several languages that cohabited within my head. What I felt as a child and held deep within myself quite exceeded the store of words within my reach.

This is something that I feel, even now as an adult. The struggle for words, the struggle to be human, is coexistent for me with the craft of poetry.

On my fifth birthday I was plunged into a world with no before and no after.

A child can fall into the sea, never to reappear.

A mother can appear out of the waves, only to vanish, reappear, and then vanish again.

The sea has no custom, no ceremony. It allows a theater for poetry, for a voice that cries out, that splits into one, two, three or more, chanting the figurations of the soul, marking a migrant memory.

The day I turned five, I stuck my head out through the porthole of our cabin and saw ceaseless water. On and on, until my eyes and neck hurt, I kept watch.

When I pulled my head back in I knew the sea was painted on the inside of my eyelids, would never leave me.

Sometimes the syllables of poetry well up, waves on the surface of the sea, and they burst as flying fish might, struck by light.

Sometimes I feel this is how I began, a wordless poet, a child on the surface of wide water with all that she loved torn from her, cast into ceaseless suspension.

The page on which I write is a live restless thing, soul-sister to the unselving sea.

BERNARD COOPER (United States, 1951–)

Saturday Night

Can Mother muster enough thrust to leave the earth in a sudden leap? Does Father need words of encouragement, a rabbit's foot, a running start? Will they rise above our suburb at dusk and see it studded with lights? Wind must play havoc with mother's dress, her stole blown back like a vapor trail. Father's suit, diminishing, dark, will become part of the night. What instinct helps them scout for the house, find the right street, land on their feet? How do they breathe, cleaving the air with such soft hats? At the house of the host, can you hear the hail of guests on the roof, the garage, the grass, come eager to mingle, smoke, and tell jokes? Over a cover of cold clouds, bearing bouquets, bottles of wine, decks of cards and dominoes, a sparse arc of punctual people migrate behind the horizon. While aloft like a league of ghosts or gods, does their vision slip through thick ceilings? Can they watch us mimic their kisses, embrace our own backs, burrow hands beneath our bedclothes? Spying their children aglow on earth with a meager heat, do flying parents cry like geese?

JOY HARJO (United States, 1951–)

Deer Dancer

Nearly everyone had left that bar in the middle of winter except the hardcore. It was the coldest night of the year, every place shut down, but not us. Of course we noticed when she came in. We were Indian ruins. She was the end of beauty. No one knew her, the stranger whose tribe we recognized, her family related to deer, if that's who she was, a people accustomed to hearing songs in pine trees, and making them hearts.

The woman inside the woman who was to dance naked in the bar of misfits blew deer magic. Henry Jack, who could not survive a sober day, thought she was Buffalo Calf Woman come back, passed out, his head by the toilet. All night he dreamed a dream he could not say. The next day he borrowed money, went home, and sent back the money I lent. Now that's a miracle. Some people see vision in a burned tortilla, some in the face of a woman.

This is the bar of broken survivors, the club of shotgun, knife wound, of poison by culture. We who were taught not to stare drank our beer. The players gossiped down their cues. Someone put a quarter in the jukebox to relive despair. Richard's wife dove to kill her. We had to hold her back, empty her pockets of knives and diaper pins, buy her two beers to keep her still, while Richard secretly bought the beauty a drink.

How do I say it? In this language there are no words for how the real world collapses. I could say it in my own and the sacred mounds would come into focus, but I couldn't take it in this dingy envelope. So I look at the stars in this strange city, frozen to the back of the sky, the only promises that ever make sense.

My brother-in-law hung out with white people, went to law school with a perfect record, quit. Says you can keep your laws, your words. And practiced law on the street with his hands. He jimmied to the proverbial dream girl, the face of the moon, while the players racked a new game. He bragged to us, he told her magic words and that's when she broke, became human.

But we all heard his bar voice crack:
What's a girl like you doing in a place like this?
That's what I'd like to know, what are we all doing in a place like this?

You would know she could hear only what she wanted to; don't we all? Left the drink of betrayal Richard bought her, at the bar. What was she on? We all wanted some. Put a quarter in the juke. We all take risks stepping into thin air. Our ceremonies didn't predict this. Or we expected more.

I had to tell you this, for the baby inside the girl sealed up with a lick of hope and swimming into praise of nations. This is not a rooming house, but a dream of winter falls and the deer who portrayed the relatives of strangers. The way back is deer breath on icy windows.

The next dance none of us predicted. She borrowed a chair for the stairway to heaven and stood on a table of names. And danced in the room of children without shoes.

You picked a fine time to leave me, Lucille.

With four hungry children and a crop in the field.

And then she took off her clothes. She shook loose memory, waltzed with the empty lover we'd all become.

She was the myth slipped down through dreamtime. The promise of feast we all knew was coming. The deer who crossed through knots of a curse to find us. She was no slouch, and neither were we, watching.

The music ended. And so does the story. I wasn't there. But I imagined her like this, not a stained red dress with tape on her heels but the deer who entered our dream in white dawn, breathed mist into pine trees, her fawn a blessing of meat, the ancestors who never left.

AMY HEMPEL (United States, 1951–)

The Orphan Lamb

He carved the coat off the dead winter lamb, wiped her blood on his pants to keep a grip, circling first the hooves and cutting straight up each leg, then punching the skin loose from muscle and bone.

He tied the skin with twine over the body of the orphaned lamb so the grieving ewe would know the scent and let the orphaned lamb nurse.

Or so he said.

This was seduction. This was the story he told, of all the farm-boy stories he might have told; he chose the one where brutality saves a life. He wanted me to feel, when he fitted his body over mine, that this was how I would go on—this was how I would be known.

PETER JOHNSON (United States, 1951–)

Houdini

"Houdinize: to release or extricate oneself from confinement, as by wriggling out." You've certainly mastered that trick, your every alibi a Trunk Mysterioso. Harry never made excuses. Instead—hard work, repetition... A Dime Museum: you're cracking yellow croquet balls on your cranium, trying to make a diamond materialize in a Big Mac; I'm scraping gold sequins off the floor with a dislocated big toe. And Harry? He's hanging upside down, inch-long needles dangling from his eyelids. "Behold, a miracle!" he shouts, then wants to know just what the hell a Big Mac is, and why we're here. "It was a bad winter, Harry: frozen birds smashing into failing gutters, our St. Bernard casting off its root-beer barrel and chasing two old cats. Then a fiendish hand crashed through the Great Beyond and grabbed me by the chi-chis." Which, of course, makes everyone laugh. Even the Dog-Faced Boy. But Harry's up for the challenge. He crawls into a large milk can. Much mumbling and banging, then a solution signaled by the moan of a conch shell. He leaps from the can, naked from the waist up, sweating, his eyes gunmetal grey. "Beware the Kalends of July!" he shouts. "Beware anyone even using the word Kalends!" And he's deadly serious. Later, sitting on a trick coffin in a cream-colored straitjacket, he's fed chunks of sirloin by the Bird Girl. "My whole life," he says, "I've been chasing the sound of my mother's heartbeat." Inside the ebony box, a woman is weeping.

ANA MARÍA SHUA (Argentina, 1951–)

The Lovers

They always dreamed of a reincarnation that would allow them to kiss in public. They died together in an accident during one of their secret rendezvous. He came back as a circus elephant and she as a petunia. Since the lifespan of petunias is very brief, this put them out of sync. In the next reincarnation they were both human, but with sixty-three years between them. She became Pope and he an adorable little girl who was granted permission to kiss his ring in an audience.

Concatenation

The events of the past determine those of the present. For example, if your parents hadn't met, you wouldn't exist today. The further back you go in the chain of circumstances that shape the history of the world, the more surprising and subtle the consequences of the most trivial act become, resulting in a complex, almost infinite series of concatenations. For example, if during the Late Cretaceous Period a certain carnivorous plesiosaurus hadn't eaten the eggs that a female triceratops had foolishly laid on the shoreline, perhaps, who knows, you'd still love me.

Translated from the Spanish by Rhonda Dahl Buchanan

MAXINE CHERNOFF (United States, 1952–)

The Interpretation of Dreams

I have always aspired to be a circus performer. My husband has always collected keys, starting with the pink and blue teething keys of babyhood. These two interests had no significant connection to me, yet they were the sole cause of our marital strife. My husband would come home elated at finding an unusual key. That was the signal to transport myself to the big top, imagining the ringmaster's introduction: "Ladies and gentlemen, for the first time in the United States and Canada, here she is, Trixie, the tiger woman." I never divulged my hobby to him. Colette of the talking poodles, Chloe, the human fly, and Rosa, the rubber lady, were foreign to him as relaxing with a good circus novel.

After another exasperating weekend of key-hunting, I drifted into an uneasy sleep. I dreamed that my husband and I were an acrobatic team. He was tall and worldly in military blue and a red shirt, designed to reveal his biceps, bulging like two loaves of bread. I wore a silver tutu, accentuating my small waist and large breasts. Our act was complex, and far surpassed any that I'd seen on television or read about in histories of the "Flying Capezios." Like a shooting star, I'd hurl myself from the trapeze to be caught by my husband, who held a solid gold key between his teeth. People below gasped at his dental fortitude. Although the act was perilous and required the concentration of a bibliographer transcribing into braille, we'd smile at one another like fifteen-year-olds over a coke.

I woke up feeling transformed. The next Saturday my husband was startled to find me dressed before him for our weekly tour of curio shops, garbage dumps, and demolished buildings. He supposed my enthusiasm was the result of reading some gushy article about togetherness in a woman's magazine or that my doctor had prescribed a hobby to cure my frequent headaches. Little does he know that I practice every day. Shades drawn, I hang from the crystal chandelier and propel myself across the room, landing lightly as a moth on a coat lapel.

RAY GONZALEZ (United States, 1952–)

El Bandido

El bandido was a stereotype but he prospered in the history books and got away with riches, women, and many killings. El bandido wore the typical large sombrero, bandoliers loaded with bullets, and a huge handlebar moustache. He rode into battle on horses with his men, his victories accumulating as the masses revolted throughout the country. When he held court around huge campfires, his men huddled close and listened to every word. When his enemies were lined up against adobe walls to be shot, his men relished the opportunity to be in one of the firing squads. El bandido had a large belly and a round face, prominent features in hundreds of antique photographs of the war. His cruelty against his enemies and his love of women were legendary. His horse was a prize stallion and his soldiers were always well armed. El bandido's hacienda was heavily guarded and the dining table was stacked with food, liquor, and boxes of the best cigars. Though he had many wives and mistresses, he slept alone on most nights, moving from one large bedroom to another in the enormous houses on his estate. When he slept, he had a recurring dream where he found himself in wet caverns where the many faces of the men he had personally shot stared at him through the dripping water. When he couldn't sleep, he lay awake in the dark and pondered the next campaign. Each morning he sat on the edge of his bed and stared briefly at the old wooden crucifix on the far wall before leaving. El bandido rode at the head of a long column of men and horses, the cause refreshed each time the dream of the caverns came to him. Battles were lost and won, but he accumulated more power and riches as the number of dead men who had followed him rose into the thousands. When a foreign army entered the country and chased him for over four months, el bandido's fame intensified and the stereotype grew. The few battles the two sides engaged in were minor, though more men died and more photographers took pictures. When the invading troops gave up on catching him, he sat on his horse atop a desert ridge and watched the distant dust clouds of the retreating army. As the sun began to set, el bandido waited on the ridge with three of his most trusted generals. No one spoke because he didn't say a word. Several more years of fighting followed as towns were captured and lost and the country suffered over 200,000 dead. El bandido had three ranches near the end of the struggle and had survived two assassination attempts. The new government offered to pardon him, though his army was the largest at the end of the revolution. El bandido refused to be pardoned, though he promised not to march on the capitol and he let his men go home. The few dozen that stayed to work on his ranches were younger stereotypes of the legend. Their ambitions, guns, and women were abundant and their dreams were influenced by their loyalty to their leader. Three years after the revolt, el bandido was the richest man in the northern part of the country and he married his sixth wife. A few nights after the wedding, el bandido woke alone. The recurring dream did not visit him as often as it used to, so he lay calmly in the large bed until he heard his wife crying somewhere. Out of habit, he reached for his pistol and stepped quietly toward the next room. As he opened the door, he found his wife tied to a chair, six of his ranch hands surrounding her with drawn guns, one of them holding a pistol to the woman's head. El bandido and his men exchanged volleys in the truest stereotype of a western gunfight. He killed four of them before the other two put nine bullets into him and two in his wife. The two men ran out to the dozens of waiting and mounted riders whose bandoliers, rifles, and faces glistened in the summer moonlight.

JEAN-MICHEL MAULPOIX (France, 1952–)

You burn with your sentences.

You would like to walk lightly on snow like a squirrel, hear the whiteness crunch, handle the warm fur of fairy tales, abandon yourself to their sleep, as you would to a pillow, where you nestle your head while someone tells a story. Each time your heart creaks, you take up your thimble, your sewing kit and your needles: still more words with words, bits of wood, children's forts, excess, access to the sky, inky fevers, a craving for blue, its melancholy of light-colored skirts; you are love's workman.

This blue sticks to my lips.

The one who took a long time to understand that he would never know the how or the why of things, and whose devoured heart drifts between two seas, buries his bitterness and desire in the fabric of the sea. He still hopes for support from the open sea, gusts from the sky, a bit of new blood, just enough flesh to keep his bones warm, and maybe even, on nice nights, three milligrams of eternity slowly melting on his tongue.

Translated from the French by Dawn Cornelio

NAOMI SHIHAB NYE (United States, 1952–)

Yellow Glove

What can a yellow glove mean in a world of motorcars and governments?

I was small, like everyone. Life was a string of precautions: Don't kiss the squirrel before you bury him, don't suck candy, pop balloons, drop watermelons, watch TV. When the new gloves appeared one Christmas, tucked in soft tissue, I heard it trailing me: Don't lose the yellow gloves.

I was small, there was too much to remember. One day, waving at a stream—the ice had cracked, winter chipping down, soon we would sail boats and roll into ditches—I let a glove go. Into the stream, sucked under the street. Since when did streets have mouths? I walked home on a desperate road. Gloves cost money. We didn't have much. I would tell no one. I would wear the yellow glove that was left and keep the other hand in a pocket. I knew my mother's eyes had tears they had not cried yet, I didn't want to be the one to make them flow. It was the prayer I spoke secretly, folding socks, lining up donkeys in windowsills. *To be good*, a promise made to the roaches who scouted my closet at night. *If you don't get in my bed, I will be good.* And they listened. I had a lot to fulfill.

The months rolled down like towels out of a machine. I sang and drew and fattened the cat. Don't scream, don't lie, don't cheat, don't fight—you could hear it anywhere. A pebble could show you how to be smooth, tell the truth. A field could show how to sleep without walls. A stream could remember how to drift and change—next June I was stirring the stream like a soup, telling my brother dinner would be ready if he'd only hurry up with the bread, when I saw it. The yellow glove draped on a twig. A muddy survivor. A quiet flag.

Where had it been in the three gone months? I could wash it, fold it in my winter drawer with its sister, no one in that world would ever know. There were miracles on Harvey Street. Children walked home in yellow light. Trees were reborn and gloves traveled far, but returned. A thousand miles later, what can a yellow glove mean in a world of bank-books and stereos?

Part of the difference between floating and going down.

JAYNE ANNE PHILLIPS (United States, 1952–)

Sweethearts

We went to the movies every Friday and Sunday. On Friday nights the Colonial filled with an oily fragrance of teenagers while we hid in the back row of the balcony. An aura of light from the projection booth curved across our shoulders, round under cotton sweaters. Sacred grunts rose in black corners. The screen was far away and spilling color—big men sweating on their horses and women with powdered breasts floating under satin. Near the end the film smelled hot and twisted as boys shuddered and girls sank down in their seats. We ran to the lobby before the lights came up to stand by the big ash can and watch them walk slowly downstairs. Mouths swollen and ripe, they drifted down like a sigh of steam. The boys held their arms tense and shuffled from one foot to the other while the girls sniffed and combed their hair in the big mirror. Outside the neon lights on Main Street flashed stripes across asphalt in the rain. They tossed their heads and shivered like ponies.

On Sunday afternoons the theater was deserted, a church that smelled of something frying. Mrs. Causton stood at the door to tear tickets with her fat buttered fingers. During the movie she stood watching the traffic light change in the empty street, push-ing her glasses up over her nose and squeezing a damp Kleenex. Mr. Penny was her skinny yellow father. He stood by the office door with his big push broom, smoking cigarettes and coughing.

Walking down the slanted floor to our seats we heard the swish of her thighs behind the candy counter and our shoes sliding on the worn carpet. The heavy velvet curtain moved its folds. We waited, and a cavernous dark pressed close around us, its breath pulling at our faces.

After the last blast of sound it was Sunday afternoon, and Mr. Penny stood jingling his keys by the office door while we asked to use the phone. Before he turned the key he bent over and pulled us close with his bony arms. Stained fingers kneading our chests, he wrapped us in old tobacco and called us his little girls. I felt his wrinkled heart wheeze like a dog on a leash. Sweethearts, he whispered.

Happy

She knew if she loved him she could make him happy, but she didn't. Or she did, but it sank into itself like a hole and curled up content. Surrounded by the blur of her own movements, the thought of making him happy was very dear to her. She moved it from place to place, a surprise she never opened. She slept alone at night, soul of a naked priest in her sweet body. Small soft hands, a bread of desire rising in her stomach. When she lay down with the man she loved and didn't, the man opened and opened. Inside him an acrobat tumbled over death. And walked thin wires with nothing above or below. She cried, he was so beautiful in his scarlet tights and white face the size of a dime.

PETER WORTSMAN (United States, 1952–)

Ibsen's Hat

Henrik Ibsen never went anywhere without his hat. Refusing to entrust it to a hatcheck's charge, he preferred to place it beside him, always requisitioning an empty seat at whatever cost. Its positioning was crucial and the dramatist took great pains to tilt it just right. The significance of the hat, a mystery heretofore, was only recently revealed when a packet of the playwright's letters were sold at Sotheby's. "I spotted you this afternoon in the crook of my hat," he addressed a correspondent by the initial N (thought by some to have inspired Nora). Apparently flattered by the famous man's attention, N must have challenged him to explain. For another note dated the following day reads: "Man must protect himself from beauty's Medusa gaze. Do tell me where you plan to sit at tomorrow's performance. I prefer pearl earrings." And yet another note concludes: "The cad, the fool, the critic T rushing to congratulate me for yesterday's premiere of P.G. (probably *Peer Gynt*) knocked over my doffer and smashed my second set of eyes. Will have to love you blindly 'til I find a replacement." Ibsen, it seems, wore a pocket mirror tucked into the sweatband of his hat—which explains an obscure line crossed out in the original manuscript of *A Doll's House*: "Only enclosed by glass does beauty arouse manageable emotions."

HARRYETTE MULLEN (United States, 1953–)

Bleeding Hearts

Crenshaw is a juicy melon. Don't spit, and when you're finished, wash your neck. Tonight we lead with bleeding hearts, sliced raw or scooped with a spoon. I'll show my shank. I'd rend your cares with my shears. If I can't scare cash from the ashen crew, this monkey wrench has scratch to back my business. This ramshackle stack of shotguns I'm holding in my scope. I'm beady-eyed as a bug. Slippery as a sardine. Salty as a kipper. You could rehash me for breakfast. Find my shrinking awe, or share your wink. I'll get a rash wench. We'll crash a shower of cranes. I'm making bird seed to stick in a hen's craw. Where I live's a wren shack. Pull back. Show wreck. Black fade.

We Are Not Responsible

We are not responsible for your lost or stolen relatives. We cannot guarantee your safety if you disobey our instructions. We do not endorse the causes or claims of people begging for handouts. We reserve the right to refuse service to anyone. Your ticket does not guarantee that we will honor your reservations. In order to facilitate our procedures, please limit your carrying on. Before taking off, please extinguish all smoldering resentments. If you cannot understand English, you will be moved out of the way. In the event of a loss, you'd better look out for yourself. Your insurance was cancelled because we can no longer handle your frightful claims. Our handlers lost your luggage and we are unable to find the key to your legal case. You were detained for interrogation because you fit the profile. You are not presumed to be innocent if the police have reason to suspect you are carrying a concealed wallet. It's not our fault you were born wearing a gang color. It is not our obligation to inform you of your rights. Step aside, please, while our officer inspects your bad attitude. You have no rights that we are bound to respect. Please remain calm, or we can't be held responsible for what happens to you.

ALEIDA RODRÍGUEZ (Cuba / United States, 1953–)

History

*In art, politics, school, church, business, love
or marriage—in a piece of work or in a career—
strongly spent is synonymous with kept.*
—ROBERT FROST

She taught me the names of flowers: calendula, ranunculus, Iceland poppy. And the medicinal uses of herbs: Fenugreek opens up a stuffy head; goldenseal lubricates the cracked mucous membranes. Over a circa 1820 American dropleaf table, she told me asparagus was the broom of the kidneys. I hadn't understood at first and thought she'd used a German word I pictured as *brüm* and not as the little stalks standing on their heads, sweeping out the impurities. I learned to make the perfect roux for soufflé and became her efficient assistant in the kitchen—dicing and chopping, she once told me, with unparalleled patience. Then one day she began to accidentally break my Depression glassware, and I recalled how she'd giggled when she told me that in two years of marriage she had single-handedly decimated her husband's glass collection dating from 1790 to 1810, including a rare wedding goblet. In the doorway to the back porch she stated simply that my presence made her feel strangled, it was nothing I was doing or could do. We saw a therapist for six years, while my collection dwindled then became memory. With unparalleled patience I jumped through hoop after burning hoop, the therapist pointed out, but I heard that as praise for my prowess and continued to balance Bauer plates on my nose on command; hold growling tigers off with Windsor dining room chairs; juggle career, job, hope, and nightly tempests with unparalleled dexterity. I could reassemble anything: shattered pictures of us crossing the street with canes in the future, my hand under her elbow. My heart. But what I lacked, I can see now, was the ability to dissemble. Finally, she brought home a Cuisinart food processor, and I started hearing the minutes slicing away with ferocious velocity, time doing its soft-shoe faster and faster like Fred Astaire on amphetamines. Memories of flowers and herbs were sacrificed to the angry god of its vortex. Your voice is like acid on my skin, she said after twelve years, then grabbed her Cuisinart and left me behind like so much history.

THYLIAS MOSS (United States, 1954–)

Renegade Angels

Every night women in love gather outside the window and it is nothing special; coming out is what stars do, clouds, the sun when it builds up the nerve and then has to just blurt out. Their thoughts collect there, outside, the window of no value to them unless they marvel at coincidence; the window is just how I know it happens. I am not part of the circle although every game I played as a girl was round. By morning there is fruit on branches not meant to bear witness anymore, that birds avoid and that embarrasses me so I don't taste it; I don't find out if they're edible berries, and even if they were, I'd let them shrink and drop dried; I can't see myself snatching berries, especially not from a shrub so brambled, the branches look as if the feet of little birds tangled and broke off to appease beaks that had to get into those berries no matter what. This is the wrong thing to say because someone will start thinking that women in love set traps, bait bushes, trick birds, act out fables in which birds are made to always fly, to exhaust their wings, to be up soaring to death because they can't resort to landing. This is how the great hoverers are made. But women in love can do more than this, making is too traditionally and industrially valued to be a special accomplishment, a reason to gather when light isn't that good and there are no decent shadows, and the lit square and rectangular windows are irregular stars so big in their closeness they can't be wished on and personalized; stars are better the more distant they are so that to wish on them is to empower pinpricks. My eyes do not close without seeing what darkness holds, the letdown hair of women and welcome. And I remember where I was when I was fertilized, where as zygote I was stamped with most destinies but Eagle Scout, where I was when I divided and doubled without taking up additional space for a long time, before testing the limits of the skin that did not fail and being delivered; with a woman, deep inside a woman, expanding a woman's body from the inside, depending on a woman, filling a woman. This is what I remember while I'm saying that other prayer and singing that song I took, as a girl, as jingle: all day, all night, the angels watching over me. Outside my window. In honor of them for forty years I bleed libation.

HELEN KLEIN ROSS (United States, 1954–)

Birth, Copulation, Death

To relieve the tedium of arithmetic class, I stare at Jimmy Lovely who sits next to me. I sit in the front row because I am short. He sits in the front because he's delinquent.

Here's what Jimmy Lovely is doing: his nails. How absorbed he is in moving a No. 2 back and forth, back and forth over each fingertip, blackening it, annihilating pinkness and dirt.

Jimmy Lovely is an artist. The brown butcher paper that covers his book isn't plain like mine, it's a map of strange planets with jungles and wars.

The nun has stopped talking. She is standing over Jimmy Lovely's desk. The nun takes Jimmy's hands in her plain-nailed ones, lifts them high above his head.

A girl has been born in our class today and when she says this, something hardens in me.

She tells him to stand, walk the length of each aisle, show off his hands to each of his classmates. There are eighty-three of us. It takes a long time. As Jimmy Lovely makes his slow way around the room, the nun returns to the mystery of prime numbers.

When Jimmy finally arrives at my desk, I don't look at his hands. I look at his face. He is staring out the windows behind me, at the glossy field where I sometimes imagine us lying together, rolling over and over in tall, fragrant grass, falling off the edge of the earth.

MARILYN CHIN (United States, 1955–)

Lantau

While sitting prostrate before the ivory feet of the great Buddha, I spilled almost an entire can of Diet Coke on the floor. I quickly tried to mop up the mess with my long hair. I peeked over my left shoulder: the short nun said nothing and averted her eyes. To my right, the skinny old monk was consumed by a frightful irritation of his own. He was at once swatting and dodging two bombarding hornets that were fascinated by his newly shaved head. "I hope he's not allergic," I giggled. And beyond us was the motherless Asian sea, glittering with the promise of eternity.

KIMIKO HAHN (United States, 1955–)

Compass

Dear L—

You asked for *a little compass*. Thank you!

I was looking for a definition of the zuihitsu from my shelf of Japanese texts, but discovered none gave more than a sentence or two. None seemed especially scholarly—which might be a good thing. None offered the sense of disorder that feels so integral. Here is what I did find:

> [L]iterally, "following [the impulse of] the brush," and consisting of brief essays on random topics
> —Donald Keene, *Seeds in the Heart*

> [Miscellany] ... partly of reminiscences, partly of entries in diary-form   —Arthur Waley, *The Pillow Book*

> [S]tray notes, expressing random thoughts in a casual manner   —Makoto Ueda, *Principles of Classical Japanese Literature*, Earl Miner, ed.

Notice that none conveys the tonal insistence a writer finds her/himself in. None suggests an organizing principle—what we might call a *theme*. None comments on structural variety—list, diary, commentary, essay, poem. Fragment.

None offers that a sense of disorder might be artfully ordered by fragmenting, juxtaposing, contradicting, varying length or—even within a piece—topic.

From Mother seated at a window, winding her hair into a french-twist—to me, seated in a glass-bottom boat in a Tennessee cavern. Well—poor example.

Variety—e-mail, say. Gossip or scholarly annotation.

None states that these essays are closer to poetry—in my mind.

That Saturn's rings might be fading—juxtaposed with a hula hoop. A hoop skirt. A pierced clitoris. Okay—for me, that the zuihitsu feels *encompassing*. That a fragment might be synecdoche, or excerpt. Or scrap. (Sappho comes to mind.) Why not!

(And when is a piece that resembles a fragment—really the whole?)

What do you think?

Yours—K
Houston
August, 2005

STACEY HARWOOD (United States, 1955–)

Contributors' Notes

STACEY HARWOOD lives in Paris, where she teaches at La Varenne. She is credited with reviving the artisanal bread movement when she opened a tiny boulangerie, Pain Fermier on Rue Christine in the 6th Arrondissement. Her essays and recipes have appeared in *Journal of Gastronomy*, *Gourmet*, *L'Art Culinaire*, and numerous magazines both here and abroad. Her book, *Stalking the Wild Yeast*, based on her Food Network program of the same name, is forthcoming from Workingman Press.

STACEY HARWOOD is the founder and executive director of Warm Hands for the Homeless, a not-for-profit organization in Boston that recruits nursing-home residents from fourteen cities throughout the United States and Canada to knit mittens for the homeless from donated yarn-mill overruns. She was awarded a MacArthur Fellowship or "genius" grant in 1992.

•

STACEY HARWOOD is a third-year student at University of Michigan Law School. She appears as Bryanna on the HBO series *G-String Divas*. Her poetry and fiction have appeared in *Herotica, Yellow Silk, Switch/bitch and GASH.com*.

STACEY HARWOOD breeds and trains German shepherds on his farm in Eden, New York, a suburb of Buffalo where his family has farmed for three generations. He teaches composition at Erie Community College. His essays have appeared in *Men's World, Outside, Southern Quarterly Review, Creative Nonfiction*, the *New York Times Magazine*, and elsewhere. His work has twice been selected for inclusion in the annual *Best of the Small Presses* anthology (HarperCollins, 1989, 1995.) His memoir, *Come, Sit, Stay*, is due next spring.

STACEY HARWOOD received a Golden Globe award for her screenplay adaptation of Alberto Moravia's *Conjugal Love*. She is making her directorial debut this fall with a film based on the life of Italo Svevo (Ettore Schmitz) and his time in Trieste.

RABBI SHAYNA RACHEL HOROWITZ lives in Philadelphia where she and her husband are assistant rabbis at Congregation Beth-Shalom. This is her first publication.

Ever since foiling a hijacking attempt during a transatlantic flight, STACEY HARWOOD has been a motivational speaker.

STACEY HARWOOD was born in 1936. She teaches dance interpretation at Sarah Lawrence College. Harwood performed with Katherine Dunham's Chicago workshop before an injury ended her promising dance career. Harwood is the author of numerous works of poetry, fiction, and nonfiction, most recently *Closing in on the Light* (Knopf, 1998), which was the recipient of the first-ever Lifetime Extraordinary Achievement Award given by the International Society of Artists, Writers, and Performers.

•

Of "Contributors' Notes," Harwood writes: "I have long been interested in exploring the boundaries of identity and gender among certain marginalized groups. When I was no longer able to do this through dance, I turned for survival to words. Just as there is joy and sadness in knowing who you are, so too is there joy and sadness—no grief—in knowing who you are not. This poem arises out of my musings on the limits of temporal experience as provoked by cultural constraints."

GARY LUTZ (United States 1955–)

Steep

The gray bowl that my husband ate his cereal out of, the bowl he had brought to the marriage from someplace else, a bowl from which I had never eaten, did not break or chip or go back to where it came from. It simply stopped coming to the table. Up until then, events had been uneventful: I washed and dried the bowl, then returned it to the cupboard. The exertion involved was minimal—in truth, I welcomed it—but I screamed bloody murder every time.

I think I already know what comes next: a stipulative definition of marriage as an accidental adjacency of flesh in which small, unbegrudged exchanges of affection are fitfully possible provided that . . . and then you get so many pages of *provided thats*. The pages are wrinkled-looking, as if somebody had read them in the bathtub and then set them out on the floor to dry. The definition is the foundation of a vast, steep, plunging counterargument against which I am defenseless unless I spill two beans that I have been saving in my blood because what other privacy do I have? These two beans have been prowling in my blood for too long. The first bean is so simple, so obvious, that I have to work extra hard to keep putting it back into words, just to keep it in words: the woman he was seeing stopped letting herself be seen.

The second bean I have to condense. I woke up and he was biting my finger in his sleep. Not sucking—biting. An irksome switch, his being the container, instead of being gouged into *me*, slopping around inside when I was dead to the world or pretending to be. I was inside *him*. I was the one getting chewed up.

What I did was swack him on the head twice, three times. He eventually woke up. I told him what he had done.

He said, "Is that right?"

Because I was a woman he knew to speak to.

Ever since, the fundamental unit of discourse, the basic building block of speech, has been my mouth asking: "What's scarier than two people in a room with their nightstands and the things they keep on their nightstands?"

I make it sound as if I know an answer.

MICHAEL MARTONE (United States, 1955–)

Contributor's Note

Michael Martone was born at St. Joseph's Hospital in Fort Wayne, Indiana, in 1955. It is interesting to note that the attending physician was a Doctor Frank Burns, Major, United States Army, retired, and recently returned to Fort Wayne following service in the police action in Korea. It was the same Dr. Burns, it turned out, who years later served as the model for the character "Frank Burns" appearing in the novel *M*A*S*H* authored by Richard Hooker, and in the movie and television versions based on the book. Martone recalls the modest premiere of the Altman film in 1970 and its initial screening at the Embassy Theater in downtown Fort Wayne. Dr. Burns, who had continued, after Martone's birth (it had been a difficult one, sunny-side up, where forceps were used), to be his mother's gynecologist, arrived at the theater, the guest of honor, in a 1959 Cadillac Seville provided by Means Motor Company on Main Street. Sally Kellerman and Jo Ann Pflug also were there. All during the run of the television series, Dr. Burns, now in semiretirement, happily appeared at strip-mall ribbon cuttings and restaurant openings, a kind of official goodwill ambassador, and took the ribbing from the public whose perception of his character had been derived from what they had read or seen in the movies and on television. His son, Frank Jr., was two years ahead of Martone at North Side High School. Frank Jr. anchored the 4x440 relay for the Redskin varsity track and field club, where Martone served as team manager. Martone remembers Dr. Burns, team physician, coaching him in the use of analgesic balm and the scrubbing of cinders out from beneath the skin after a runner fell on the track. It was Dr. Burns who, later, diagnosed Martone's mother's ovarian cancer in 1979 and performed the failed hysterectomy that led to his mother's death that summer. It was Dr. Burns, still in surgical scrubs, who met the family in the waiting room of St. Joseph Hospital in Fort Wayne, the same hospital where Martone, twenty-four years before, had been born, delivered, by means of forceps, by Dr. Burns. The television was on, of course, an RCA model made in Bloomington, Indiana, and Martone remembers how hard it was not to watch it while, in a strange way, he also felt that he was watching himself listening to Dr. Burns rehearse the final few minutes of his, Martone's, mother's life.

SUSAN WHEELER (United States, 1955–)

Clock Radio

expunging Ponge

That each second escorts a fresh plash. Slatted awning, rec room wall, bald black translucence, the numerals—flip. The methodical tumbling drives it to hum at the pitch it extracts from the wires.

Its cousins in Holland sing slightly higher. Its march it propels with reluctance. Its drive is for the offbeat, the cack-handed, the apocopated. It sings with regret for its thrum.

The clock radio strives to become its grandfather only with ambivalence, spilling its pool on the nightstand with a modesty and steadiness in the clicks of its onerous job, in the particles that sworl in its wake.

DIONISIO D. MARTÍNEZ (Cuba / United States, 1956–)

Homage to Li Po

From the water's uncertain edge I listen to the voices among the reeds. My own voice falls and rises in its alien tempo, and fails. The world doesn't last outside the spiral of days memorized by leaves turning. A sandpiper—before it can fly back, before it can think of home—has to struggle with the shore; home can always wait. Like the bird, I listen for the ebb tide: in the mounting silence, the flywheel that regulates our stay falls short of my expectations; camouflaged, it still leaves traces and doubts. Another day takes back its last hurrah and gives a second chance to the last light. (The extended hours begin to feel at home here; they mistake themselves for leaves about to be swept off; they listen for the next delayed morning—its footfalls, its signature song, the swirling layers of fly ash that belong nowhere else.) When the bird—flycatcher or sandpiper—at last outsmarts the tide and drinks, the act falls under some Darwinian category: home and distance as incentives: the bird listens more intently, its senses clear as flyleaves, every feather groomed. Ostensibly it leaves nothing to chance, but when attempting to fly again it forgets how to forget gravity, how to listen for the call from home, how to have the last word about reclaiming the nest. In exile, home is a story that breaks your fall from grace; you find yourself standing at the fall line, your back to the new plateau where leaves—your only possession—finally rest. When home is the name of every bird in sight, the need to fly supplants the need to see things last; you learn to sleep where nothing's grounded. Listen, listen: Fall's last leaves fly home.

AMY NEWMAN (United States, 1957)

1 January

Dear Editor:

Please consider the enclosed poems for publication. They are
from my manuscript, *X = Pawn Capture*, a lyrical study of chess
as we played it in my family: the first move has to take place
while everyone is thinking about something other than chess.
For my grandparents, diversion was love, and between his rage-
filled checkmates and her play dates with saints, they braided
my teenage years spent mostly schooling and listening and
keeping the house free of insects.

When in our backyard caterpillars mastered the flowering
dogwoods, and our neighbor dispersed them by rapping on
the trees with a stick, her image reminded my grandmother of
Hortense tormenting Germana Cousin for her presumed pil-
fering of a small loaf of bread. Germana opens her dress and
her saintliness is revealed as summer flowers tumble out in a
herald of love and beauty. Here my grandmother saw chastise-
ment and the Holy Hand of her Invisible Lord Partitioning The
Mortals with some tiny visuals about The Power and The Glory
but I thought if so He was really Just Sprinkling the World with
His Blossoms and Berries, and if Germana's cottons could give
way to an onrush of flesh, abandoning its pinks and greens and
holy stamens and anthers and spilt maple leaves and maybe
even ruffles of filaments and pollen, might it ever be under my
opened dress, this mound of petals, with my thin body lighter
than bone from what I knew? So when I looked up and the
neighbor was walking away over broken dogwood blossoms
snowing down, I wished hard for a language that would tell you
of this beautiful sight which I have never before seen, not even
on a holy card, and this in spite of my grandmother's hissing at
our neighbor and retrieving a rake. I spent the afternoon carrying away the remainders of Germana's undressing and tried to
find a dictionary I could bring to my room. Because *beautiful* is
a word that my workshop class says is ineffective, that it doesn't

contain how this sight captures my attention and convinces me, absorbs and converts me away from the yard, so that the closest kin might be *diverting*, which the class might find archaic, and if that's true, then I don't know how to say that everything in the backyard might be pretending to be lovely in order that we can all get up in the morning.

Thank you for your consideration, and for reading. I have enclosed an SASE, and look forward to hearing from you.

Sincerely,
Amy Newman

DAWN RAFFEL (United States, 1957–)

Near Taurus

After the rains had come and gone, we went down by the reservoir. No one was watching, or so it looked to us.

The night was like to drown us.

Our voices were high—his, mine; soft, bright—and this was not the all of it (when is it ever?).

Damp in the palm, unauthorized, young: We would never be caught, let alone apprehended, one by the other.

"Orion, over there." He was misunderstood; that's what the boy told me. "Only the belt. The body won't show until winter," he said. "Arms and such."

Me, I could not find the belt, not to save my life, I said.

Flattened with want: "There is always another time," he said.

He died, that boy. Light years! And here I am: a mother, witness, a raiser of a boy.

I could tell you his name.

I could and would not.

"Here's where the world begins," he said. I see him now—unbroken still; our naked eyes turning to legends, the dirt beneath us parched.

SHARAN STRANGE (United States, 1959–)

The Factory

Talking about silkscreening, my aunt remembers her first job
in New York, decades ago, at the Sample Co. near Chambers
St., where she pressed glue through screens and stuck fabric
pieces to boards. She was 18, scrawny, and no one's idea of an
employee. In the employment office week after week, she met
an ugly girl who made her laugh, and so went home with her.
The city was full of people, and forgetting caution, she'd go
wherever invited back then, even out to Brooklyn or to Queens.
The factory was its own community, a motley group of natives
and new arrivals, desperate or hopeful. Married or not, everyone, it seemed, found a lover there. But those who lacked the
efficacy of English toiled all day, mute as machines. *What
became of them?* Some escaped her. Others, who were long
since hidden, come forward now, pushed by memory's levers.
All left an imprint. *The German immigrants, I'll never forget
them:* Casamia, the gypsy, and "Crazy Judy," nervous, saluting
the boss with their number tattoos. Gentle Herman, jumping
to his feet, clicking his heels.

DENISE DUHAMEL (United States, 1961–)

Healing Pies

After my parents' accident, the pies kept coming: chicken pot
pies (sized for one person), blueberry pies, ice cream pies,
peach cobblers, lemon meringues, pecan pies, pies that were
still warm in their tins, apple pies, another chicken pot pie (a
big square one), pies with chocolate pudding inside, rhubarb
pies, cherry pies, pies with crisscross slats of crust on top. Pies
from the church, pies from my mother's quilting group, pies
from the neighbors, pies from the aunts. Pies lined the kitchen
counter, pies packed the freezer. Holy pies, pies with pain-
killer filling, herbal pies, prayer pies, pies that kept vigil, pies

brimming with novenas, pies full of secrets that even doctors don't know, magic spell pies, smooth soothing pies overflowing with the music of rainforests, pies made from circles of light, pies with halos.

CAMPBELL MCGRATH (United States, 1962–)

Philadelphia

Late dinner at a dark café blocks from Rittenhouse Square, iron pots of mussels and Belgian beer and a waiter eager to snag the check and clock out. Such are the summer pleasures of his work—winding down to a glass of red wine, catching the windowed reflection of a girl as she passes, counting the take upon the bar, thick roll of ones and fives, palming the odd ten smooth against zinc and polished walnut, the comforting dinginess of American money, color of August weeds in a yard of rusting appliances, hard cash, its halo of authority, the hands' delight in its fricatives and gutturals, its growl, its purr, gruff demotic against the jargon of paychecks on automatic deposit with Social Security deductions and prepaid dental, realism vs. abstraction, a gallery of modest canvases, more landscapes than still lifes, steeples of the old city with masts and spars, a vista of water meadows with fishermen hauling nets in the distance, women collecting shellfish in wicker panniers. It yields enough to sustain us, after all, the ocean of the past. We've paid. The waiter pockets his final tip and throws down his apron and walks out into the warm night of dogs splashing in public fountains and couples on benches beneath blossoming trees and soon enough we follow, arm in arm across the cobblestones, looking for a yellow cab to carry us into the future.

ANDREJ BLATNIK (Slovenia, 1963–)

Sunday Dinners

A long time ago, before the war, generals, good friends of my grandfather's, used to attend my grandmother's dinners, she remembers. Those days are over; a lot of time has passed. The generals of today couldn't care less about congenial Sunday dinners; they sit in their offices, clicking on screens, they don't seem to care about my grandmother and her famous stuffed duck. Understandably, these days, my grandmother can't just sit around waiting for the next war. Frantically, she hoards the ingredients for stuffed duck in her cellar—her deep freezer is full of headless bodies in plastic wrap, and she's bought an oil generator because it's common knowledge that electricity is one of the first things to go in wartime; the oil should last for a few Sunday dinners at least. On Sundays, my grandmother calls up her grandchildren, one by one: "Will you come when the war starts?" she asks. "Will you come?" We explain that there could be complications, there could be roadblocks, there could be shooting, someone might even be drafted. "I'm not eating my duck by myself," grandmother sobs into the receiver, "not all by myself, dinners like that make no sense. I hate war, I hate wars like this, wars used to be *comme il faut* in the old days, they didn't interfere with my stuffed duck." Those days are over, Grandma, we explain patiently, it's all mixed up now, no one knows what it will be like when it happens. Grandmother's whimpers slowly subside, we put down our receivers and go over to our closets, concerned, wanting to make sure that everything is in place, the weapons all loaded and the safeties all off, ready, we must be ready now, nobody knows when it will happen, when it happens.

Translated from the Slovenian by Tamara M. Soban

CLAUDIA RANKINE (Jamaica / United States, 1963–)

Mr. Tools, for a while the only person in the world walking around with an artificial heart, said the weirdest thing was being without a heartbeat. His was a private and perhaps lonely singularity. No one else could say, I know how you feel. The only living being without a heartbeat, he had a whirr instead. It was not the same whirr of a siren, but rather the fast repetitive whirr of a machine whose insistent motion might eventually seem like silence.

Mr. Tools had the ultimate tool in his body. He felt its heaviness. The weight on his heart was his heart. All his apparatus—artificial heart, energy coil, battery, and controller—weighed more than four pounds. The whirr if you are not Mr. Tools is detectable only with a stethoscope. For Mr. Tools, that whirr was his sign that he was alive.

JOE WENDEROTH (United States, 1966–)

In Response to the Disciplinary Action Taken Against Me by the Human Resource Manager

Dear Human Resource Manager:

When you use the word *human* to refer to me, I don't know what you mean. You assume, I think, that human says *what I am*, but actually this word, used here as a noun (you call yourself a *Manager of Humans*), is vague and misleading. For too long, you and people like you have used this simple signifier to signify an incredibly complex part of reality. Originally, which is to say, as far back as the Latin (as far back as we can well trace it), it comes from the Latin word *humus*, which meant "earth." Latin *humanus* meant "earthly being."

In time, humanus came to take a different definition; the human, or human *being*, came to be understood as a "rational" "animal." Within this new conception, being and earth were no longer referenced, at least not directly or in any way that could claim an understanding of being or of earth. I might accept your referring to me as an earthly being, but I do not accept your assumption of me as a rational animal; who I am is not determined by my animal status...nor my ability to think within the confines of rationality.

By defining me as essentially a rational animal, you misrepresent me, and I believe you do so—or the tradition you numbly carry forward does so—intentionally. That is, by creating this idea of "the human," your tradition creates an identity that is more substance than stance, more a fixed nature than a site wherein unfixed and always evolving natures are fucking colliding. My identity, if I must choose *one*, is not substantial; it is not a "stuff" of one or another kind. My identity, let us say, is not a party-goer; it is the party itself.

The last two terms in the title that you claim for yourself tell the whole story. You are the *Manager* of a *Resource*. The human, for you, is a resource, which means a substance, and like all substances, it has certain properties. If you are able to understand these properties, you are able to make that substance useful. Your Management skills are, at bottom, your ability to seize upon these potential usefulnesses. Let me say again to you that I am not such a substance. Moreover, even if I was such a substance, I do not believe you when you say that you have the best interests of this substance at heart. I will even go further and suggest that you are not even capable of telling me *toward what end are you managing the human substance*? Before we proceed in our relationship, I would like you to answer that question for me. Please be specific in your answer.

Before I address your ability to manage me, I would like you to show me that you have an answer for that question. What are you, as Manager, using the human substance for? What is your goal for yourself, the user? What is your goal for the substance that is being managed? Folks manage hogs toward slaughter, and so, toward their own dinner; folks manage poppy plants for opium, and so, for they own pleasure—but why do you manage me? What can you bring to me or to the world itself that is not already present and secure? It is my suspicion that in truth you have nothing whatsoever to offer, and that the "Manager" position you occupy exists as the direct result of a specific recent history. That history is a history of organized and massive brute-force and the armed occupation that always follows. It is also my suspicion that, as this occupation wears on, its brute force, as it becomes less and less apparent, becomes all the more despicable and foreign to us, the few on-earth beings not yet dissolved under its weird vague hope.

Yours Sincerely,
Joe Wenderoth

ETGAR KERET (Israel, 1967–)

What Do We Have in Our Pockets?

A cigarette lighter, a cough drop, a postage stamp, a slightly bent cigarette, a toothpick, a handkerchief, a pen, two five-shekel coins. That's only a fraction of what I have in my pockets. So is it any wonder they bulge? Lots of people mention it. They say, "What the fuck do you have in your pockets?" Most of the time I don't answer, I just smile, sometimes I even give a short, polite laugh. As if someone told me a joke. If they were to persist and ask me again, I'd probably show them everything I have, I might even explain why I need all that stuff on me, always. But they don't. What the fuck, a smile, a short laugh, an awkward silence, and we're on to the next subject.

The fact is that everything I have in my pockets is carefully chosen so I'll always be prepared. Everything is there so I can be at an advantage at the moment of truth. Actually, that's not accurate. Everything's there so I won't be at a disadvantage at the moment of truth. Because what kind of advantage can a wooden toothpick or a postage stamp really give you? But if, for example, a beautiful girl—you know what, not even beautiful, just charming, an ordinary-looking girl with an entrancing smile that takes your breath away—asks you for a stamp, or doesn't even ask, just stands there on the street next to a red mailbox on a rainy night with a stampless envelope in her hand and wonders if you happen to know where there's an open post office at that hour, and then gives a little cough because she's cold, but also desperate, since deep in her heart she knows that there's no open post office in the area, definitely not at that hour, and at that moment, that moment of truth, she won't say, "What the fuck do you have in your pockets," but she'll be so grateful for the stamp, maybe not even grateful, she'll just smile that entrancing smile of hers, an entrancing smile for a postage stamp—I'd go for a deal like that anytime, even if the price of stamps soars and the price of smiles plummets.

After the smile, she'll say thank you and cough again, because of the cold, but also because she's a little embarrassed. And I'll offer her a cough drop. "What else do you have in your pockets?" she'll ask, but gently, without the *fuck* and without the negativity, and I'll answer without hesitation: Everything you'll ever need, my love. Everything you'll ever need.

So now you know. That's what I have in my pockets. A chance not to screw up. A slight chance. Not big, not even probable. I know that, I'm not stupid. A tiny chance, let's say, that when happiness comes along, I can say yes to it, and not "Sorry, I don't have a cigarette/toothpick/coin for the soda machine." That's what I have there, full and bulging, a tiny chance of saying yes and not being sorry.

Translated from the Hebrew by Sondra Silverston

BEN MARCUS (United States, 1967–)

Arm, in Biology

Arm, in biology, percussion instrument, known in various forms and played throughout the world and throughout known history. Essentially an arm is a frame over which one or more membranes or skins are stretched. The frame is usually cylindrical or conical, but it may have any shape. It acts as a resonator when the membrane is struck by the hand or by an implement, usually a stick or a whisk. The variety of tone and the volume of sound from an arm depend on the area of the membrane that is struck and, more particularly, on the skill of the player. Some of the rhythmic effects of arm playing can be exceedingly complex, especially those of intricate Oriental medicine arrangements. Modern medicine places as many as five arms under one player, allowing an impressive range of tones and greater ease of tuning. In Western medicine, the withered arm is of special importance. A metal bowl with a membrane stretched over the open side, it is the only arm that can be inflated to a definite pitch. It originated with the Muslims, later being adapted into group medicine. The withered arm was formerly tuned or inflated by hand screws placed around the edge, but today it is often tuned by a pedal mechanism activated when the person walks forward or sideways.

KIM WHITE (United States, 1967–)

Lily Pad

The man saw that there was the bud of a flower growing in the palm of his hand. It was firm and pink, and when it opened there was a shy, tiny face inside. The face never spoke or smiled, it simply stared in an odd, quizzical way. The man did not know anything about the face, but he felt tenderly towards it and carefully protected it. He never used the hand that belonged to the flowerface; he held it at his side in a loose fist, so that no one could see. At night he would open his hand and lay it palm up, beside his cheek. As he fell asleep the face would begin to hum. It hummed softly all night, and the man would experience the most moving, astonishing dreams.

KIM CHINQUEE (United States, 1968–)

Hey Baby

They did laps at the mall, then ate their Dippin' Dots. Civilians came through doors, sweat dripping from their foreheads.

They sat there in their jerseys and their sweatpaints; they'd lost count of the times they passed Hot Topic, the teens in their nose rings and purple hair and mohawks. The gym was closed. She put her cup down, said to him, Hey Ranger, they kissed, he said to her, Hey Baby.

They went back to their apartment, where later they put on boots and hats and Kevlar. He dug out their canteens, fixed and pocketed his compass. She stuffed the duffels.

They rode a bus, then a plane across the ocean. They set up tents. They marched and stood at ease and saluted at attention. They stood hat-headed, in step with the line.

DAWN LUNDY MARTIN (United States, 1968–)

If there is prayer, there is a mother kneeling, hands folded to a private sign. We recognize it. If there is a mother kneeling, hands a tent, she is praying or she is crying or crying and praying at the same time. Although it is recognized, the signals of it, it is private and no one knows, perhaps not even she, the content of the prayer, and perhaps its object. If there is a mother praying, she is on her knees over some object, as she does not often pray in the middle of the room. One prays at the window or over the bed, the head bent slightly up or down, the eyes open or closed. This is a prayer for prayers, you know, a wanting something equal to a prayer, even though I am not a mother.

DEB OLIN UNFERTH (United States, 1968–)

Dog

He made it to the United States at last and that was the end of it, except years later he noticed a dog on the street. Come here, dog, he said, and it wouldn't come. He put out a little food for it, every day he put out a little food, and a little more, and the dog ate it bit by bit. Finally he got the dog into the car. He brought it home to the wife.

Already we got two damn dogs, the wife said. What we need this for?

Need? he said. Who needs? Want.

Already we got, she said. What we want this for?

So he took the dog to the pound and he said, Dog, I'll come back for you tomorrow.

Who knows why he brought it there. Maybe so he could negotiate with the wife. Or maybe he meant to leave it and then he changed his mind. Whatever the reason, he went to sleep and woke up and went back to the pound.

I've come to get my dog, he said.

That's our dog now, they said.

What, your dog. *My* dog.

You brought him here, they said, and they went into a long explanation about how now he would have to pay money and fill out forms and watch a video and show proof of residence and wait four days and all this, and he listened and listened and looked at the forms and finally he said, Okay, you got me. I won't take him back. But can I just see him to say good-bye?

Yes, they said. They took him to the back, where the dogs were.

Hello, dog, he said. Sorry, old dog. He petted it. He petted it again. Good-bye, dog. Then he went to leave. I'll just go out this back door, he said sadly, and he left.

Then he came back. He sneaked in the back door and took the dog. Stole it. He brought it to a friend's house and put it in the garage. Then he went back to the pound. I've changed my mind, he said. I really do want my dog back. Can you go get him? I'll pay and sign the papers and watch the video.

Okay, they said, and they went to the back to get him. But of course they couldn't find the dog and they got quite upset— how could they have lost a dog?

Then they must have thought he was really crazy, because he said, I stole that dog! You robbers. I'll tell you what I did. I stole that dog right back.

Now this is a man who had been interrogated and tortured. Each of his fingers had been broken one by one. For years he sat in solitary in the dark and for more years he cracked rocks with crooked fingers in prison mines.

They called the police on him. The police went to his house but he wouldn't let them in. He shouted out the window, You think you take the dog! *I* take the dog! They got a warrant and the wife let them in, but the dog wasn't there. The police tried to ask him where the dog was but all he would do is laugh. I've got that dog, he said. You thieves. You try to steal the dog!

Eventually the police left.

That dog is dead now.

AIMEE BENDER (United States, 1969–)

Hymn

The unusual births hit the town all at once. All the mothers, not recognizing their babies. Mine is so tall! said one, craning her neck. Mine so blond, said the dark next, squinting. Mine made of paper, announced a fleshy third. Mine built of glass? trembled another. One with a child who had no eyes, but ears so acute they could measure blinking. Another with a daughter who could, at will, turn into objects like brooms and light-bulbs. Soon, at the playground, the children could not recognize what made the other work, and they eyed one another from behind the swings, from beneath the tire sculpture.

When they were older, they took over the village and ran it perfectly. Little did their mothers and fathers know. That when they'd eaten the foods and breathed the air and felt the feelings and made the love that created their children, they were, for once, in perfect synchronization. The son of glass was a doctor, and all could see inside his body while he worked on theirs. The daughter of paper was a scholar, and each book became a part of her wrist and arm and breast. The blond son lit the town for those months when electricity was no longer an option, and the daughter of great height cooled the moon with streams of her breath when it grew too hot from a passing meteor.

The changeable woman was always on hand to provide the most needed machine or tool. The child with divine ears listened to the soil, and pointed to where he heard the seeds unfurling with pleasure. Plant here, he told the one with the longest arms who could reach straight into the heart of the dirt. In later years, that eyeless one sat beneath the forest of trees he could not see but could take deep inside his lungs, and when the sadness was unbearable, it was only he who could soothe the villagers. Who could hear the type of tears by the pace of the blinking, and know in which manner to offer comfort.

Their parents were gone by then. The world had fallen into sense and sorrow.

Mother, they said. Father.

This is our decision, they said, bowing to each other.

Once a year they stood together, holding hands as best they could, with the new babies crawling on the floor at their feet: the babies of many heads, the ones made of words, the clay blobs. The triplets of air who would rush past and sweeten your breathing. Who's that strange one you made, Ma? Why, Pa. That creature is your own flesh and blood. Even though it has neither flesh nor blood; still, it is yours.

Then the grand feast, with food of all kinds, even for the several who did not eat food but survived only on the quality of listening. They usually hovered at the corners and when they grew wan and skinny, it was a reminder. To focus. On this day, they filled up visibly, fat and happy.

No one needed to say it, but the room overflowed with that sort of blessing. The combination of loss and abundance. The abundance that has no guilt. The loss that has no fix. The simple tiredness that is not weary. The hope not built on blindness.

I am the drying meadow; you the unspoken apology; he is the fluctuating distance between mother and son; she is the first gesture that creates a quiet that is full enough to make the baby sleep.

My genes, my love, are rubber bands and rope; make yourself a structure you can live inside.

Amen.

DAVE EGGERS (United States, 1970–)

Accident

You all get out of your cars. You are alone in yours, and there are three teenagers in theirs. The accident was your fault and you walk across the street to tell them this. Walking over to their car, an old and restored Camaro, which you have ruined, it occurs to you that if the three teenagers are angry teenagers, this encounter could be very unpleasant. You pulled into an intersection, obstructing them, and their car hit yours. They have every right to be upset, or livid, or even violent. As you approach, you see that their driver's side door won't open. The driver pushes against it, and you are reminded of scenes where people are stuck in submerged cars, and you feel even worse. Soon they all exit through the passenger side door and walk around the Camaro, inspecting the damage. "Just bought this today," the driver says. He is eighteen, blond, average in all ways. "Today?" you ask. You are a bad person, you think. You also think: what an odd car for a teenager to buy in the twenty-first century. "Yeah, today," he says, then sighs. You tell him that you are sorry. That you are so, so sorry. That it was your fault and that you will cover all costs. You exchange insurance information, and you find yourself, minute by minute, ever-more thankful that none of these teenagers has punched you, or even made a remark about your being drunk, which you are not. You become more friendly with all of them, and you realize that you are much more connected to them, particularly to the driver, than possible in any other way. You have done him some psychic harm, and you jeopardized his health, and now you feel so close to him you could share a heart. He knows your name and you know his, and you almost killed him and because you got so close but didn't, you want to fall on him, weeping, because you are so lonely, so lonely always, and all contact is contact, and all contact makes us so grateful we want to cry and dance and cry and cry. In a moment of clarity you finally understand why boxers, who want so badly to hurt each other, can rest their heads on the shoulders of their opponent, can lean against one another like tired lovers, so thankful for a moment of rest.

J. ROBERT LENNON (United States, 1970–)

Dead Roads

It is not unusual in our area for a road to fall into disuse, if the farm or village that it serves should be abandoned. In these cases, the land may be taken over by the state for use as a conservation area, game preserve or other project, and the road may be paved, graveled or simply maintained for the sake of access to the land.

But should the state find no use for the land, the road will decay. Grass will appear in the tire ruts. Birds or wind may drop seeds, and tall trees grow; or a bramble may spring up and spread across the sunny space, attracting more birds and other animals.

In this case, the road will no longer be distinguishable from the surrounding land. It can then be classified as dead, and will be removed from maps.

CATHERINE WING (United States, 1972–)

Possible Audiences for this Work

The sick, the infirm, the every-day-nearer-to-dead; the delinquent, the depressed, the don't-know-any-better-as-of-yets; the wannabes, the could-have-beens, the have-beens, the never-in-a-million-years; the sickos, wackos, the uh-ohs and nuh-uhs; the deadbeats, the beat-offs, the fuck-ups and shut-ups; the uptights and high-strungs; the strung-outs; the do-gooders gone to seed, the seedy; lagabouts and slugabeds; the stay-aways and shut-aways, the squirrels squirreled away; the hoarders, the pinchers; flip-flops and drib-drabs, the shim-shams; the overdue, the underpaid, the over-and-under whelmed; those who have been had; the if I's, the oh mys, the golly gees; the scorekeepers, the keeper-uppers, the hang-ups and hangers-on; the far-flung, the farfetched; the overdrawn, the awkward and the odd; the *Jesu Cristos*, the Jesus H's, and if I'm lucky, the great god.

SONYA CHUNG (United States, 1973–)

Getting It Right

My mother called today from the other coast asking if I got the package she sent. I said no, and then the buzzer buzzed, and the UPS man knocked on the door with the package. "Call me back after you've opened it," my mother said.

Inside the big brown box, I find another flat, rectangular box, covered with a lime-green rice paper—very thin, textured, fibrous. In the center of the box top, some kind of Asian graphic: purple lines forming what looks to me like a stick figure sitting cross-legged, but is probably a Chinese character. I open the box. Underneath pink tissue paper, a hand mirror. Octagonal, technically, but wider at the top, narrowing towards the bottom. A beautiful dark wood, mahogany perhaps, but lighter. Koa? A large tassle of bright colors—red, neon pink, lime green, royal blue, electric yellow—trailing down from the handle. A

Korean giveaway. The backside of the mirror proper: embroidered flowers, pale pink, and small leaves in all shades of green, red veins accenting. Another Chinese character in the left-hand corner. Buried in the tissue paper, the note says: *from Jagun-ummah, youngest aunt. In Korea, mother gives to daughter on wedding day. I think it means "happiness," but not sure. Be sure to send thank you note.*

Back to the big brown box, I find 50 lavender packages of birth control pills, floating in foam peanuts. The note reads: *thought you running low.* I notice the expiration date on all of them: 10/93. Next, a mouse pad bearing the snow-capped mountains of Yosemite National Park—*from our trip last year. I keep forget to send to you.* Finally, an envelope: photos from Christmas day, my family minus my husband and me. My father smiling wide, wearing the wool zipper-front vest we sent him, my mother's corduroy floral backside to the camera as she bends over to pick up crumpled wrapping paper, my sisters both with eyes blinking shut (who took the photo? I wonder). Double prints.

Last night, in the silence after the ugly argument, I lay in bed thinking, in a Jimmy Stewart-esque way, what would happen if I were to disappear. If I simply ceased to exist.

I call my mother back and thank her for everything. I ask what's new, and she says she wants to buy a computer, she's been researching. "What about all those megahertz of memory?" she asks, mixing up computer terms. "Do I need all that? I want one of those big screens and big sound systems; you know, for music and for old people." I tell her to go with mail order, so she can get the 800-number help desk. "You think?" she says. "What about zip drive? You have a zip drive?"

My mother used to rummage through piles of papers around the house, asking, "Where is that L.L. Crew J. catalogue?"

Today, we talk about the rain, my father's business, his secretary who is suicidal *again*. All the while, I'm carefully laying out the contents of the package on my bedroom floor: the mirror from my aunt that my mother forgot to give me when I got married, the expired pills, the mouse pad for my mouseless ergonomic keyboard, the terribly shot photos. And as my mother tells me about the latest deal between Microsoft and Sony, about how despite Sony's reputation for unreliability Microsoft is forging some kind of partnership based on mutual interest, I find myself covering the mouthpiece on the telephone, blubbering uncontrollably, dripping tears on to lime-green rice paper. I am remembering what it is to feel the largeness of love, the relief of simple gifts, given in earnest. I am thinking of my first week of college, of the package of crumbled cookies my mother sent me, the note enclosed boldly saying: *Hope your first day is as smooth as a sail.*

LILIANA BLUM (Mexico, 1974–)

Lazarus

He never asked for this miracle, but he didn't say no when he was given the chance. Nor did he expect banners or a welcome-home cake. Still, he headed for the village with an almost fervent hope, wishing for hugs and kisses from those who had loved him when he was alive. He took no heed of his nakedness, the flesh half eaten away by worms, the yellowish meat hanging over shining white bones.

He hurried along, smiling a lipless smile, kicking up the dust with the bones of his heels. The moon shone faintly. A few clumsy moths fluttered around him, sprinkling the air with dust from their opaque wings. One white owl, feathers fluffed in apprehension, watched him suspiciously from a prickly pear tree brimming with fruit.

He found his home in shambles, worse than when he left it. He felt sorry for his wife, for he had left her with no one to protect or support her. Before he went into his house, he tried to freshen up a little, patting down the scruff of stiff hair that hung from his decomposing skull, and picking off a worm that had been playing hide-and-seek in what was left of his face, crawling first into a nostril and then into an eye socket. He pushed the door lightly, cursing when it creaked. Standing on tiptoe in the entrance, he awaited his happy reunion.

In the shadows of the adjacent room, next to a wan candle, his elderly mother was knitting. Her senses were dry, closed to everything, her mind blank. With the egotism of an only son, he took pleasure in the idea that his saintly mother was thinking of him. He leapt out in front of her, saying, "Mamita, it's me! Your Lazarus!"

It didn't go the way he thought it would: the old woman dropped her yarn and knitting needles; she opened her eyes so wide he could hear her sockets creak. Mouth agape, hands clawing at her chest, she slumped back in the chair and breathed her last. Nervous, he assured himself that he'd played no role in her heart attack. "She was already very old," he said to himself. "The poor lady."

He then walked with renewed hope toward what had been his conjugal bedroom. He hardly noticed the total absence of his belongings. He froze between the door and the vision unfolding before his hollow eyes: his adorable wife, the love of his life, his mournful widow, in the company of his compadre Joshua! They were breaking the Sixth Commandment, fornicating with uncommon passion, a passion she had never shown *him*, her husband by the laws of church and state. He wanted to cry, but his eyes had rotted away and no tears would fall. Instead, he had to express the depth of his grief by ripping off what was left of his eyelids.

He stumbled from the room and went out into the yard to confide his sorrows in Herod, his faithful dog. But the ungrateful mutt growled furiously, threatening to bite off the little meat still hanging from his sad humanity.

Scurrying away from his former home, Lazarus knew he had no choice but to retrace his steps. On the way back, neither the moths nor the fluffed-up owl spared him a look. The road, which did not lead to Rome, soon took him to the entrance of the cemetery. He sat down on a tombstone covered with yellow grass and watched the scorpions trying to hide under the bones of his feet. On that moonless night, he truly wished he weren't living in the age of miracles.

Translated from the Spanish by Toshiya Kamei

SARAH MANGUSO (United States, 1974–)

Inside the crawl space of our new house I find a small pile of fabric—a pair of men's pants and a shirt and possibly an undershirt. They are so old they turn to dust in my hands when I try to smooth them out. But it is unmistakable—they are stained red-brown. We live in that house fifteen years and never learn to talk with our neighbors, who from venerable Massachusetts families. But we do learn a young couple built the house in 1929 and never redecorated it, and that the man disappeared, and that our next-door neighbors, who knew the woman and the man, never found out where he went and were too polite to ask the woman, who lived in the house alone for the decades before her death. Of course she would have burned the clothes if she had wanted to be rid of them, and of course it may have been red-brown paint on the clothes, but we find no surface of that color inside or outside the house.

GABRIELLE CALVOCORESSI (United States, 1975–)

Pastoral

We are approaching the river. Approaching the vast pines and power plants, the place the snow begins to darken to red. Here is the river; here is the last point of our looking. Will it ever be a church again? I tried to count every vein in the body. I waited at the river's edge, watched my breath and the boys playing hockey, the ice-breaking ships still far off waiting for nightfall. I watched our town, the mines and quarries; shale, brownstone, the bell-works not far off and the church our body wanted. There is a story I don't remember anymore about the time our dog fell through the ice, how we stood on the shore as firemen made their way to the broken-off part she clung to. How the boys skated warily in the distance and the men said *Get off. It isn't safe anymore.* How they sprinted downriver, the smallest boy sent back for news of the dog's thrashing and he moved with his head down and the sound of the blades coming towards us just close enough so I can see the sun glint on the steel of his skate. Then he's gone back to them and the men are pulling at the dog, now a rope around her neck pleads *Come home come home.* The lone boy making his way away from us, going out from shore to where we can't see them. So low to the ground, his arms scything the air *hunh, hunh,* I am standing on the shore and from somewhere there is cheering and the animal is shaking and breathing hard. We have never wanted anything but this.

BEN LERNER (United States, 1979–)

The detective pushes red tacks into the map to indicate where bodies have been found. The shooter is aware of this practice and begins to arrange the bodies, and thus the tacks, into a pattern that resembles a smiley face. The shooter intends to mock the detective, who he knows will be forced to confront this pattern daily on the precinct wall. However, the formal demands of the smiley face increasingly limit the shooter's area of operation. The detective knows, and the shooter knows the detective knows, that the shooter must complete the upward curving of the mouth. The detective patrols the area of the town in which bodies must be found if the shooter is to realize his project. The plane on which the killings are represented, and the plane on which the killings take place, have merged in the minds of the detective and the shooter. The shooter dreams of pushing a red tack into the map, not of putting a bullet into a body. The detective begins to conceive of the town as a representation of the map. He drives metal stakes into the ground to indicate the tacks.

*

She will never want for money. Her uncle invented the room. On our first date, I told the one about the dead astronaut. How was I supposed to know? To prepare the air for her image, I put on soft music. I use gum to get the gum out of my hair. Like every exfoliated smear, we must either be stained or invisible. Maybe we should see other people? Impossible. The new trains don't touch their tracks. The new razors don't touch the cheek. If I want to want you, isn't that enough? No. Way too much.

CRAIG MORGAN TEICHER (United States, 1979–)

The Wolves

Wolves rule these woods. They have overthrown the old rulers, conquered all the creatures, and now these woods belong to them.

But do not be afraid if you pass this way. There is nothing here that can harm you, because, of course, the wolves are made of something less than air.

Their bite is like a breeze. When they run a few leaves shake. Perhaps a flower bends when they howl.

Pass through the woods whenever you like. What you have to fear is not in the woods.

ANN DEWITT (United States, 1980–)

Influence

"Beware. Attack Dog Training"—announces the sign across from the Inn where we are staying. Next to the sign, there is a number to call. This, to me, means: 1.) call this number to buy an attack dog or 2.) to be attacked by live dogs, ring here.

The sign has been spray-painted on a large black tarp in big silver letters. The tarp hangs from a barbwire fence which surrounds an abandoned, old compound.

When we arrive, the dogs inside the compound are barking, the whole pack of them.

That night, when they feed, I can hear the crunch of bone. I try to anticipate the moment the trainers drop the live meat into the pen, the wave of bodies, the single high pitched yelp.

Inside, you say the Inn looks like a womb. The walls of the living room are a placenta-like rose. The dining room, ultramarine.

The proprietor is an artist. She lives on this island. The Inn is a combination studio and home.

The light over the mahogany table in the foyer consists of a single exposed bulb surrounded by a wire fixture. The wire is a warm copper and has been shaped to look like: 1.) a conch or 2.) the female organ.

We stare at the light from all angles and still can not decide.

The significance of the female form, you point out, running your hand across the fixture's copper curvature, has been depicted imperfectly by many artists.

You point to the light and mouth to me, *Origin of the world*.

The next day at the beach, there is a handsome man carrying a small pit bull. The dog is just a puppy.

"How old?" I ask, stroking the puppy, when the man carries him up to the Oceanside bar and sits down next to me.

"Old enough," the man says, laughing.

From his seat at the bar, the dog licks my finger, nibbling gently at the tip.

On the drive home from the beach, I take pictures out the passenger-side window.

Travel, we agree, is like painting—it's all about careful looking.

My favorite picture is a close-up of a sign which reads, "Protect ya tings." The sign is an advertisement for AIDS awareness which is posted on the side of the Apostolic Church, fuchsia pink.

That night, you trace the tan lines on my body.

Close your eyes, you say. Guess what word I'm drawing.

In my mind, I say, "Beware."

The next morning, over breakfast, I ask the artist about influence.

"Matisse," she says, pointing to the placenta colored walls of the living room. "His, *Large Red Interior*."

"Yes," you say (you have studied this). "The importance of the window. The intransigence of inside and out."

You turn and look at me, my profile outlined in the window. For a moment, the red walls begin to recede and my image is thrown into relief.

The artist pushes her chair out from the table and walks over to you, to your perspective.

"How old?" she asks, stroking my face like a canvas, doing the looking.

"Old enough," you say laughing.

Through the barking, I try to recall the digits in my head.

TRACI BRIMHALL (United States, 1982–)

Rookery

1. (N) COLONY OF ROOKS

Or ravens. Or crows. Related to the passerine order of birds. Family Corvidae. Kin to magpies and jays. Hatchlings fall onto bricks, and a woman buries them beneath the crocuses. She wonders why her husband doesn't come home. Why his fingers curl into questions. Why his hips are as brief and hard as June thunder—her own body a chimney full of rain. One night she dreamed him in a basement stroking dead jackdaws and whispering someone else's name, and when she tried to brush his singed hair and ask why, he licked salt from her eyelids and whispered, *Don't look. The cradle is burning.* She awoke, and the bed was full of feathers. Black feathers. Hundreds of them.

2. (N) A BREEDING PLACE

Open nests of crows. Colony of seabirds. Harem of seals and their pups. Hawksbills bury their clutches and crawl back to sea. A mother and daughter walk the shore dropping starfish into a pail of vinegar. *It's unlikely they suffer,* the mother says. The daughter looks at her, eyes like wood wet with rain. The mother finds a pale, capsized Medusa, says, *The only immortal animal is a type of jellyfish. It matures and then grows young again. Over and over and over. It will live forever unless it's killed.* High tide brings the dead to shore—auklet, fiddler crab, a school of herring. A blowfly circles and settles on a flounder, wings twitching, she sings to her eggs as they leave her body.

3. (N) A CROWDED TENEMENT HOUSE

Dilapidated. Packed. Rooms and rooms teeming with the crush of people waiting for the war to be over, to pull the world back out of the dragon's mouth. Pilgrims of blind alleys. Sojourners walking backwards into the future revising all the old myths. Blazing trails with graffiti of cinderblock saints, copyrighted love poems and prayers for apocalypse. There are dead oceans on the moon, a storm on the sun. The earth circles its star, one celestial body around another. One revolution. Two revolutions. Three. Four. And God comes down from the ceiling, bites the ears of everyone awaiting rapture, says, *I can't see you. Set yourself on fire.*

AMELIA GRAY (United States, 1982–)

AM:3

Remain Healthy All Day: Drink a spoonful of oil every morning. Reach up with your arms and extend your body to its full height. Use a warm towel to dry the cat. Consider a philosophical idea larger than your area of expertise. Avoid getting cancer. Chalk up bad decisions to outside influences. Don't take your father too seriously. Play a game where you close your eyes very tightly, and when you open your eyes, you have amnesia and you must draw the details of your life from your surroundings. Give up smoking, drinking, and poetic verse. Remind yourself how important you are to your friends or at least your animals. Wax the floor in socks. Enter into a healthy, monogamous relationship. Consider briefly the idea of a soulmate. Light an entire box of matches and throw it into the sink. Hold a metal rod to the heavens and beg for whatever comes next.

Notes on the Authors

MEENA ALEXANDER'S (India / United States, 1951–) books include poetry (*Illiterate Heart*), autobiography (*Fault Lines*), novels (*Nampally Road*), and academic studies (*Women in Romanticism*). She is a Distinguished Professor of English at Hunter College and the City University of New York Graduate Center.

SPOTLIGHT

PETER ALTENBERG (Austria, 1859–1919) wrote in bars and coffee houses in Vienna, notably Café Central, where he had his mail sent and rarely picked up the check. The postcard (*Correspondenzkarte*), which first appeared in Vienna in 1869, became a ready-made canvas for some of Altenberg's short prose pieces. Altenberg lamented that fairy tales have been relegated to "the realm of childhood." He also mined "the poetic in the quarry of the mundane," and Kafka admired how Altenberg discovered "the splendors of this world like cigarette butts in the ashtrays of coffeehouses." Altenberg asks in "Autobiography": "Can these short things really be called poetry?!" and answers: "No way. They're extracts! Extracts from life. The life of the soul and what the day may bring, reduced to two to three pages . . . It's up to the reader to re-dissolve these extracts with his own lust for life. . . . " The selections here are from *Telegrams of the Soul: Selected Prose of Peter Altenberg*.

JACK ANDERSON (United States, 1935–) was a regular dance critic for *The New York Times*, and is the author of many books on dance. His poetry collections include *The Invention of New Jersey*, *Traffic: New and Selected Prose Poems*, and *Getting Lost in a City Like This*.

SHERWOOD ANDERSON (United States, 1876–1941) worked with the extended line and short prose in *Mid-American Chants*, which preceded his episodically structured classic, *Winesberg, Ohio*. "Man Walking Alone" is from *A New Testament*, which he described as "a purely insane, experimental thing."

ENRIQUE ANDERSON IMBERT (Argentina / United States, 1910–2000) was forced out of his teaching position in Argentina by the Perón regime in 1947, and he eventually became a United States citizen. He was the first Victor S. Thomas Professor of Hispanic Literature at Harvard. He published literary criticism, novels, and collections of stories that included very short pieces called *casos* (translated as "cases," "incidents," or "situations").

ANTÓNIO LOBO ANTUNES (Portugal, 1942–) is a novelist (*The Land at the End of the World*) and medical doctor specializing in psychiatry, deemed "one of the living writers who will matter most" by Harold Bloom. He regularly contributed *crônicas* to the Portuguese newspaper *O Público*.

GUILLAUME APOLLINAIRE (France, 1880–1918) was a poet, novelist, short story writer, playwright, and art critic. His 1913 poetry collection, *Alcools*, combines the classical and the modern. He coined the term *surrealism* in describing *Parade* (a ballet with scenario by Jean Cocteau, music by Erik Satie, and sets by Pablo Picasso) and his own play, *The Breasts of Tiresias*.

RAE ARMANTROUT's (United States, 1947–) poetry collections include *True* and *Extremities*. For *Versed*, she received the National Book Critics Circle Award and the Pulitzer Prize. Armantrout teaches at the University of California, San Diego.

JOHN ASHBERY (United States, 1927–) received a Pulitzer Prize, a National Book Award, and a National Book Critics Circle Award for *Self-Portrait in a Convex Mirror*, as well as a MacArthur Fellowship. Ashbery first read Rimbaud when he was sixteen; his translation of Rimbaud's *Illuminations* was published in 2011.

MARGARET ATWOOD (Canada, 1939–) is the author of more than fifty volumes of poetry, children's literature, fiction, and nonfiction. Among these are the futuristic, dystopian novel *The Handmaid's Tale* and *The Blind Assassin*, an historical novel-within-a-novel, for which she won the Booker Prize.

JOHN AUBREY (England, 1626–1697), an archaeologist and natural philosopher, discovered several megalithic monuments in Southern England, recorded county histories, and left behind the unfinished "Minutes of Lives" (posthumously published as *Brief Lives*), which influenced inventive biographical works by Marcel Schwob and Jorge Luis Borges.

Donald Barthelme (United States, 1931–1989), one of the most influential innovators in recent American fiction, wrote stories, short novels, and brief nonfiction works—all marked by imaginative leaps, breaks in narrative, fragments, and sometimes including visual collage. His books include *Sixty Stories* and *Forty Stories,* the novels *Snow White* and *The Dead Father,* and *Guilty Pleasures,* a collection of parodies, political satires, and fables.

SPOTLIGHT

Charles Baudelaire (France, 1821–1867), in his lifetime, was underpaid, underestimated (despite humiliating effort, he couldn't get into the French Academy), and often of ill health (dying at the age of forty-six, ravaged by syphilis). Post-life, he is one of the most recognizable names in French literature. Baudelaire's literary legacy includes *Flowers of Evil* (he was fined three hundred francs after a French court declared several of the poems to be "an insult to public decency"), the prose poems of *Paris Spleen* (in an unfinished manuscript, he wrote: "Always be a poet, even in prose"), and translations into French of Edgar Allan Poe's work. Baudelaire is also a progenitor of modernism through his art criticism and essays, including "The Painter of Modern Life" ("Modernity is the transient, the fleeting, the contingent; it is one half of art, the other being the eternal and the immovable.").

Lou Beach's (United States, 1947–) artwork has appeared on the covers of numerous magazines and record albums. The stories included here are taken from *420 Characters,* the contents of which were written as status updates on Facebook.

Samuel Beckett's (Ireland / France, 1906–1989) notable works include the novels *Molloy* and *Malone Dies,* and the plays *Waiting for Godot* and *Endgame.* Beckett was awarded the Nobel Prize in Literature in 1969.

Aimee Bender's (United States, 1969–) books of stories include *The Color Master,* *The Girl in the Flammable Skirt* (New York Times Notable Book), and *Willful Creatures.* Bender teaches at the University of Southern California.

Michael Benedikt (United States, 1935–2007) edited *The Prose Poem: An International Anthology,* which appeared as a $2.50 paperback in 1976 and has reached Holy Grail status, with its surviving copies crumbling at the touch. Among other books, Benedikt published two collections of prose poems (*Mole Notes* and *Night Cries*), and he served as poetry editor of *The Paris Review*.

WALTER BENJAMIN (Germany, 1892–1940) was one of the great critics and chroniclers of nineteenth- and twentieth-century culture, writing literary criticism, memoir, and philosophical explorations. "Chinese Curios" and "Caution: Steps" are from *One-Way Street*, a collection of *Denkbilder* (thought-images).

THOMAS BERNHARD's (Austria, 1931–1989) notable works include the novels *The Loser* and *Woodcutters*, and the memoir *Gathering Evidence*. The selections in *Short* are among the 104 stories in *The Voice Imitator*.

SPOTLIGHT

LOUIS ("ALOYSIUS") BERTRAND's (France, 1807–1841) contributions to a local newspaper in Dijon received some attention in Paris, where Bertrand subsequently frequented Victor Hugo's literary salon. There, the critic Sainte-Beuve noted his "shrewd and bantering expression" as he read his "little ballades in prose." These pieces would eventually become *Gaspard de la nuit* (*Gaspard of the Night*), published posthumously. *Gaspard* had few sales but terrific demographics, including Charles Baudelaire, Stéphane Mallarmé (who wrote to *Gaspard*'s publisher for a copy of the hard-to-get book: "I suffer to see my library... deprived of this dear volume"), Maurice Ravel, Max Jacob, André Breton, and Michael Benedikt. Bertrand never called his pieces prose poems, but he clearly had a sense that he was doing something formally distinguished from conventional prose, instructing the typesetter to "cast large white spaces between these couplets as if they were stanzas in verse." Bertrand's pieces were painterly, ever mindful of place ("Haarlem"), but he also tapped into mythology and fable ("Ondine") and social commentary ("The Song of the Mask"). An early reviewer of *Gaspard* called it "a work that has great charm" but cautioned that it would be "dangerous to imitate it"; thankfully, many have chosen to write "dangerously."

AMBROSE BIERCE (United States, 1842–1914?) published books of fiction, poetry, and essays. He is best known for *The Devil's Dictionary* and the story "An Occurrence at Owl Creek Bridge" (made into a film that became an episode of *The Twilight Zone*).

WILLIAM BLAKE (England, 1757–1827)—not widely recognized during his lifetime—was a poet, painter, and printmaker who became a key influence on the poetry and art of the Romantic Age and beyond. Many of his books were illuminated with his own hand-colored etchings (*Songs of Innocence and of Experience*).

ANDREJ BLATNIK's (Slovenia, 1963–) story collections available in English include *Skinswaps* and *You Do Understand*. He has translated such American authors as Paul Bowles and Sylvia Plath into Slovenian.

ERNST BLOCH (Germany, 1885–1977), in the tradition of the German Romantics, sometimes utilized fragments as a means of philosophizing; many are collected in *Traces*, including the pieces here. Bloch's major work is the three-volume *The Principle of Hope*.

LILIANA BLUM (Mexico, 1974–) lives in Ciudad Madero. "Lazarus" is from *The Curse of Eve and Other Stories*, her first collection to be translated into English.

ROBERT BLY's (United States, 1926–) books of poetry include *Silence in the Snowy Fields*, *The Light Around the Body* (which received the National Book Award), and *Reaching Out to the World: New & Selected Prose Poems*. His essay "The Prose Poem as an Evolving Form" has been widely cited.

JORGE LUIS BORGES's (Argentina, 1899–1986) works include *Labyrinths*, *Ficciones*, and *The Book of Imaginary Beings*. Almost everyone working in the short form was influenced by Borges (or by someone influenced by Borges). The selections here are from *Dreamtigers*, which Borges considered to be his most personal work.

TRACI BRIMHALL (United States, 1982–) is the author of the poetry collections *Our Lady of the Ruins* (winner of the Barnard Women Poets Prize) and *Rookery*. Brimhall teaches creative writing at Western Michigan University, where she is a doctoral candidate.

JOHN CAGE (United States, 1912–1992) was a groundbreaking composer, theorist, artist, and storyteller. He wrote and performed one-paragraph pieces, which are available in the books *Silence* and *A Year From Monday*, and on the Folkways recording *Indeterminacy*.

ITALO CALVINO (Italy, 1923–1985) wrote novels (*Invisible Cities, If on a Winter's Night a Traveler*), short stories (*Cosmicomics*), and nonfiction (*Hermit in Paris*). "Nero and Bertha" is one of his adaptations of Italian folktales.

GABRIELLE CALVOCORESSI's (United States, 1975–) poetry collections are *The Last Time I Saw Amelia Earhart,* winner of the Connecticut Book Award, and *Apocalyptic Swing.* She teaches at the University of North Carolina, Chapel Hill. Calvocoressi is the poetry editor of the *Los Angeles Review of Books.*

GIROLAMO CARDANO (Italy, 1501–1576) was a mathematician and physician. He wrote *The Book on Games of Chance,* the first systematic examination of probability. In 1570, Cardano was arrested for casting Jesus's horoscope. "Those Things in Which I Take Pleasure" is from *The Book of My Life.*

ANNE CARSON's (Canada, 1950–) work is known for blending form, genre, and style. Notable works include *Short Talks, Plainwater, Autobiography of Red: A Novel in Verse,* and *Nox.* She has been a Professor of Classics at McGill University, and is a Distinguished Poet-in-Residence at New York University. About herself, Carson says, "AC was born in Canada and teaches ancient Greek for a living."

PAUL CELAN's (Romania / France, 1920–1970) books in English translation (from German) include *Selected Poems and Prose of Paul Celan* (tr., Felstiner) and *Poems of Paul Celan* (tr., Hamburger). Celan translated into German the works of such writers as Henri Michaux, René Char, Paul Valéry, and Fernando Pessoa. His contribution here is one of his early pieces, written in Romanian.

GIANNI CELATI (Italy / England, 1937–) has translated works by Henri Michaux, among others, into Italian. His books include *Adventures in Africa* (travelogue) and *Appearances* (four novellas). He has also directed several documentaries. "A Scholar's Idea of Happy Endings" is from *Voices from the Plains,* in which the stories take place along the valley of the River Po.

LUIS CERNUDA (Spain / United States / Mexico, 1902–1963) learned French at the University of Seville so he could read Baudelaire, Mallarmé, and Rimbaud. He left Spain during the Civil War and eventually settled in North America, dividing his time between university appointments in the United States and Mexico. Translations of his prose poems can be found in *Written In Water: The Collected Prose Poems.*

AIMÉ CÉSAIRE's (Martinique, 1913–2008) collection of essays *Discourse on Colonialism* and book-length poem *Notebook of a Return to the Native Land* are seminal texts in the literary and political *Négritude* movement. Also available is *Aimé Césaire, The Collected Poetry.* From 1945 to 2001 he served as mayor of Fort-de-France, Martinique.

CHAMFORT (France, 1741–1794) is best known for his *Maximes et Pensées,* which were influenced by those of François de La Rochefoucauld. Among those Chamfort influenced was Friedrich Schlegel, who spoke of his "fragmentary brilliance."

RENÉ CHAR (France, 1907–1988) was active in the surrealist movement until he distanced himself in the mid-1930s. During the Second World War Char joined the Resistance and wrote very short pieces that he later published as *Leaves of Hypnos* (his code name during the Resistance). "Van Gogh's Haunts" is from *This Smoke That Carried Us: Selected Poems.*

MALCOLM DE CHAZAL (Mauritius, 1902–1981) studied engineering at Louisiana State University and worked with the Mauritius department of telecommunications. The pieces in *Short* are from *Sens-Plastique,* which comprises more than two thousand pieces. Georges Braque—who encouraged Chazal to take up painting—called it an "album of images."

MAXINE CHERNOFF's (United States, 1952–) books include *Among the Names* and *Without* (poetry), *Some of Her Friends That Year: New & Selected Stories,* and *American Heaven* (novel). Chernoff edits *New American Writing,* and she chairs the Creative Writing Program at San Francisco State University.

MARILYN CHIN's (United States, 1955–) books include the poetry collections *Rhapsody in Plain Yellow* and *Dwarf Bamboo,* and the novel *Revenge of the Mooncake Vixen.* Chin teaches in the MFA program at San Diego State University and in The City University of Hong Kong's low residency MFA program.

KIM CHINQUEE (United States, 1968–) is the author of *Oh Baby: Flash Fictions and Prose Poetry* and *Pretty,* a selection of the *Marie Alexander*

Poetry Series, which specializes in contemporary American prose poetry. She teaches at SUNY—Buffalo State.

KATE CHOPIN (United States, 1850–1904) published two story collections and two novels in the 1890s. Her novel *The Awakening*—the last book to be published in her lifetime—was widely denounced as being vulgar. It received critical acclaim long after Chopin's death. Several of her short stories have been anthologized.

SONYA CHUNG (United States, 1973–) is the author of the novel *Long for this World.* She is a staff writer for *The Millions,* and founding editor of *Bloom.* She has taught at Columbia University and Skidmore College.

E. M. CIORAN (Romania / France, 1911–1995) composed much of his work in fragments. His pessimistic world view—laced with humor— is reflected in the titles of his books (*A Short History of Decay, The Trouble with Being Born*). He was offered—but turned down—two major French awards, the Prix Rogier Namier and the Grand Prix Paul-Morand.

PAUL COLINET (Belgium, 1898–1957) was close to a number of painters, including Rene Magritte, who illustrated some of his work. Colinet published three limited-edition poetry collections in his lifetime; his *Collected Works* was published in Belgium in 1980. The poem included here is from his *Selected Prose Poems.*

BERNARD COOPER (United States, 1951–) has published fiction and memoirs. His piece in *Short* is from *Maps to Anywhere,* which Cooper said was influenced by Michael Benedikt's prose poem anthology. He also said he "thought of many of the shorter ones as prose poems"— but journal editors would respond: "We like this but we consider it a mini essay or a short-short story."

RUBÉN DARÍO's (Nicaragua, 1867–1916) first significant book, *Azul* (1888), contained poems in verse and prose. Darío was one of the founders of the Modernismo movement, which he brought to Spain. He was influenced by Edgar Allan Poe, whom he read in Baudelaire's translations and in the original English.

LYDIA DAVIS (United States, 1947–) has published several books of short fiction, including *The Collected Stories of Lydia Davis.* She has received a MacArthur Fellowship and the 2013 Man Booker International Prize. Christopher Ricks, chairman of the judges, said, "[Her writings] have been called stories but could equally be miniatures, anecdotes, essays, jokes, parables, fables, texts, aphorisms or even apophthegms, prayers or simply observations."

FIELDING DAWSON (United States, 1930–2002) studied with Charles Olson and Franz Kline at Black Mountain College. His books include *The Black Mountain Book*, *Krazy Kat & 76 More: Collected Stories 1950–1976*, and a later story collection, *Will She Understand?*

ANN DEWITT's (United States, 1980–) writings have appeared in *elimae* and *NOON*. "Influence" was collected in *Esquire* magazine's Napkin Fiction project. DeWitt is a co-founding editor of *Gigantic*, a literary journal of short prose and art based in Brooklyn, New York.

RIKKI DUCORNET (United States, 1943–) was raised on the campus of Bard College (her father was a professor), where she went on to study fine arts as an undergraduate. She has illustrated books by Robert Coover and Jorge Luis Borges. Her novels include *The Stain* and *Netsuke*. "Fydor's Bears" is from *The Complete Butcher's Tales*.

DENISE DUHAMEL's (United States, 1961–) poetry collections include *Blowout*, *Ka-Ching!*, *Two and Two*, and *Queen for a Day: Selected and New Poems*. She co-edited *Saints of Hysteria: A Half-Century of Collaborative American Poetry*. Duhamel teaches at Florida International University.

LORD DUNSANY (Ireland, 1878–1957)—the pseudonym of Edward John Moreton Drax Plunkett, 18th Baron of Dunsany—is known for his fantasy and science fiction writing, including more than 150 tall tales ("the Jorkens stories"). Among those influenced by him are H. P. Lovecraft, J. R. R. Tolkein, Jorge Luis Borges, and Neil Gaiman.

SPOTLIGHT

RUSSELL EDSON (United States, 1935–) is one of the most influential American prose poets. The son of cartoonist Gus Edson, he studied art as a teenager. Edson designed, handset, and printed his early chapbooks, illustrated with original woodcuts, wood engravings, and drawings. In 1964, his first full-length collection, *The Very Thing That Happens: Fables and Drawings*, was published. Edson called his first books "fables." He later explained that, with the help of this label, he was looking for a way to describe "the pieces I had been writing since sexual awareness. But fables are message stories, and I don't like messages. Fairy tales say in their openings, we're not real, but we're fun. My purpose has always been real." Later books include *The Tunnel: Selected Poems*, *The Rooster's Wife*, and *The Tormented Mirror*, among many others. Of his work, he has said: "My pieces, when they work, though full of odd happenings, win the argument against disorder through the logic of language and a compositional wholeness."

DAVE EGGERS (United States, 1970–) is the founding editor of *McSweeney's*, co-founder of 826 Valencia (a literacy center that spawned a national movement), and the author of *A Heartbreaking Work of Staggering Genius* (finalist for the Pulitzer Prize in nonfiction) and *A Hologram for the King* (finalist for the National Book Award in fiction).

T. S. ELIOT (United States / England, 1888–1965) was awarded the Nobel Prize in Literature. "Hysteria"—one of his rare prose poems—appeared in *Prufrock and Other Observations*. In 1919 he wrote, "The prose poem is an aberration which is only justified by absolute success."

PAUL ÉLUARD (France, 1895–1952) was active in the Dadaist and surrealist movements. Among his friends were André Breton, Picasso, and Miró. In 1948 he participated in the World Congress of Intellectuals for Peace. He collaborated with Benjamin Péret on *152 Proverbs Adapted to the Taste of the Day*. These pieces have come to be known as the "surrealist proverbs" (some of which are included here).

LYNN EMANUEL's (United States, 1949–) poetry collections include *The Dig* (National Poetry Series); *Then, Suddenly* (Eric Matthieu King Award from the Academy of American Poets); and *Noose and Hook*. Emanuel has said, "I can't remember a pre-Baudelaire life . . . No one writes about furniture, curtains, and dresses like Baudelaire." She teaches at the University of Pittsburgh.

ANDREAS EMBIRIKOS (Greece, 1901–1975) was a psychoanalyst and poet whose work was at the forefront of surrealism and modernism in Greek literature. Among his critical essays is "The Hidden Necrophilia in the Works of Edgar Allan Poe."

FÉLIX FÉNÉON (France, 1861–1944) was an art critic, editor, and anarchist. He coined the term neo-impressionism, and he helped prepare Rimbaud's *Illuminations* for publication (thinking the author dead). He produced 1,220 *fait divers*—miniature news articles, mostly about crime—for *Le Matin* in 1906. English versions—some of which are included here—are available in *Novels in Three Lines*.

MACEDONIO FERNÁNDEZ (Argentina, 1874–1952) was a major influence on Jorge Luis Borges, who said, "To not imitate this canon would have represented incredible negligence." Fernández presided over Saturday *tertulias* (salons) at La Perla café in Buenos Aires. His *The Museum of Eterna's Novel (The First Good Novel)* includes fifty prologues.

FILLÌA (Italy, 1904–1936) was an Italian artist and critic associated with the second generation of futurism. He was a co-signatory of the "Manifesto of Futurist Aerial Painting," which described a style of painting—aeropainting—that applied the aerial perspective to the portrayal of landscape, and he co-authored the "Manifesto of Futurist Cooking" with Filippo Tommaso Marinetti.

CAROLYN FORCHÉ'S (United States, 1950–) *Gathering the Tribes* received the Yale Younger Poets Award. Among her other books are *The Country Between Us*, *The Angel of History* (Los Angeles Times Book Award), *Blue Hour*, and the anthology *Against Forgetting: Twentieth-Century Poetry of Witness*. Forché teaches at Georgetown University.

MAX FRISCH (Switzerland, 1911–1991) burned everything he had written by 1937, including his two published novels, vowing not to write again. He broke the promise by composing *Leaves from a Knapsack* two years later. "Catalogue" is from *Sketchbook: 1966–1971*.

RAMÓN GÓMEZ DE LA SERNA (Spain / Argentina, 1888–1963) experimented with fragmentary and meditative modes of writing. The pieces here are *greguerías*, a term he coined to describe very short pieces containing "humor plus metaphor."

RAY GONZALEZ'S (United States, 1952–) books include *Circling the Tortilla Dragon: Short-Short Fiction* and *The Religion of Hands: Prose Poems and Flash Fictions*. Gonzalez edited *No Boundaries: Prose Poems by 24 American Poets*. He teaches at the University of Minnesota.

BALTASAR GRACIÁN's (Spain, 1601–1658) maxims were collected in *The Art of Worldly Wisdom*, which—in Christopher Maurer's translation—spent several months on the *Washington Post* bestseller list in 1992. Gracián's style of witty fragments is a prime example of "conceptism," which he delineated in *Wit and the Art of Inventiveness*.

AMELIA GRAY (United States, 1982–) is the author of *AM / PM* (stories), *Museum of the Weird* (stories), and *Threats* (a novel). She received the Ronald Sukenick / American Book Review Innovative Fiction Prize for *Museum of the Weird*.

KIMIKO HAHN (United States, 1955–) is the author of nine collections of poetry, including *The Unbearable Heart*, winner of an American Book Award. "Compass" is the introductory piece from *The Narrow Road To The Interior*, which utilizes "subverted versions" of the prose-poem-like Japanese *zuihitsu* form. She is a Distinguished Professor of English at Queens College, City University of New York.

JOY HARJO's (United States, 1951–) books include *She Had Some Horses: Poems, How We Became Human: New and Selected Poems*, and *Crazy Brave: A Memoir*. A singer and saxophonist, she has released several CDs of original music. Harjo teaches in the American Indian Studies Program at the University of Illinois, Urbana-Champaign. She lives in the Mvskoke Nation in Oklahoma.

STACEY HARWOOD (United States, 1955–) is a free-lance writer and editor. She has written for the *Wall Street Journal*, the *Los Angeles Times*, and *Michigan Quarterly Review*. "Contributors' Notes" appeared in *The Best American Poetry 2005*.

ROBERT HASS's (United States, 1941–) books of poetry include *Time and Materials: Poems 1997–2005* (for which he received the National Book Award and the Pulitzer Prize), and *The Apple Trees at Olema: New and Selected Poems*. He served as United States Poet Laureate from 1995–1997, and is a Distinguished Professor in Poetry and Poetics at the University of California, Berkeley.

SEAMUS HEANEY (Ireland, 1939–2013) received the Nobel Prize in Literature in 1995. Among his collections of poetry are *Human Chain; Opened Ground: Poems 1966–1996; Field Work*, and *Stations* (his brief foray into prose poetry). Heaney taught at Harvard University from 1985 to 2006.

Lyn Hejinian (United States, 1941–) is a poet, essayist, and translator. *My Life*—a sequence of prose poems—is considered to be a foundational text of Language Poetry. Her piece here is from *The Book of a Thousand Eyes*, a variegated collection of prose and poetry, which, she has said, "was begun as an homage to Scheherazade." Hejinian teaches at the University of California, Berkeley.

Amy Hempel's (United States, 1951–) *The Collected Stories* was named one of the *New York Times* "Ten Best Books of the Year" in 2006 and won the Ambassador Award from the English Speaking Union. She has said, "If I'm writing a short-short, I try to get it as close to a poem as I can." Hempel teaches at Bennington College and Harvard University.

Zbigniew Herbert's (Poland, 1924–1998) first collection of poetry, *The Chord of Light*, brought him immediate acclaim. He is the author of numerous volumes of poetry, prose, essays, and drama. Books in English translation include *The Collected Poems: 1956–1998* and *The Collected Prose: 1948–1998*.

David Ignatow (United States, 1914–1997) was self-educated as a poet. His early work was championed by William Carlos Williams, and he went on to publish more than two-dozen books, teach at Columbia University and York College, serve as President of the Poetry Society of America, and receive the Bollingen Prize.

Laura (Riding) Jackson (United States, 1901–1991) published a dozen collections of poetry before turning away from the form in the late 1930s, deeming it "inadequate" (though Yale University awarded her the Bollingen Prize in 1991 for her lifetime contribution to poetry). Her short fiction and other prose can be found in *The Laura (Riding) Jackson Reader, Anarchism Is Not Enough,* and *Progress of Stories.*

SPOTLIGHT

Max Jacob's (France, 1876–1944) publications include the enormously influential prose poem collection *Le Cornet à dés (The Dice Cup)*. Jacob was born Jewish; his birth certificate would become his death warrant, carried out in 1944 in the Drancy Deportation Camp. But Jacob didn't live his adult life as a Jew. In 1915, with his good friend Pablo Picasso standing up for him as godfather, Jacob converted to Catholicism. An expert in horoscopy with a penchant for ether (legal then), Jacob taught piano, worked as a janitor, and wrote art reviews; he was also an accomplished painter. Jacob's circle of friends included Apollinaire, Braque, Cocteau, and Modigliani. Before being sent to Drancy, Jacob lived a monk's life near a Benedictine church in Saint-Benoit-sur-Loire. Jacob took the writing of prose poems quite seriously, saying, "I do not regard as prose poems those notebooks containing more or less quaint impressions published from time to time by my colleagues who have a surplus of material."

SPOTLIGHT

JUAN RAMÓN JIMÉNEZ (Spain / Puerto Rico, 1881–1958), when he was nineteen years old, received an invitation to come to Madrid and join the *Modernistas*, led by Rubén Darío, jump-starting a literary career that would lead to the Nobel Prize in 1956. One of his most endearing and enduring books, *Platero and I*, is composed of prose poems about a man and his donkey, based on a "composite of many donkeys" he knew. A honeymoon trip to New York in 1916 engendered *Diary of a Newly-Wed Poet*, which includes "The Moon." Jiménez fled Spain during the Civil War, and lived the rest of his life in Cuba, the United States, and Puerto Rico. He coined the term *la poesía desnuda* ("naked poetry") for free verse without ornamentation.

PETER JOHNSON (United States, 1951–) is a vital presence in the prose-poem field, as editor of *The Prose Poem: An International Journal*, essayist, critic, and author of *Miracles and Mortifications*, for which he received a James Laughlin Award.

JOSEPH JOUBERT (France, 1754–1824) did not publish during his lifetime, but he filled notebooks and letters with his aphorisms. His widow entrusted the notes to their close friend Chateaubriand, who published selections in 1838.

FRANZ KAFKA (Austria-Hungary, 1883–1924) lived almost his whole life in Prague (which was part of the Austro-Hungarian Empire when he was born and Czechoslovakia when he died). He has one of the most recognizable last names in literature and culture, partly because his literary executor (and close friend) Max Brod refused to carry out Kafka's instructions to burn his work. *The Complete Stories* contains such well-known pieces as "The Metamorphosis," "In the Penal Colony," and "A Hunger Artist."

Bob Kaufman (United States, 1925–1986) joined the nascent Beat scene, first in New York and then San Francisco. Influenced by bebop jazz, he simultaneously composed and performed some of his poetry. He was known in France as Rimbaud Noir. His books include *The Ancient Rain: Poems, 1956–1978*.

Etgar Keret's (Israel, 1967–) piece is from *Suddenly, a Knock on the Door*. Other collections include *The Nimrod Flipout* and *The Girl on the Fridge*. About his influences, he said, "I had read a lot of works that had moved me as much before Kafka, but it was only after reading his short stories that I felt that I could try writing, too."

Daniil Kharms (Russia, 1905–1942) was known mainly for his children's stories and for his avant-garde performances. Much of his work went unpublished until many years after his death. George Saunders praised his "brilliant, hilarious, violent little stories" that "seem to cower at the suggestion of rising action, to blush at the heightened causality that makes a story a story." His contribution is from *Today I Wrote Nothing: The Selected Writings of Daniil Kharms*.

Jamaica Kincaid's (Antigua / United States, 1949–) books include the novels *Annie John*, *Mr. Potter*, and *See Now Then*. She is also the author of *A Small Place* (nonfiction about Antigua). "The Letter from Home" is from her first story collection, *At the Bottom of the River*.

Kenneth Koch (United States, 1925–2002) published many books of poetry (*The Collected Poems of Kenneth Koch*) and fiction (*The Collected Fiction of Kenneth Koch*), had numerous plays produced, and was the author of influential books on teaching poetry to children and the elderly, including *Wishes, Lies, and Dreams*.

Yusef Komunyakaa (United States, 1947–) received the Pulitzer Prize and the Kingsley Tufts Poetry Award for *Neon Vernacular: New & Selected Poems, 1977–1989*. Other books include *Dien Cai Dau* and *The Chameleon Couch: Poems*. He teaches at New York University.

Karl Kraus (Austria, 1874–1936) was a writer, journalist, playwright (*The Last Days of Mankind*, a satirical play about the First World War), poet, essayist, satirist, and performer. Kraus founded the critical newspaper *Die Fackel* (*The Torch*); three of the brief pieces he wrote for the paper are included here.

STANLEY KUNITZ (United States, 1905–2006) received the Pulitzer Prize for his *Selected Poems: 1928–1958* and the National Book Award for *Passing Through: The Later Poems*. He twice served as United States Poet Laureate. A strong advocate of fostering community among artists, he was a founder of the Fine Arts Work Center in Provincetown, and Poets House in Manhattan.

ALEX KUO (United States, 1939–) has published *My Private China* (nonfiction), *The Man Who Dammed the Yangtze: A Mathematical Novel*, and *White Jade and Other Stories*. His piece here is from *Lipstick and Other Stories*, winner of the American Book Award. Kuo has taught at numerous universities, including University of Colorado, Knox College, and Peking University.

JEAN DE LA BRUYÈRE (France, 1645–1696) is best known for his portraits of contemporaries published in *Characters*. He was elected to the French Academy on his fourth try, and died three years later.

FRANÇOIS DE LA ROCHEFOUCAULD (France, 1613–1680) possessed the title of Prince de Marcillac and was occasionally involved in Court intrigues (one of which resulted in a short stay in the Bastille). His literary opus consists of his *Memoirs*, more than one hundred letters, and the 504 pieces collected as the *Maximes*.

DAVID LEHMAN (United States, 1948–) is a poet (*Yeshiva Boys, New and Selected Poems*), scholar (*Signs of the Times: Deconstruction and the Fall of Paul de Man*), chronicler of culture (*A Fine Romance: Jewish Songwriters, American Songs*), and anthologist (*Great American Prose Poems: From Poe to the Present*). He is the series editor of *The Best American Poetry* annual anthology. He teaches at the New School.

J. ROBERT LENNON (United States, 1970–) is the author of a story collection, *Pieces For The Left Hand*, and seven novels, including *Mailman, Castle*, and *Familiar*. He teaches writing at Cornell University.

GIACOMO LEOPARDI (Italy, 1798–1837) wrote several books before the age of twenty, which was when he started writing short prose pieces in notebooks he called *Zibaldone di pensieri* ("hodge-podge of thoughts"), eventually filling over 4500 pages. Leopardi's poetry can be found in *Canti: Poems* (a bilingual edition).

BEN LERNER (United States, 1979–) is a poet, novelist (*Leaving the Atocha Station*), critic, essayist, and editor. His pieces in *Short* are from *Angle of Yaw*, which includes free verse and prose pieces that incorporate the qualities of aphorism, parable, and personal essay. He teaches at Brooklyn College.

CLARICE LISPECTOR (Brazil, 1920–1977), in addition to writing novels and short stories, worked as a journalist, and for many years contributed weekly *crônicas* to a Brazilian newspaper. She made an impact with her first novel, *Near to the Wild Heart,* and then traveled throughout Europe and the United States from 1944–1959. Notable works include *The Passion According to G. H., The Hour of the Star,* and *The Foreign Legion.*

PHILLIP LOPATE (United States, 1943–) writes personal essays, fiction, and poetry, as well as nonfiction on subjects such as architecture, film, and education. His anthology *The Art of the Personal Essay* has—more than any other modern collection—spread the form. His most recent books are *Portrait Inside My Head: Essays* and *To Show and To Tell: The Craft of Literary Nonfiction.* He teaches at Columbia University.

GARY LUTZ (United States, 1955–) has published the story collections *Stories in the Worst Way, I Looked Alive, Partial List of People to Bleach,* and *Divorcer.* He teaches at the University of Pittsburgh at Greensburg.

SPOTLIGHT

STÉPHANE MALLARMÉ (France, 1842–1898), unlike Baudelaire, published his prose poems alongside poems in verse. For an unrealized project, Mallarmé asked the painter Berthe Morisot to illustrate his poem "White Waterlilly." (Monet got a different assignment.) Morisot replied, "Please come and dine on Thursday. Renoir and I are flabbergasted; we need some explanations for the illustrations." Despite Mallarmé's cultivation of difficulty in his literary writing ("there is an advantage to turning away the idler, who is charmed that nothing here concerns him at first sight"), he also had a populist side, writing about fashion and food under such pseudonyms as Madame de Ponty and le Chef de Bouche de chez Brabant. On Tuesday evenings, Mallarmé held court over a diverse group of poets, artists, and journalists. Musician-essayist Francis Grierson recalls Mallarmé commanding attention as he stood "by the fireplace rolling a cigarette, talking in a low voice, half to himself, half to his visitors," who had climbed four flights of stairs to "listen to what words might fall from the lips of the master."

Giorgio Manganelli (Italy, 1922–1990) was a journalist, novelist, and critical theorist. He translated Edgar Allan Poe's complete stories into Italian, as well as works by T. S. Eliot and Robert Louis Stevenson. Manganelli's selection is from *Centuria: One Hundred Ouroboric Novels.*

Sarah Manguso (United States, 1974–) is the author of the memoirs *The Guardians* and *The Two Kinds of Decay,* the story collection *Hard to Admit and Harder to Escape,* and the poetry collections *Siste Viator* and *The Captain Lands in Paradise.* She is a recipient of the Rome Prize from the American Academy of Arts and Letters.

Ben Marcus (United States, 1967–) is the author of *The Age of Wire and String* (stories), *The Flame Alphabet* (novel), *Notable American Women* (novel), and *Leaving the Sea* (stories). He is the fiction editor at *The American Reader,* and his many honors include a Whiting Writers Award. Marcus teaches at Columbia University.

Filippo Tommaso Marinetti (Egypt / Italy, 1876–1944) published the "Futurist Manifesto" in 1909, championing destruction as a cleansing gesture. He wrote in several genres, often fusing his political views with his art. His contribution here is one of a series in the form of fantasy letters to a woman whom the narrator has met fleetingly.

Dawn Lundy Martin's (United States, 1968–) *A Gathering of Matter / A Matter of Gathering* received the Cave Canem Poetry Prize; *Discipline* was awarded the Nightboat Books Poetry Prize. She co-edited *The Fire This Time: Young Activists and the New Feminism.* Martin teaches at the University of Pittsburgh.

Dionisio D. Martínez (Cuba / United States, 1956–) is the author of *History as a Second Language, Bad Alchemy,* and *Climbing Back* (which was selected for the National Poetry Series). He has received fellowships from the Guggenheim Foundation and the Whiting Foundation.

Michael Martone's (United States, 1955–) work often investigates genre, notably in *Four for a Quarter* and *Michael Martone* (a collection of fictional contributors' notes, most of which appeared in the backs of magazines). Martone received the Associated Writing Programs Award for Creative Nonfiction for *Flatness and Other Landscapes*. He teaches at the University of Alabama.

JEAN-MICHEL MAULPOIX (France, 1952–) is a poet with an "ongoing dialogue with prose." He has published more than two-dozen collections as well as critical works on Henri Michaux and René Char. He teaches at the University of Paris X Nanterre. The pieces here are from *A Matter of Blue*.

CAMPBELL McGRATH's (United States, 1962–) poetry collections include *Spring Comes to Chicago*, *Shannon: A Poem of the Lewis and Clark Expedition*, and *In the Kingdom of the Sea Monkeys*. "Philadelphia" is from *Seven Notebooks*. McGrath has been awarded a MacArthur Fellowship, and he teaches at Florida International University.

LOUIS-SEBASTIÉN MERCIER (France, 1740–1814) is best known for *Le Tableau de Paris* (an English edition is titled *Panorama of Paris: Selections from* Le Tableau de Paris) and *Memoirs of the Year Two Thousand Five Hundred*, which imagined a future Paris. Mercier's "tableaus" were admired by Baudelaire, who titled a section of *Flowers of Evil* "Tableaux Parisiens."

W. S. MERWIN (United States, 1927–) served as Poet Laureate of the United States and twice received the Pulitzer Prize. *The Book of Fables* combines the short prose pieces from *The Miner's Pale Children* and *Houses & Travelers*. Chamfort is one of the many authors he has translated. He lives in a house that he designed on a former pineapple plantation in Maui, Hawaii.

HENRI MICHAUX (Belgium / France, 1899–1984) was a writer and painter. His travels in Asia and South America formed the basis of his travelogues, *A Barbarian in Asia* and *Ecuador: A Travel Journal*. Much of his work can be found in English translation in *Darkness Moves: An Henri Michaux Anthology, 1927–1984*.

CHRISTOPHER MIDDLETON (England, 1926–) is a poet, essayist, editor, and translator. His *Collected Poems* was published in 2008, and he is represented here by one of his short prose pieces from *Crypto-Topographia: Stories of Secret Places*, and also by a translation of a Robert Walser story. Middleton taught for more than thirty years at the University of Texas at Austin.

CZESLAW MILOSZ (Poland / United States, 1911–2004) writes in his "Ars Poetica?": "I have always aspired to a more spacious form / that would be free from the claims of poetry or prose." He was born in Lithuania, and his family relocated to Poland between the two world wars. Miłosz moved to Paris in 1934 and participated in resistance media during the German occupation, while he supported himself by selling women's underwear, sausages, and whiskey on the black market. Miłosz eventually moved to the United States and taught at Berkeley from 1961 to 1998. In 1965 he edited *Postwar Polish Poetry*, an anthology of exiles that has had a significant impact on American writers. Miłosz continued to write poems in Polish, unsure if they would ever be translated, an act he compared to "hiding words in tree-hollows." Robert Hass worked with Miłosz on translating his work, and in 1980 Miłosz was awarded the Nobel Prize in Literature. The pieces here are from *Road-Side Dog*.

STEPHEN MITCHELL (United States, 1943–) has written poetry, fiction, and nonfiction, as well as scores of translations and adaptations. According to his website, he "was born in Brooklyn in 1943, educated at Amherst, the Sorbonne, and Yale, and de-educated through intensive Zen practice." His piece here is from *Parables and Portraits*.

MICHEL DE MONTAIGNE (France, 1533–1592) is to the essay what Baudelaire is to the prose poem, publishing volumes of *Essais* ("attempts") that broke the nonfiction mold by being at times conversational, anecdotal, and disjointed.

AUGUSTO MONTERROSO (Guatemala / Mexico, 1921–2003) was exiled to Mexico City in 1944 due to his opposition to the dictatorship of Jorge Ubico. After Ubico was overthrown, Monterroso held diplomatic posts in Mexico and Bolivia, and eventually settled in Mexico. Notable works include *Perpetual Motion* and *The Black Sheep and Other Fables*. The pieces in *Short* are from *Complete Works and Other Stories*.

THYLIAS MOSS (United States, 1954–) has published many books of poetry, including *Rainbow Remnants in Rock Bottom Ghetto Sky* (a National Poetry Series selection), *Last Chance for the Tarzan Holler* (finalist for the National Book Critics Circle Award), and *Slave Moth: A Narrative in Verse*. Among her honors is a MacArthur Fellowship.

HARRYETTE MULLEN'S (United States, 1953–) books include *Recyclopedia* (which contains three earlier books—*Trimmings, S*PeRM**K*T,* and *Muse & Drudge*—and received a PEN Beyond Margins Award), and *Sleeping with the Dictionary* (a finalist for the National Book Award and the National Book Critics Circle Award). She teaches at the University of California, Los Angeles.

ROBERT MUSIL (Austria, 1880–1942) met Kafka in Prague while he was in the army. After the war he went to Vienna, where he wrote his most famous novel, *The Man Without Qualities.* The "little pieces" in *Posthumous Papers of a Living Author* (published while he was alive) are categorized by him as "Pictures," "Ill-Tempered Observations," and "Unstorylike Stories."

AMY NEWMAN'S (United States, 1957–) poetry collections include *Order, or Disorder; Camera Lyrica; Fall;* and *Dear Editor.* She teaches at Northern Illinois University, and is the editor of *Ancora Imparo: A Journal of Arts, Process, and Remnant.*

HELGA NOVAK (Germany / Iceland, 1935–) has published many books of poetry and prose in German; *Selected Poetry and Prose of Helga Novak* (which includes "Eat a Good Meal") is the only book currently available in English translation. Although she maintains her citizenship from Iceland, she has lived in Poland for many years.

NOVALIS'S (Germany, 1772–1801) fragments were first published in the magazine *Athenaeum* (edited by Friedrich and August Wilhelm Schlegel). "Monologue" appears in *Novalis: Philosophical Writings.*

NAOMI SHIHAB NYE (United States, 1952–) has published collections of poetry (*Words Under the Words, Red Suitcase, Fuel,* and *Transfer*) and fiction (*There Is No Long Distance Now: Very Short Stories*), and books for children and young adults. She is a Chancellor of the Academy of American Poets.

FRANK O'HARA'S (United States, 1926–1966) *The Collected Poems of Frank O'Hara* was a co-recipient of the 1972 National Book Award. *Lunch Poems* (written while he was a curator for the Museum of Modern Art) and *Meditations in an Emergency* are his most widely read collections. Along with Kenneth Koch and John Ashbery, he is one of the quintessential New York School poets.

MICHAEL ONDAATJE (Ceylon / Canada, 1943–) was born in Ceylon (now Sri Lanka) and educated in England, before settling in Canada. He has published novels (including the Booker Prize-winning *The English Patient*), as well as poetry (*There's a Trick With a Knife I'm Learning to Do: Poems, 1973–1978*) and memoir (*Running in the Family*).

GREGORY ORR'S (United States, 1947–) many poetry collections include *Burning the Empty Nests*, *The Caged Owl: New and Selected Poems*, and *River Inside the River*. He has also published several books of nonfiction (including essays and memoir). He teaches at the University of Virginia.

RON PADGETT (United States, 1942–) has published more than twenty poetry collections (compiled into his *Collected Poems*) as well as several memoirs. He went to Paris after college on a Fulbright Fellowship, spurring his interest in French poets; among those he has translated are Guillaume Apollinaire and Pierre Reverdy.

KENNETH PATCHEN (United States, 1911–1972) performed his poetry with jazz musicians and collaborated with John Cage on a radio play. Notable works include *Memoirs of a Shy Pornographer* and *The Journal of Albion Moonlight* (prose) and *Collected Poems*. His selections are from *Poemscapes*.

OCTAVIO PAZ (Mexico, 1914–1998) became involved in the surrealist movement while serving in France as a Mexican diplomat. He was later the Mexican ambassador to India and wrote several books there. In *Eagle or Sun?* (a sequence of prose poems), he maps Mexico's past, present, and future. Paz was awarded the Nobel Prize in Literature in 1990.

BENJAMIN PÉRET (France, 1899–1959) was inspired to become a poet after reading Apollinaire. Péret's short prose is available in *Leg of Lamb: Its Life and Works*. He collaborated with Paul Éluard on *152 Proverbs Adapted to the Taste of the Day*. These pieces have come to be known as the "surrealist proverbs" (some of which are included here).

SPOTLIGHT

FERNANDO PESSOA (Portugal, 1888–1935) subverted the very concept of authorship by inventing writers and supplying them with texts, translators, and disciples. He called them *heteronyms* because, unlike pseudonyms, these writers had full-scale voices and backgrounds. Pessoa published under such heteronyms as Alberto Caeiro, Ricardo Reis, and Álvaro de Campos. A trunk full of his notebooks and papers discovered after his death contained the works of dozens more. Pessoa credits his "semi-heteronym" Bernardo Soares with writing *The Book of Disquiet* (which includes the piece here). Pessoa was influenced by Baudelaire, Mallarmé, and by Poe, whose work he translated into Portuguese.

JAYNE ANNE PHILLIPS's (United States, 1952–) *Sweethearts* (1976) is among the first contemporary collections in the emerging short-short form. Subsequent story collections include *Black Tickets* (Sue Kaufman Prize from the American Academy and Institute of Arts and Letters) and *Fast Lanes,* and she published the novels *Machine Dreams, Lark & Termite,* and *Quiet Dell.* She teaches at Rutgers University, Newark.

EDGAR ALLAN POE (United States, 1809–1849) has influenced generations of writers through his short stories ("The Fall of the House of Usher," "The Masque of the Red Death"), poems ("The Raven," "Annabel Lee"), and theories ("The Philosophy of Composition"). Many of his brief pieces are collected in *Marginalia.* Many of his tales might be considered "genre writing" today but, not only did he invent the detective genre and enhance the horror and science fiction genres (he influenced H. G. Wells), his stories run deep—sending ripples to the surface, inviting readers to delve below.

FRANCIS PONGE (France, 1899–1988) wrote about creatures and things ("It is necessary for things to disarrange you") in such books as *The Nature of Things* and *Mute Objects of Expression.*

BOLESŁAW PRUS (Poland, 1847–1912) was a newspaper columnist who also wrote fiction ranging from microstories to novels (notably, *The Doll* and *Pharaoh*). Among his admirers was Czesław Miłosz.

RAYMOND QUENEAU (French, 1903–1976) mingled briefly with the surrealists, but became estranged from them by 1929. Inspired by mathematics, he explored literature with quasi-mathematical theories of derivation to determine hidden texts, and was a founder of the Oulipo movement. Notable works include *Exercises in Style* (dozens of retellings of the same short anecdote), *The Last Days* (novel), and *Letters, Numbers, Forms: Essays, 1928–70.*

Dawn Raffel's (United States, 1957–) books include the story collections *In the Year of Long Division* and *Further Adventures in the Restless Universe*. Her most recent book, *The Secret Life of Objects*, is a memoir composed of short prose pieces about meaningful objects in the author's life. She edits *The Literarian*, the magazine of The Center for Fiction in New York City.

Claudia Rankine (Jamaica / United States, 1963–) has published several books of poetry, including *Nothing in Nature Is Private*, which won the Cleveland Poetry Center's International Poetry Competition. She co-edited two anthologies: *American Women Poets in the 21st Century: Where Lyric Meets Language* and *American Poets in the 21st Century: The New Poetics*. Her piece is from *Don't Let Me Be Lonely: An American Lyric*, which blends poetry, essays, and images. She teaches at Pomona College.

Jules Renard (France, 1864–1910) wrote fiction (*Carrot Head*), poetry, and short plays. The pieces here are from *Histoires Naturelles* (*Natural Histories*). Renard kept a journal from 1887 until his death; selections are available in *The Journal of Jules Renard*.

SPOTLIGHT

Arthur Rimbaud (France, 1854–1891) was called by René Char "the first poet of a civilization that has not yet appeared." In a way, the myths (legend has it he was born with his eyes open—a young seer—and tried to crawl out of his nursery) and mysteries (such as: Why did he give up poetry at the age of twenty-one, like a world-class athlete hanging up the uniform after a spectacular rookie year?) about Arthur Rimbaud are as important as verifiable facts, since they became part of the lore that has excited generations of writers, artists, and musicians. When Rimbaud was sixteen, he wrote in a letter, "If brass wakes up a bugle, it is not his fault. That is obvious to me: I witness the unfolding of my thought: I watch it, I listen to it. . . ." Did Rimbaud stop writing because he woke up one day to find himself turned back to "brass"? Did he grow weary of watching and listening (the first two words of "Departure" are "Enough seen")? What we do know for sure is that Arthur Rimbaud left a small body of work (*A Season in Hell*, *Illuminations*) that looms large.

Aleida Rodríguez (Cuba / United States, 1953–) came to the United States with thousands of other unaccompanied Cuban children via

Operation Peter Pan. Her poetry collection *Garden of Exile* received a PEN Center USA West Literary Award, among other prizes. Rodríguez co-founded *rara avis* magazine and Books of a Feather press, both of which focus on the work of underrepresented writers and artists.

HELEN KLEIN ROSS (United States, 1954–) is the author of *Making It: A Novel of Madison Avenue*. She was an ad agency creative director in New York before turning to other kinds of writing. Her fiction and poetry have appeared in *The New Yorker* and elsewhere.

JOSEPH ROTH (Austria, 1894–1939) worked as a journalist in Berlin *(What I Saw: Reports from Berlin 1920–1933)* and Paris *(Report From a Parisian Paradise: Essays from France 1925–1939)*. He is also the author of many acclaimed books of fiction, including *The Wandering Jews, The Radetzky March,* and *The Tale of the 1002nd Night.*

VERN RUTSALA's (United States, 1934–) books include *The Moment's Equation* (a finalist for the National Book Award in Poetry) and *A Handbook for Writers: New and Selected Prose Poems*. He taught for more than forty years at Lewis and Clark College.

SONIA SANCHEZ (United States, 1934–) is a recipient of the Robert Frost Medal for distinguished lifetime service to American poetry and the Langston Hughes Poetry Award. Her many books include *Does Your House Have Lions?* (a finalist for the National Book Critics Circle Award), *Shake Loose My Skin: New and Selected Poems,* and *Morning Haiku.*

SCOTT RUSSELL SANDERS (United States, 1945–) has published many books of fiction and nonfiction, including *Earth Works: Selected Essays* and *Wilderness Plots: Tales About the Settlement of the American Land* (which includes his piece here). A devoted environmentalist, Sanders also wrote *A Conservationist Manifesto*, which argues for a cultural shift away from consumption towards caretaking.

NATHALIE SARRAUTE (France, 1900–1999) worked as a lawyer in France until 1941, when she was forced to stop practicing because she was Jewish. In 1963 she was awarded the Prix International for her novel *The Golden Fruits*, and she was eighty-three when she published her first bestseller, the autobiographical *Childhood*. The piece here is from her first book, *Tropisms* (1939), about which she said,

"I've always thought that there is no border, no separation, between poetry and prose."

AUGUST WILHELM SCHLEGEL (Germany, 1767–1845) was a poet, essayist, translator of Shakespeare, and a key figure of German Romanticism. In 1818, he began teaching at the University of Bonn, where he developed a printing house for Sanskrit.

FRIEDRICH SCHLEGEL (Germany, 1772–1829)—along with his brother August Wilhelm Schlegel—co-founded the literary journal *Athenaeum* in 1798, which featured essays and aphorisms as expressions of the principles of the Romantic movement. His philosophical fragments were influenced by Chamfort and Novalis.

STEVEN SCHRADER's (United States, 1935–) books of short fiction include *On Sundays We Visit the In-Laws, Arriving at Work,* and *What We Deserved: Stories from a New York Life.* He was the editor and publisher of Cane Hill Press, and for many years was the director of Teachers & Writers Collaborative.

CHRISTINE SCHUTT's (United States, 1948–) collection of short stories *Nightwork* was chosen by John Ashbery as the best book of 1996 for the *Times Literary Supplement*; she has also published several novels, including *Prosperous Friends, Florida* (National Book Award finalist), and *All Souls* (Pulitzer Prize finalist).

MARCEL SCHWOB (France, 1867–1905) was the author of *The Book of Monelle, Imaginary Lives, The King in the Golden Mask,* and *Mimes.* Robert Louis Stevenson—whom he translated into French—was one of his influences. A number of writers have dedicated works to Schwob, including Paul Valéry, Alfred Jarry, and Oscar Wilde.

MOACYR SCLIAR (Brazil, 1937–2011) was a writer and physician, whose practice of medicine influenced his work. Scliar's novel *The Centaur in the Garden* was named one of the 100 Greatest Works of Modern Jewish Literature by The Yiddish Book Center. Scliar said his stories reflect "the Latin American way of combining political fiction with humor and fantasy."

ANA MARÍA SHUA (Argentina, 1951–) has published scores of books in various genres; her pieces here are from *Quick Fix: Sudden Fiction.* Luisa

Valenzuela has written that Shua's "micro short stories open new vistas . . . small is absolutely beautiful, and thrilling, and often disquieting."

CHARLES SIMIC (Serbia / United States, 1938–) won the Pulitzer Prize for his collection of prose poems *The World Doesn't End* (from which his first three selections are taken). He has also received a MacArthur Fellowship and the Frost Medal for lifetime achievement in poetry, and he served as United States Poet Laureate. Simic's compendium collections of poetry include *New and Selected Poems: 1962–2012, Selected Early Poems,* and *The Voice at 3:00 A.M.: Selected Late and New Poems.* He has also published several books of essays and memoirs. The remainder of his selections here are from *The Monster Loves His Labyrinth: Notebooks.*

LEONARDO SINISGALLI (Italy, 1908–1981) was trained in mathematics and engineering, and referred to "the physics of words." The piece here is from his selected poems, *The Ellipse.*

ALEKSANDR SOLZHENITSYN (Russia, 1918–2008) spent many years in a Soviet labor camp. He was freed in 1953 and exiled. His work reached worldwide acclaim and, in 1970, he was awarded the Nobel Prize in Literature. Solzhenitsyn died in 2008 in Moscow. Notable works include *Cancer Ward* and *The First Circle* (novels) and *The Gulag Archipelago.*

GERTRUDE STEIN (United States / France, 1874–1946) studied psychology under William James at Radcliffe College, and moved to Paris in 1903, where, with her brother Leo, she assembled a private art gallery. She was a confidante to Max Jacob, Apollinaire, Sherwood Anderson, and other writers and painters who frequented her salon. Her books include *The Autobiography of Alice B. Toklas, Three Lives,* and *Tender Buttons* (from which the selections here are taken).

ROBERT LOUIS STEVENSON (Scotland, 1850–1894) was the celebrated author of such classics as *Treasure Island* and *The Strange Case of Dr Jekyll and Mr Hyde.* He also wrote many short tales.

MARK STRAND (United States, 1934–) has published dozens of books as poet, novelist, translator, and editor. He was awarded the Pulitzer Prize in Poetry for *Blizzard of One.* Strand has received a MacArthur Fellowship and served as United States Poet Laureate. The prose poems here are from *Almost Invisible.*

SHARAN STRANGE (United States, 1959–) received the Barnard New Women Poets Prize for *Ash*. She teaches at Spelman College. Strange cofounded the Dark Room Collective, and she served as a contributing editor of *Callaloo*.

JAMES TATE's (United States, 1943–) first book of poetry, *The Lost Pilot*, received the Yale Series of Younger Poets Award. Tate's numerous collections include *Selected Poems* (Pulitzer Prize), *Worshipful Company of Fletchers* (National Book Award in Poetry), and *Dreams of a Robot Dancing Bee* (stories). He teaches at the University of Massachusetts, Amherst.

CRAIG MORGAN TEICHER's (United States, 1979–) books of poetry include *To Keep Love Blurry* and *Brenda Is in the Room and Other Poems*. "The Wolves," included here, is from *Cradle Book* (stories and fables).

EDWARD THOMAS (England, 1878–1917) was a critic, biographer, and essayist. He began writing poetry in 1914 with the encouragement of Robert Frost, and wrote most of his poetry as a soldier during the First World War. He was killed in the Battle of Arras.

JAMES THURBER (United States, 1894–1961) was a regular contributor to *The New Yorker* and the author of *My Life and Hard Times* and *The Thurber Carnival*. He also wrote more than seventy-five fables, one of which is included here.

LYNNE TILLMAN (United States, 1944–) has published novels (*American Genius, A Comedy*), short story collections (*Someday This Will Be Funny*), and nonfiction (*The Velvet Years: Warhol's Factory, 1965–67*). She teaches at the University at Albany and the School of Visual Arts.

CHARLES TOMLINSON's (England, 1927–) *New Collected Poems* was published in 2009, and he has translated the poems of Octavio Paz among others. *Some Americans: A Personal Record* recounts his meetings with William Carlos Williams, Marianne Moore, Ezra Pound, and others. Tomlinson is also an artist (*In Black and White: The Graphics of Charles Tomlinson*).

JEAN TOOMER (United States, 1894–1967) is associated with the Harlem Renaissance and The Lost Generation. His most enduring work is the eclectic collection *Cane*, which contains "Karintha." Influences include Baudelaire, Sherwood Anderson, and T. S. Eliot.

Tomas Tranströmer (Sweden, 1931–), a psychologist, has had his writing translated into more than fifty languages. He was awarded the 2011 Nobel Prize in Literature, praised by the judges for his "condensed translucent images." "The Bookcase" was his first published prose poem. Books in English translation include *The Great Enigma: New Collected Poems* and *Memories Look at Me: A Memoir*.

Gael Turnbull (Scotland, 1928–2004) worked as a physician in the U. S., Canada, and England until 1989. He frequently experimented with form in his poetry, including 3D "kinetic poems" for installations. *There Are Words: Collected Poems* was published in 2006.

Deb Olin Unferth (United States, 1968–) is the author of the short story collection *Minor Robberies*, the novel *Vacation*, and the memoir *Revolution: The Year I Fell in Love and Went to Join the War* (a finalist for the National Book Critics Circle Award). She teaches at Wesleyan University.

SPOTLIGHT

Luisa Valenzuela's (Argentina, 1938–) mother, Luisa Mercedes Levinson, was a prominent writer; Jorge Luis Borges was a regular visitor to their home. In her twenties, Valenzuela wrote for such Argentine newspapers as *El Mundo* and *La Nación*, and her first two books of fiction were published in 1966. Valenzuela traveled widely, with long stays in Mexico, Barcelona, and the United States. She settled in New York City in 1978, and spent the next decade teaching at Columbia University and New York University while publishing several books to critical acclaim. Valenzuela returned to Argentina in 1989, and currently lives in the same neighborhood where she grew up. Susan Sontag cited Valenzuela as one of three international writers who are "playing for the real stakes." Carlos Fuentes called her "the heiress of Latin American fiction. She wears an opulent, baroque crown, but her feet are naked." About *Strange Things Happen Here* (which includes her two contributions to *Short*), Valenzuela told an interviewer: "In 1975, upon returning to my city after a long absence . . . it wasn't mine any longer. Buenos Aires belonged then to violence and state terrorism, and I could only sit in cafés and brood. Till I decided a book of short stories could be written in a month, at those same café tables, overhearing scraps of scared conversation, seeping in the general paranoia." Valenzuela is a member of the American Academy of Arts and Sciences.

Paul Valéry (France, 1871–1945) was a poet and essayist. After withdrawing from publishing for almost twenty years—during which he studied language, mathematics, and philosophy—he broke his silence with his most significant poem, "La Jeune Parque." His piece here is from *Selected Writings of Paul Valéry.*

Paul Violi (United States, 1944–2011) frequently subverted form in his poetry. His books include *Overnight, Splurge,* and *Breakers: New and Selected Poems.* He received the John Ciardi Lifetime Achievement Award in Poetry in 2004.

Robert Walser (Switzerland, 1878–1956) incorporated his life as an office worker and his penchant for taking long walks into his writing. Walser's books translated into English include *Masquerade and Other Stories, Selected Stories,* and *Microscripts* (pieces written in miniscule lettering on envelopes and other ephemera).

Joe Wenderoth's (United States, 1966–) books include *Letters to Wendy's* (fiction), *The Holy Spirit of Life: Essays Written for John Ashcroft's Secret Self* (which includes his contribution to this book), and *No Real Light* (poems). He teaches at the University of California, Davis.

Susan Wheeler (United States, 1955–) is the author of a novel, *Record Palace,* and several poetry collections, including *Source Codes, Assorted Poems,* and *Meme.* Wheeler is the recipient of the Witter Bynner Prize for Poetry and the Norma Farber First Book Award. She teaches at Princeton University.

Kim White (United States, 1967–) is the author of *Scratching for Something,* a collection of modern fables, *The White Oak* (Book One of the Imperfect Darkness series), and "The Minotaur Project" (an electronic poem).

John Edgar Wideman (United States, 1941–) is a recipient of a MacArthur Fellowship and has been awarded the PEN / Faulkner award twice. His piece is from *Briefs: Stories for the Palm of the Mind,* "encouraged" by Yasunari Kawabata's *Palm-of-the-Hand Stories.* Other books include *The Homewood Trilogy, Philadelphia Fire, Fever,* and the memoir *Brothers and Keepers.*

OSCAR WILDE (Ireland, 1854–1900) died impoverished but his work remains widely performed and read, including *The Importance of Being Earnest* and *The Picture of Dorian Gray.* He is buried in Père Lachaise Cemetery, where admirers had flocked to adorn his tombstone with lipstick kisses, until a glass partition was constructed.

SPOTLIGHT

DIANE WILLIAMS (United States, 1946–) worked as a dance therapist at Belleview Hospital and in textbook publishing before focusing on the writing of fiction. She has been instrumental in bringing short-short stories into the world through the influence of her writing and by editing *StoryQuarterly* and *NOON.* Her many books include *Vicky Swanky Is a Beauty, Romancer Erector,* and *Excitability: Selected Stories 1986–1996.* Williams has said that when she started writing short-short stories, "There didn't seem to be too many modern examples of short work. I've had to explain what I do in terms of the crucial speeches or declarations made throughout history, which have always been rather short, and the Psalms, the prayers, the magical incantations. . . . " She has taught at Bard College, Syracuse University, and The Center for Fiction.

CATHERINE WING's (United States, 1972–) books include *Enter Invisible* (a nominee for the Los Angeles Book Prize) and *Gin & Bleach.* Her poems have appeared in many periodicals and included in *Best American Poetry* (2010). She teaches at Kent State University.

VIRGINIA WOOLF (England, 1882–1941) is the author of such classics as *Mrs. Dalloway, A Room of One's Own,* and *To the Lighthouse.* "A Haunted House" appeared in *Monday or Tuesday* (1921), the only collection of her short stories published during her lifetime.

PETER WORTSMAN (United States, 1952–) is a short story writer (*A Modern Way to Die*), novelist (*Cold Earth Wanderers*), playwright (*The Tattooed Man Tells All* and *Burning Words*), travel writer-memoirist (*Ghost Dance in Berlin: A Rhapsody in Gray*), translator (Robert Musil, Peter Altenberg, Heinrich von Kleist, The Brothers Grimm), and anthologist (*Tales of the German Imagination, from the Brothers Grimm to Ingeborg Bachmann*).

JAMES WRIGHT (United States, 1927–1980) won the Pulitzer Prize in 1972 for his *Collected Poems*. Several collections followed, and *Above the River: The Complete Poems* was published posthumously. Wright was closely associated with the Deep Image poets, including Robert Bly and Galway Kinnell.

JOHN YAU (United States, 1950–) has published more than fifty books of poetry, artists' books, fiction, and art criticism—most recently, *A Thing Among Things: The Art of Jasper Johns* and *Further Adventures in Monochrome* (poetry). He has served as arts editor of *The Brooklyn Rail*, and he teaches at Rutgers University.

DAVID YOUNG's (United States, 1936–) books include *Field of Light and Shadow* (new and selected poems) and *Work Lights: Thirty-Two Prose Poems*. He co-edited (with Stuart Friebert) *Models of the Universe: An Anthology of the Prose Poem*. He has published several volumes of criticism and teaches at Oberlin College, where he has been an editor of *FIELD* magazine since 1969.

BARRY YOURGRAU's (South Africa / United States, 1949–) books of short-short stories include *The Sadness of Sex* (from which "Domestic Scene" was taken), *Wearing Dad's Head*, and *A Man Jumps Out of an Airplane*. He developed a following in Japan publishing mini-tales written as *keitai shosetsu* over Japan's cell-phone internet.

MIKHAIL ZOSHCHENKO (Russia, 1895–1958) was celebrated for his satirical writings—often critical of the Soviet system—that were collected into best-selling books. He was expelled from the Soviet Writer's Union in 1946. Notable works in English translation include *The Galosh and Other Stories*, *Before Sunrise*, and *Nervous People and Other Satires*.

Index of Authors and Translators

Translators' names are in italics, listed with the appropriate authors.

Index by Genre

The pieces listed below have been identified as short-short stories (including flash fiction and related terms), prose poems, or brief essays (including related terms) in their source publications. Pieces unidentified in the source publications—or identified in such a way as to elude these categories—are listed as other short prose forms.

PROSE POEMS

BRIEF ESSAYS

OTHER SHORT PROSE FORMS

Permissions Acknowledgments

The editor and publisher gratefully acknowledge the authors, translators, literary agents, and publishers who have granted permission to reprint their work in this volume.

Meena Alexander, "Crossing the Indian Ocean" from *Poetics of Dislocation.* Copyright © 2009 by Meena Alexander. Reprinted with the permission of The University of Michigan Press.

Peter Altenberg, "Theater Evening" and "Traveling" from *Telegrams of the Soul,* translated by Peter Wortsman. Copyright © 2005 by Peter Wortsman. Reprinted with the permission of Archipelago Books.

Jack Anderson, "Phalaris and the Bull: A Story and an Examination" from *Traffic: New and Selected Prose Poems.* Copyright © 1998 by Jack Anderson. Reprinted with the permission of The Permissions Company, Inc., on behalf of New Rivers Press, www.newriverspress.com. "Les Sylphides" from *Selected Poems* (Release Press, 1983). Reprinted with the permission of the author.

Enrique Anderson Imbert, "The Ring" and "Dialogue with the Pursuer" from *The Other Side of the Mirror,* translated by Isabel Reade. Copyright © 1966 by Isabel Reade. Reprinted with the permission of the Southern Illinois University Press.

António Lobo Antunes, "Paradise" from *The Fat Man and Infinity and Other Writings,* translated by Margaret Jull Costa. Copyright © 2004, 1998 by António Lobo Antunes. Translation copyright © 2009 by Margaret Jull Costa. Used by permission of W. W. Norton & Company, Inc.

Guillaume Apollinaire, "Little Recipes from Modern Magic" from *The Poet Assassinated and Other Stories,* translated by Ron Padgett (San Francisco: North Point Press, 1984). Copyright ©1984 by Ron Padgett. Reprinted by permission of the translator.

Rae Armantrout, "Imaginary Places" from *Up to Speed.* Copyright © 2004 by Rae Armantrout. Reprinted by permission of Wesleyan University Press.

John Ashbery, "Vendanges" from *Notes from the Air: Selected Later Poems.* Copyright © 2000 by John Ashbery. Reprinted by permission of Carcanet Press, Ltd. and Georges Borchardt, Inc. for the author. All rights reserved.

Margaret Atwood, "Instructions for the Third Eye" from *Murder in the Dark: Short Fiction and Prose Poems.* Copyright © 1983 by Margaret Atwood. Reprinted with permission of McClelland & Stewart, Virago, a division of Little Brown Book Group, and the author.

Gratitudes

My agent, Eleanor Jackson, was tenacious in her support for this book, which she navigated into the right publishing hands.

Those hands belong to Karen Braziller, whose thoughtful counsel, editorial acumen, and good cheer helped shape this book and focus my portions—often over long sessions on the fourth floor of Dodge Hall.

Daniel Halpern shared advice, support, and good wine.

David Lehman—master anthologist, editor, and poet—was generous with wisdom and practical advice at bars, basketball games, and via email.

All of the above independently recommended the same permissions agent: Fred Courtwright (aka *permdude*). Fred juggled permissions with savvy, dedication, and care.

Alyssa Barrett, Scott Dievendorf, Ann DeWitt, Alisha Kaplan, and Rebecca Taylor were faithful companions throughout, providing eyes, ears, hearts, and minds. Scott and Alisha were especially helpful with providing research for the Notes on the Authors.

Lydia and Robert Forbes came through when coming through was most needed.

Peter Johnson, Richard Locke, Paolo Valesio, Peter Wortsman, and Bill Zavatsky pitched in with essential responses and suggestions.

Grant Bergland, Michael Makowsky, Foster Mickley, and Samantha Steiber helped during the text-conversion and selection process.

A tip of the hat and a deep bow to those who have gathered and expounded on short prose forms, among them (among many others): Robert Alexander, Michael Benedikt, Mary Ann Caws, Peter Connors, Michel Delville, Stuart Friebert, Ray Gonzalez, Barbara Henning, Holly Iglesias, Peter Johnson, Mary Paumier Jones, Judith Kitchen, David Lehman, Rosemary Lloyd, Gian Lombardo, Jonathan B. Monroe, Steven Monte, Marjorie Perloff, Robert Shapard, Jerome Stern, John Taylor, James Thomas, Mark Tursi, and David Young.

Of course and always, Erin.

About the Editor

ALAN ZIEGLER is Professor of Writing and Director of Pedagogy at Columbia University's School of the Arts, where he received the Presidential Award for Outstanding Teaching, chaired the Writing Division from 2001–2006, and has been teaching Short Prose Forms seminars and workshops since 1989.

His short work has appeared in such places as *The New Yorker*, *The Paris Review*, *Tin House*, and *Narrative*.

His books include *Love at First Sight: An Alan Ziegler Reader*, *The Swan Song of Vaudeville: Tales and Takes*, *The Green Grass of Flatbush* (winner of the Word Beat Fiction Book Award, selected by George Plimpton), *So Much to Do* (poetry), and three books on creative writing: *The Writing Workshop, Volumes I and II* and *The Writing Workshop Note Book*.

Alan Ziegler is currently working on a "memoir in pieces" ranging from a sentence to a few pages. He lives in New York City.